JOHN RUSKIN'S LABOUR

JOHN RUSKIN'S LABOUR

A study of Ruskin's social theory

P. D. ANTHONY

University College, Cardiff

CAMBRIDGE UNIVERSITY PRESS

Cambridge

London   New York   New Rochelle
Melbourne   Sydney

Published by the Press Syndicate of the University of Cambridge
The Pitt Building, Trumpington Street, Cambridge CB2 1RP
32 East 57th Street, New York, NY 10022, USA
296 Beaconsfield Parade, Middle Park, Melbourne 3206, Australia

First published 1983

Printed in Great Britain at the University Press, Cambridge

Library of Congress catalogue card number: 83–8803

British Library Cataloguing in Publication Data

Anthony, P. D.
John Ruskin's labour.
1. Ruskin, John – Sociology
I. Title
301′.092′4 HM24

ISBN 0 521 25233 4

TM

FOR DANIEL

Contents

Acknowledgements

I must thank my colleagues who have, wittingly or otherwise, helped to develop the ideas I have expressed. Foremost among them are George Thomason, Tom Keenoy, David Simpson, Mike Reed, John Whitehouse and Haroon Saad. Others, whom I have not named, will detect their own influence and deserve my gratitude. Anton Zijderveld made helpful and stimulating suggestions about the importance of the comic and the grotesque. I owe a particular debt to Richard Read who, under no particular obligation as friend or colleague, read a draft of this work and sent me a detailed and informed commentary which repaired many errors, omissions and misunderstandings. Those that remain are the result of my own incapacity and my gratitude to him and to the others implies no shared responsibility on their part. Finally, I must thank Mrs Mair Price who patiently typed several versions of what follows.

REFERENCES

All the references to Ruskin's work are to the Library Edition: E. T. Cook and A. Wedderburn (eds.), *The works of John Ruskin* (39 vols., London, George Allen, 1903–12). Specific references are given to the name of the work followed by the volume number and page number, thus: Ruskin, *Sesame and Lilies*, 18, p. 146.

Introduction

Ruskin has suffered lately from a superfluity of writers and a
deficiency of readers so that, although Ruskin needs no apology,
another book about him requires at least an explanation. The
popular desertion of a good writer always produces a measure of
attention from acolytes who would win back the lost flock. Although
interest in Ruskin is not quite as low as it was when Sir Kenneth Clark
wrote of booksellers who told him that, when they bought job lots,
Ruskin was thrown out like dog-fish from the catch, he is still not
widely read. One of the reasons often given for their foolhardiness by
writers upon him is a worthy desire to restore him to wider public
knowledge and attention. The same ambition explains a well-known
tendency among them (which I share) to quote from him too
extensively. It stems from a wish to show off his astonishing style and
is, at the same time, an acknowledgement by the writer of his
inescapable addiction to it.

Like the readership, the number of writers upon Ruskin has
considerably diminished. There were once shoals of them, following
the current of his vast and popular reputation and paying their own
earnest homage to 'the master'. There may be more interest now in
the United States, in France (possibly the legacy of Proust) and in
Japan, than there is in England. The nature of the interest has
changed from time to time as different aspects of Ruskin have
attracted attention. His work has always appeared to present two
sides and the interest shown in each has alternated with the other. His
contemporary Victorian reputation lay largely in his art criticism, in
the author of *Modern Painters*, *The Stones of Venice*, and *The Seven Lamps
of Architecture*. This was also the Ruskin whose prose style was so loved,
the prose poet and master of the English language. The work of social
criticism to which he turned as he escaped from his parents' influence
was an embarrassment to much of this audience. As the fortunes of
Victorian aesthetics declined and as Victorian taste came to be

derided Ruskin's art work diminished in standing, quite unfairly because he was the severest critic of contemporary artistic judgment. After 1918, when social reform, radicalism, socialism, communism all became respectable and fashionable, Ruskin's social criticism began to be taken seriously while his other work was consigned to the musty vaults of the Victorian heritage. By now both Ruskin and Victorian art are restored to favour, the contemporary interest in him is largely in his aesthetics. Socialism and communism are now, if not discredited, intellectually unfashionable, and Ruskin's social work is not much read. This also is an unfair association because he was one of the severest critics of socialism. Those who now comment on his social criticism often have to apologise for it, acknowledging that some of it is quite unsuitable for a modern audience.

So, when one Ruskin is in the other seems to be out. One particular reason for the current decline in the fortunes of the social Ruskin is that, paradoxically, while communism is no longer fashionable, Marxism has come to be almost synonymous with a radical criticism of capitalism; it has come to be believed that any consistent attack upon it must be launched from a Marxist base. One illustration of this view is the strange tale (which we must postpone) of the rehabilitation of William Morris. Not so long ago, Morris was often regarded as a good designer whose political theory was, to put it at its kindest, unsound. Now Morris is regarded as unique among British critics of capitalism. His canonisation coincides with the argument that he is a Marxist, the claim is made that 'with Morris the final step was taken . . . The final step involved the discovery and absorption of Marx, and the realisation of the proletariat as the sole revolutionary force capable of breaking through all the existing contradictions.'[1] Until Morris could be claimed for Marxism he could not be treated seriously or saved from political oblivion. Once the claim has been made, Morris is admitted to the pantheon of serious social critics.

But no one could make this claim for Ruskin. Ruskin was not a socialist, not a Marxist, not even a democrat. So, Ruskin's social theory remains a subject for apology, not to be taken very seriously, or the subject of considerable condescension, since seriousness and significance have come to be equated with Marxism.

One reason for returning to Ruskin's views about society and work entails a criticism of this assumption and a challenge to what might be described as Marxist intellectual imperialism. Another reason for

---

[1] Jack Lindsay, *William Morris, his life and work* (London, Constable, 1975), p. 381

returning to a writer who is no longer widely read must always be the conviction that he has something to say worth listening to and the hope that those who are not prepared to listen may be persuaded that they are mistaken. Ruskin is certainly worth listening to, but his speech is somewhat prolix for the times we live in and, although the greatest of writers, the newcomer to him may need a little practice. Hence, once again, the lengthy quotation in what follows: the best outcome to be hoped for is that some readers may have the opportunity for practice before they begin the much more proper and enjoyable activity of reading Ruskin himself.

A second reason for this account of Ruskin's social theory is, although important in itself, trivial and personal in its inception. A reviewer who was kind enough to notice *The ideology of work* was irritated by what he saw as the steadfast refusal of its author to get off the fence. Having exposed, as he would hope, the various attitudes to and appeals for hard work which have been made from time to time, we deserve to be told, said the reviewer, what his own attitude is but, apart from some alarming evidence that he takes William Morris seriously, the author tells us nothing. The reviewer was quite right. Although I had hoped to have explained my own reticence in the body of the work by suggesting that postures and attitudes were always loaded with self-interest and by the rather limp contention that the whole business of work was not only a business, but extraordinarily complicated, something more does seem to be required. In order to provide it, it seemed sensible to turn to that writer who has achieved the most subtle and sensitive understanding of the meaning of work, to John Ruskin. He succeeds at least in explaining why work cannot be easily understood because it contains and expresses so much of the complexities and contradictions, the pleasure and the pain of the human condition. His explanation is important because he understands that the experience of work is at the heart of the social, the economic and the political problems of the world, and that it occupies this central position because the questions it raises are essentially moral.

I have previously suggested that there is a clear difference between the classical attitude to work in which medieval European thought reflected an Athenian scepticism about work and the modern view in which men were convinced by every means available that work was the most important thing in their lives. Classical scepticism suggested that work carried out for some other person entailed a loss of freedom which was akin to slavery. Work, therefore, conferred no status on the worker, although the citizen's occupation in quite menial tasks entailed no loss of dignity as long as he was free of economic dependence. The Church continued to regard economic activity and the pursuit of gain as morally doubtful activities and work as morally valuable only because it was unpleasant, as a discipline imposed by the fall. This classical tradition hardly survived the onslaught of the reformation, the triumph of reason in the renaissance, the development of capitalism and industrialisation. The old world was dead and the attitudes born with the new seemed to be natural and innate, universal and unchallengeable. Even the challenges to economic orthodoxy, the radical alternatives, shared the same economic assumptions, achieving an appearance of bitter hostility by schematic division within a binding faith.

But the old tradition never quite died. Ruskin probably represents its first and most articulate expression in the modern world. His classical and biblical learning and his concern with aesthetic values enabled him to transcend and question the economic ends so often taken to represent terminal social values within the nineteenth century. Ruskin raised fundamental questions about work and the condition of workers. How closely did the condition of the industrial worker correspond to the slave? Was it right to condemn slavery and promote industrial labour? For what purpose was industrial labour employed and should we regard the extension of its employment as always beneficial? Should the consumers of luxuries which entailed suffering in their production be held responsible for that suffering? Was it unavoidable that industrial work should mean lives of misery for workers? Ruskin tried to derive the answers to these and other fundamental questions from Christian principles and biblical teaching, not from economic theory. His first conclusion was that we could not look to economic theory for answers as it rested upon false and immoral assumptions, false because they were un-Christian and immoral because they subordinated human good to selfish and pleasure-seeking ends. It was because Ruskin subjected economics itself, by now the touchstone of human affairs, to wider and more universal principles of inspection that he was able to break out of the trap which had so effectively enclosed the greater part of the debate about work and its direction. For the same reason his criticisms of capitalism seem to have an originality and a vigour which distinguish them from Marxist derivatives and even from Marx himself. Ruskin is outside the orthodoxy which bound nineteenth-century capitalists and their critics.

That independence is by now more widely recognised in William Morris whose reputation as a critic of capitalism now stands high. One of the suggestions I hope to elaborate is that William Morris was almost entirely what Ruskin made him. My admiration for Ruskin should be sufficiently obvious already to make it apparent that this view proposes no damage to the reputation of Morris. Morris is in no way diminished by the claim that his criticisms of capitalism derive from Ruskin rather than from Marx, although it must be acknowledged that the number of acolytes would be seriously reduced if that claim were to be firmly established.

The attempt to establish it has one other purpose, although not central to this account as it is not a political work. There was once a British radical tradition, undeniable if difficult to define. Its beginning might be determined in Gerard Winstanley, its end in William Morris. Both are communists. They are separated and uneasily related by a diversity of critics and opinions, Cobbett and Owen, Carlyle, Southey and the tory radicals, by Ruskin. The tradition is English in its avoidance of theoretical consistency and dogma and, perhaps, in its decency and empiricism. It was given in its last years a somewhat un-English zeal by Methodist energy and Scottish and Welsh enthusiasm. It achieved practical consequence in the formation of the Labour Party and a degree of intellectual respectability in Fabianism. And there it ended. The intellectual tradition became outmoded, stuffy, and eventually, quaint. It was left to express itself most vigorously in Guild Socialism which offered a consistent and influential programme but which never recovered from the economic depression of the 1930s and was, by the end of the second world war, abandoned by the trade unions. Other minority movements like distributism or the green shirts, while maintaining something of that vigour, disappeared as effective criticisms of existing society. The main political tradition suffered two disabling blows, in the Attlee government of 1946 – the first in that it carried out its reformist programme, achieved a great measure of nationalisation and founded the Welfare State. There seemed to be nothing left to do but to run the new Jerusalem. This task represented the second blow: the emptiness of achievement was succeeded by the boredom of administration, socialist aspiration was exhausted. The nonconformist conscience, that considerable contribution to British socialism, was left with nothing officially to object to. The Fabian tradition, largely captured by the rational social administration of the Webbs, was left to squabble about the size and content of the shopping bag for nationalisation. The Labour Party, its last populist leader disgraced by his defence of nuclear weaponry, was left without direction or intention, its only claim to electoral approval that it was a more effective administration of a semi-capitalist or a corporatist society. The indices of its performance in future were not to be justice, equality, health, culture or art, but the GNP, the balance of payments, the Retail Price Index, the employment figures and the *Financial Times* Share Index.

The exhaustion of the British Labour Party represented the end of the British socialist tradition, not the end of socialism. The decline of nonconformist energy and the poverty of Fabian theory could be challenged only from the left. The result has been the infiltration of the Party by Marxism which has become so much the concern of British politicians. It is easy to dismiss this tale as the most recent version of a conspiracy theory or as journalistic sensationalism. The emergence of Marxism need not be the result of a sinister plot financed by the Kremlin or of a deliberate intention to subvert the constituencies. It is the inevitable result of the absence of any theoretical alternative, the Marxist influence exists because there is nothing else; as things stand, either the Labour Party must cease to exist as a representative of socialist intention or it must become Marxist. The only obstacle to that conclusion is the trade union movement, the sturdy independence of which, rests upon pragmatism rather than opposing theory. Indeed, the steadfast refusal of British trade unions to engage in intellectual activity of any kind has not only saved it from Marxist domination, it may be necessary to its own effective opposition to Marxism in the affairs of the Labour Party. As long as the unions avoid theory they can concentrate on short-term adjustments and equivocations, concerned only with the immediate interests of their members and their own continued representation of them. And as long as they succeed in the pursuit of those two interrelated objectives the unions remain as the despair of Marxists and the only effective alternative influence in the Labour Party.

This cannot continue as a satisfactory state of affairs, however, because the unions cannot be regarded as a permanently reliable opposition. Unchallenged theoretical domination has an ultimate effect, even on the English proletariat. A serious threat to the influence of the unions within the Labour Party comes, paradoxically, when Labour is in power and when the unions come to see themselves as a responsible arm of government; the role of the unions within the Party is best exercised during Conservative administrations. Neither the Party nor the unions can be expected to seek permanent opposition out of a conviction that this is the only way to keep in check the theoretical influence of Marxism. So, reluctantly, the Labour Party must look for a theoretical alternative. My suggestion is that the only direction available for examination is the English radical tradition all trace of which has by now all but been obliterated. Ruskin (and Morris) represents the last statement of that tradition and for that reason alone it is worth some critical discussion.

Ruskin was not a socialist and Morris was a communist or an anarchist. They each contributed a denunciation of capitalism so total as to rule out the possibility of the replacement of private enterprise by public ownership based upon the same economic principles. Ruskin, in particular, makes the truly revolutionary proposal that, to avoid the consequences of capitalism, we must turn our moral values on their head. Ruskin demands no mere political revolution, the workers of the world have seen that that sort of turn leaves them in the same place. Ruskin tells us that this is bound to be the case unless we change our attitude, our moral outlook and our behaviour. The means he advocates to bring about such radical change are themselves radical and often unpalatable. Whether they are practical or not, Ruskin reminds us of the distance we have travelled from a society that can be recognised as good, decent and honourable and of the very great effort that has to be made to return to virtue. He insists that the change is so thorough that it cannot be brought about by legislation or insurrection. It must be accomplished, if it can be done at all, by changing the intentions and values of individual men and women. If it cannot be done or if we choose not to do it, Ruskin has still left us with a vision of a truly alternative society. That alternative has two politically important features. It is based on a passionate conviction of the responsibilities of leadership and of its conception of just and honourable relationships between men. It is also concerned to establish the meaning of work and the realisation of the burdens which governors, purchasers and employers necessarily impose upon those who have to endure it. Ruskin acknowledged that the burden is unavoidable but he tells us that at least we must impose it with care, even with love.

Ruskin is not a socialist because he believed that socialist intentions were misguided and irrelevant. His criticisms of capitalism, his moral insight into its corruption, his revolutionary alternative and his sympathetic understanding of the meaning of work are all necessary ingredients in socialism and his warning that a socialist alternative is likely to perpetuate the same indecencies as capitalism is particularly timely. Whether we can achieve or wish to attempt the moral revolution which Ruskin advocated, his advice remains as a template to measure the degree of social corruption which we have chosen as an alternative to it. The theocracy which has recently been established in Iran suggests to us that a complete transformation in social values cannot be accomplished without suffering and bloodshed. Ruskin would probably have acknowledged that but would have argued that to perpetuate the alternative of permanent moral corruption could never produce happiness or fulfilment in any social form.

My purpose then, is to try to suggest an outline of Ruskin's alternative to our present social relationships so that we may use it to measure our performance within a social and economic structure which has become, as Max Weber predicted it would, an iron cage, the constraints of which have become so familiar as to be barely noticeable.

Two disclaimers are necessary before we begin. The purpose of this book is to examine Ruskin's social criticism but part of the argument to be developed is that this grows from and is inextricably related to his work on art and architecture. For that reason we must begin with the wider context of his work before we get to his views on society, economics and labour. Apart from the difficulty that it will take some time before we reach our real subject, the reader may have concluded by then that the author does not know what he is talking about or, at-least, that he has no special claim for attention in the matter of aesthetics. The only way of avoiding this difficulty is that specialists confine themselves to one of the two 'sides' of Ruskin. Generally speaking, they do, but that contributes to the belief that there are two Ruskins and our case is that there is only one. The only alternative is to face the difficulty and to do one's best to elucidate a subject in which one has no special competence, foolhardy though the attempt may be, before minding one's own business and sticking to one's last.

The second is that it seems to me to be unnecessary to include in this account anything but the barest biographical information. There is no shortage of reliable accounts of Ruskin's life, the only aspect of which still seems to attract some speculative enquiry being the question of his marital relations. Fortunately, this seems to be by now both a settled question and utterly irrelevant to the matter at hand.

1

The laws of right

There is only one Ruskin. Not only has there been no writer like him in the English language but his work presents a unity which has not always been recognised. It was a convenient failure of recognition for those Victorians who chose to idolise the aesthete and to ignore the prophet of social doom. Ruskin recognised this distinction amongst his readers and protested that he would write no more pretty prose because 'many people thought of the words only and cared nothing for their meaning' so that he would write in future with great plainness.[1]

His safer work in art and architectural criticism was republished in popular editions and given as school prizes. His social criticism was republished by the revolutionary anarchist William Morris and copied out by hand by working readers. He also smarted at the sneer (a sexual sneer) at the gentle refinement of his style: 'I'm not going to let them have any more fine "language" to call me a "mad governess" for.' It was easy to say that there were two Ruskins, easier still as the divisions seemed to occupy different parts of the writer's life. The division could be made to coincide with his tragic madness. The aesthetic Ruskin was young, brilliant and sane. The social Ruskin was old, morose and mad. Ruskin's work itself does not always suggest unity. His writing was sometimes prolix in style, and occasionally bewilderingly ill-directed in intention. Ruskin liked to explain that the more labyrinthine turns and diversions in his argument were all part of a grand design, that all would be revealed as logically and systematically related, but his occasional apologies for past digressions which set out to show that 'true love is inconsistent with railways, with joint-stock banks . . . with grouse shooting, with lawn tennis'[2] suggest that his performance and his intentions were sometimes at odds.

[1] Ruskin, *Sesame and Lilies*, 18, p. 146
[2] Ruskin, *Fors Clavigera*, 29, p. 445

9

If the apparent divisions of his life were complicated by differences in his style, the whole impression of disunity was compounded by the extraordinary range of subject matter which his work encompassed. He wrote about everything or, at least, as Mrs Meynell said, he wrote about everything except music.[3] To catalogue his subject matter would be tedious, but he actually claimed expert knowledge and superior critical understanding in the distinct fields of art, architecture, economics, geology, botany and ornithology.

The appearance of a scattered lack of direction of his work and life is misleading. Ruskin's work presents an unusual unity: 'the whole of Ruskin's opus is an uninterrupted dedication to the Oneness of many'.[4] Whatever field demands his attention, his endeavour is to demonstrate its manifestation of a general law and, therefore, its relationship to other fields equally subsumed under that law and expressive of it. Ruskin was never able to arrive at a systematic expression of this law; he might have acknowledged that such a task was beyond the puny capacity of any human being. The best that could be accomplished through human endeavour, if it were honestly and purposefully directed by good men, was the insight into manifestations of that law. Insight was possible for some men; understanding was impossible because the law was God's. Ruskin's conviction can be explained by his birth and his background, by the Presbyterian education provided by his parents, by his 'marsupial upbringing' as Quentin Bell describes it. Ruskin's Christian faith developed and broadened as he grew older. At one time it showed signs of weakening but it was only to transcend his earlier Protestant bigotry in achieving a deeper and wider religious understanding.

It is possible to argue that Plato's idealism contributed to the unity of Ruskin's understanding. Hardly a day passed, he said, when he did not read Plato. Rosenberg rejects Plato as a source of Ruskin's ideas of beauty because, he says, Plato regarded sense experience as illusory and as leading away from the ideal.[5] But Ruskin, too, although the most steadfast advocate of strict and accurate observation of nature, entered the severest warnings against the slavish copying of the evidence provided by the senses. Sensation is not sufficient: 'the truth

[3] Mrs Meynell made the interesting comment that Ruskin was unnecessarily preoccupied with the question of the imitation of and selection from nature because of his 'lack of music, and in default, therefore, of a sense of the separateness of an art that imitates nothing' (*John Ruskin* (Edinburgh, Blackwood, 1890), p. 37). Ruskin liked music but did not have a lot to say about it.

[4] John D. Rosenberg, *The darkening glass* (London, Routledge and Kegan Paul, 1963), p. 42
[5] *ibid.*, p. 20

of nature is a part of the truth of God; to him who does not search it out, darkness, as it is to him who does, infinity'.[6] Sensation is not sufficient, partly for physiological and partly for moral reasons. To convey truth in art, sensation must be worked upon by perception, allied to educated judgment and sensibility and informed by the love of nature.

The matter was put plainly in a discarded manuscript version of Chapter IV of *The Stones of Venice* in which Ruskin goes back to his discussions of ideas of truth, beauty, and relation in *Modern Painters*. His purpose had been, he said, 'to show that the Truth of greater art was that which the soul apprehended, not the sight merely; that the Beauty of great art was in like manner that which the soul perceived, not the senses merely'.[7] Ruskin's art criticism is preoccupied with aspects of truth and moral purpose rather than with the recording of sense data. He is not sufficiently enslaved by sensation to be separated from the influence of Plato and the affinity he often shows for ideal forms of beauty and for the close relationship between beauty and truth positively attest Plato's influence.

But the dominant influence is the Christian God and the Christian European tradition. No one can understand Ruskin without acknowledging this domination. The various avenues in which he directed his work were not empirical attempts to arrive at general theory, nor the accretion of evidence upon which to build an inductive edifice. Everything that Ruskin did was a deduction from first, Christian principles. God and moral order informed all of nature and all of human affairs. It follows that any study of nature or humanity will demonstrate that order. The relationship of his specific studies to his general principles explains several characteristics of Ruskin's work. It explains his confidence in undertaking the study of unfamiliar fields and his apparently arrogant willingness to challenge the acknowledged authorities in any of them. He more than once acknowledged the accuracy of the observation that he set out to write a book in order to learn about its subject. But the observation is only true in part. In a sense, Ruskin always knew what he wanted to say and knew what he was about to discover. Sometimes the result was the paradox that has been observed between the meticulous truth of his descriptions of nature, art or building, and the dogmatism and confusion which may attend his use of these to illuminate his general theme. Ruskin

[6] Ruskin, *Modern Painters*, 3, p. 141
[7] Ruskin, *The Stones of Venice*, 11, p. xix

observed with clinical accuracy but often in order to illustrate perversely his grand design.

This confidence or faith is related to other characteristics. Ruskin is sometimes dogmatic and almost always didactic (despite his warnings against the uselessness of didactic art). The most ardent of his admirers have always had to acknowledge that most of his work abounds 'with arbitrary opinions, extravagances of enthusiasm, prejudiced judgments, and sudden vehement outbursts of arrogant condemnation'.[8] Ruskin was always laying down the law, sometimes the law seemed to take a perverse form but Ruskin always insisted that his readers should understand it. Unfortunately the truths that he would have his readers understand seemed sometimes to take contradictory forms. Ruskin acknowledged it. He never felt, he said, that he had dealt adequately with a subject unless he had contradicted himself three times in its discussion. But it was aspects or manifestations of the law rather than the law itself that was contradictory. He put the matter plainly in the first volume of *Modern Painters*:

The laws of the organization of the earth are distinct and fixed as those of the animal frame, simpler and broader, but equally authoritative and inviolable. Their results may be arrived at without knowledge of the interior mechanism; but for that very reason ignorance of them is the more disgraceful, and violations of them more unpardonable. They are in the landscape the foundation of all other truths, the most necessary, therefore, even if they were not in themselves attractive; but they are as beautiful as they are essential, and every abandonment of them by the artist must end in deformity as it begins in falsehood.[9]

Ruskin's subject is always the laws of organisation which, if understood, will clearly serve to discriminate between truth and falsehood. He began the study of these laws in painting. There is an inescapable sense in which the start was fortuitous and unplanned. His first intention, apart from a general resolve to write and to make his way in the world, was, after Oxford, to write a pamphlet in response to attacks on Turner in *The Literary Gazette* and *The Athenaeum* of 14 May 1842, but he found himself compelled 'to amplify what was at first a letter to the editor of a Review into something very like a treatise on art'.[10] The treatise on art expanded to fill five volumes, the first published in 1843 when Ruskin was twenty-four

[8] Derrick Leon, *Ruskin, the great Victorian* (London, Routledge and Kegan Paul, 1949), p. 76
[9] Ruskin, *Modern Painters*, 3, p. 425
[10] *ibid.*, p. 3

years of age, and the fifth in 1860 when he was forty-two. The work is largely concerned to establish the reputation of Turner, to argue that in respect of the truth of their observation and the honesty of their work, painters of the nineteenth century were often superior to classical painters and to establish, no less, canons of authentic judgment and criticism. But grand as was this original design, there are the earliest signs that it was not sufficient for Ruskin's purpose. Art, however satisfying, has often unsettled the Protestant mind and Ruskin announced at the beginning of the first volume that he had a higher end in view 'than mere insight into the merits of a particular master, or the spirit of a particular age'.[11] It was rather 'a question which, in spite of the claims of Painting to be called the sister of Poetry appears to me to admit of considerable doubt, whether art has ever, except in its earliest and rudest stages, possessed anything like efficient moral influence on mankind'.[12] This was so because 'That which ought to have been a witness to the omnipotence of God, has become an exhibition of the dexterity of man.'[13] Art is more than technique and more than the copying of what it deals with, 'it must never exist alone, never for itself, it exists only when it is the means of knowledge or the grace of agency for life'.[14]

Two essential characteristics concern the subject matter of art and its treatment. All beauty resides in nature and cannot be found elsewhere: 'Forms are not beautiful *because* they are copied from Nature: only it is out of the power of man to conceive beauty without her aid.'[15] The message is consistent: 'The Art of Man is the expression of his rational and disciplined delight in the forms and laws of the Creation of which he is a part.'[16] In order to express this right relationship between the greatest painters and nature, Ruskin devoted over 250 pages of his third volume of *Modern Painters* to the principles of geological structure, of compact and slaty crystallines, compact coherents and lateral ranges. In an Epilogue to the work, published in 1888, Ruskin said that everything he had said was summarised in the aphorism, 'All great Art is Praise.'

As to the treatment of nature by the artist it is important that the artist should not set out to exhibit his own dexterity, 'the skill of the artist, and the perfections of his art are never proved until both are

[11] *ibid.*, p. 20
[12] *ibid.*, p. 21
[13] *ibid.*, p. 22
[14] Ruskin, *Lectures on Art*, 20, p. 96
[15] Ruskin, *The Seven Lamps of Architecture*, 8, p. 60
[16] Ruskin, *The Laws of Fesole*, 15, p. 351

forgotten. The artist has done nothing until he has concealed himself; the art is imperfect which is visible; the feelings are but feebly touched, if they permit us 'to reason on the methods of their excitement . . . The power of the masters is shown by their self-annihilation.'[17] It is because the older painters have exhibited their own technique that they have filled the world with honour of themselves and not of God. This was a particular form of a paradox, incidentally, which was to recur time after time in Ruskin's work, a paradox in which a desirable objective is obtainable only by a steadfast refusal to pursue it. In this case, Ruskin's paradox suggests that the reputation of a Master can be attained only by concealing the attributes of a Master; in other versions we will see that pleasure in work is to be achieved only if it is not made the object of work.

Ruskin's early work was preoccupied with art but with art as a moral instrument. The close relationship between art and morality is the explanation of the relationship between Ruskin's art work and his social criticism; it is why there are not two or twenty Ruskins, but one. His editors, rebutting the common view that his life and work divided about 1860, that he was previously a writer on art and subsequently a writer on social questions, said that 'Ruskin's interest in social, political and economic questions had for many years been developing, that it was a direct outcome of his artistic studies, and that it dated back at least to the years 1849–1851–1853'.[18] Social criticism grew out of art criticism because of the view which he took of art as essentially a moral activity and the evolution or growth can be seen in two transitional stages. The first concerns the close connection which Ruskin saw between art and national character or historical mood. The second concerns his work on architecture and the explanation of his decision to turn to architecture as a field of study.

The steps connecting art, the moral character of men and the moral character of nations and societies are clearly taken in a passage in *The Seven Lamps of Architecture*. Most of us, Ruskin says, are afflicted by a false life of custom and accident, overlaid by the weight of external things. We are all of us likely to be frost-bitten in some degree, the best of us resisting this dead encumbrance from time to time 'but, with all the efforts that the best make, much of their being passes in a kind of dream, in which they indeed move, and play their parts sufficiently, to the eyes of their fellow dreamers, but have no clear consciousness of

---

[17] Ruskin, *Modern Painters*, 3, pp. 22–3
[18] Ruskin, editors' introduction, 16, p. xxii

what is around them, or within them; blind to the one, insensible to the other'.[19] He goes on to compare the lives of men and of nations and says that nations can be afflicted by a similar deadness which is clearly revealed in their architecture. What people like is determined by what they are and if their taste is formed so, inevitably, is their character. For this reason the object of true education is not simply to make people do the right things but to make them enjoy the right things. Because of this intimate connection between public taste and public character, 'the art of any country is the exponent of its social and political virtues . . . the art, or general productive and formative energy, of any country, is an exact exponent of its ethical life'.[20] The character of men and of nations can be read in their art.[21]

There is nowhere in which this character may be read more easily than in the architecture of nations. It was for this reason that Ruskin turned to undertake a study of architecture even more extended and intensive than his examination of painting. He was still, as he would always be, concerned with determining 'some constant, general and irrefragable laws of right' which span the 'entire horizon of man's action',[22] but he set out, in *The Seven Lamps of Architecture* (1849), to discover the particular application of these laws in architecture. In teaching the principles of architecture as he did in this work and in *The Stones of Venice*, Ruskin actually spoke of teaching his readers how to read buildings as they might read books. The content of these volumes in stone would reveal the values, character and ambitions of the people in whose societies those buildings had been raised.

Good architecture is, quite simply, the work of good men, but not of a few good men unrepresentative of their society: 'every great national architecture has been the result and exponent of a great national religion. You can't have bits of it here, bits there – you must have it everywhere or nowhere.'[23] This particular judgment was delivered in a lecture given in the Town Hall, Bradford, in 1864 when he had been asked to talk about the design of the new Exchange building. An impossible task, said Ruskin, because nobody cared about it, neither he nor his audience: 'you cannot have good architecture merely by asking people's advice on occasion. All good architecture is the expression of national life and character and is

[19] Ruskin, *The Seven Lamps of Architecture*, 8, p. 193
[20] Ruskin, *Lectures on Art*, 20, p. 39
[21] *ibid.*, p. 83
[22] Ruskin, *The Seven Lamps of Architecture*, 8, p. 21
[23] Ruskin, *The Crown of Wild Olive*, 18, p. 444

produced by a prevalent and eager national taste, or desire for beauty.'[24]

Architecture is singularly instructive as the mirror of social character; it is 'the distinctively political art'.[25] In *The Stones of Venice* (1851) Ruskin argues with a precision that is both characteristic and fallible that the architecture of Venice can be taken as an example of the reflection in architecture of social and moral characteristics. One of the ways in which Ruskin is widely known to have transformed Victorian taste is in the change he brought about in the appreciation of Venice. Before Ruskin, Venetian gothic was largely ignored while her renaissance architecture was admired; Ruskin restored the gothic to favour if he did not succeed in utterly discrediting the renaissance. The greatness of Venice, he said, coincided with her faith and her architecture proclaimed it. The moral decline of Venice set in in 1418 precisely with the death of Carlo Zeno. The gothic style reflected the greatness of Venice, the renaissance its corruption. We must postpone a discussion of the opposition of styles and the social and political significance which Ruskin attached to them because it is such a central part of his teaching that it demands more careful attention. Architecture has a special significance as the political art because, although all art for Ruskin is informed with moral significance, architecture retains this characteristic of art in general and has special features. Its decoration signifies moral features but architecture is an especially social art. Its manifestation in buildings requires social organisation and it also exhibits in the clearest possible form, social values. Architecture is, in fact, a monument to social values.

The significance of architecture in this respect is revealed in *The Seven Lamps of Architecture*. Architecture is 'that art which, taking up and admitting, as conditions of its working, the necessities and common uses of the building, impresses on its form certain characters venerable or beautiful, but otherwise unnecessary'.[26] The seven lamps are general principles which govern this unnecessary activity. The lamp of sacrifice is the spirit in which precious and expensive materials are used, it involves self-denial for the sake of self-discipline or the desire to honour and please others by the costliness of the sacrifice. This principle is 'the opposite of the prevalent feeling of modern times which desire to produce the largest results at the least cost'. Ruskin responds to the familiar criticisms of the inutility of

[24] *ibid.*, p. 434
[25] Ruskin, *The Seven Lamps of Architecture*, 8, p. 20
[26] *ibid.*, p. 28

sacrifice and self-denial: 'it is just because we do not enough acknowledge or contemplate it as good in itself, that we are apt to fail in its duties when they become imperative, and to calculate with some partiality, whether the good proposed to others measures or warrants the amount of grievance to ourselves, instead of accepting with gladness the opportunity of sacrifice as a personal advantage'.[27] The same habit of precise and careful calculation is castigated in terms of labour: 'all old work [in architecture] nearly has been hard work . . . Ours has as constantly the look of money's worth, of a stopping wherever and whenever we can, of a lazy compliance with low conditions . . . Let us have done with this kind of work at once, cast off every temptation to it: do not let us degrade ourselves voluntarily, and then mutter and mourn over our shortcomings.'[28] The relationship between a moral principle (self-denial) and social good is hinted at in these passages and clearly established by his denunciations of decorations which have become 'foolishly and apathetically habitual' and upon which depend whole trades of pleasureless work. Luxury in our own houses should imply that we have sufficiently provided for others and that there is enough left for luxury. Self-sacrifice implies a moral habit: the choice 'is not between God's house and His poor . . . It is between God's house and ours.' The social implications of this principle are as clear as the implicit criticism of utilitarianism and the economic calculation of self-interest.

The second principle is Truth. Here Ruskin made his very influential criticism of deception in architecture by the intention to suggest a different structure from the real one or by the imitation of false surfaces (graining or marbling in paint work was a particular abomination). Ruskin reveals his preference for structural functionalism; the greatest buildings are those which reveal their structure to an intelligent eye. This principle of Truth is certainly a moral one but it has little to do with social purpose or intention (although, as we shall see, the connection is soon to be established), but even here he seeks a connection. It concerns decoration rather than structure. There are two reasons for the agreeableness of ornamentation, the first for the abstract beauty of its forms, the second because of the sense conveyed of human labour spent upon it. Our response to carving 'results from our consciousness of its being the work of poor,

27 *ibid.*, p. 31
28 *ibid.*, p. 44

clumsy, toilsome man'.[29] This sense of sympathy with manual labour which some forms (primarily the gothic) of architecture seemed to enhance and some forms (renaissance) to suppress, was to become an important part of his doctrine.

The third principle, Power, moves back toward the social. Architecture takes one of two forms: it is derived from or it imitates natural forms, or it is majestic, when it depends upon arrangement emanating from the human mind, sublime to the extent of the power of the mind it expresses. 'All building, therefore, shows man either as gathering or governing; and the secrets of his success are knowing what to gather, and how to rule.'[30]

The Lamp of Beauty returns to a discussion of the useful and the decorative in building and Ruskin asserts that the two must be separated, ornament should not be mixed with business. Things associated with action, occupation or business should not be decorated, 'where you can rest, there decorate, where rest is forbidden, so is beauty'.[31] The violation of this principle, common in nineteenth-century building, has the direst effect, says Ruskin: it is valueless, it gives no pleasure, it satiates the senses and vulgarises forms. This most tireless of travellers (although invariably, at this time, by coach) adds that the whole system of railroad travelling is addressed to people who 'being in a hurry, are therefore, for the time being, miserable'. The design of railways and railway buildings should be directed at reducing their misery by shortening the time taken in their journeys.

In the fifth principle, called the Lamp of Life, Ruskin says that beauty depends upon the expression of vital energy in organic things. The effect of architecture depends very much upon the pleasure taken in the vivid expression of intellectual life in working upon, moulding and organising the inert substances of which building is composed. Ruskin makes the distinction we have already noticed between the true or vital life of man and a false or habitual life. Architecture can come to represent this false and habitual life, it can represent the moral decay of a whole society. And then Ruskin takes one of his farthest steps so far from art across the bridge of morality to social concern. The essential question concerning ornament concerns the state of mind of the man who produced it: 'was it done with enjoyment – was the carver happy while he was about it? It may be the hardest work possible, and the harder because so much pleasure

[29] *ibid.*, p. 82
[30] *ibid.*, p. 102
[31] *ibid.*, p. 105

was taken in it, but it must have been happy too, or it will not be living. You cannot get the feeling by paying for it – money will not buy life.'[32]

The sixth principle is Memory. Ruskin asserts the importance of a tradition, of a veneration for the works left us by our fathers and the necessity of conviction that we are working and building for our children. By this standard of respect for what is handed down to us, Ruskin deplores the contemporary classic building of his own day: 'there must be a strange dissolution of natural affection, a strange unthankfulness for all that homes have given and parents taught, a strange consciousness that we have been unfaithful to our father's honour, or that our own lives are not such as would make our dwellings sacred to our children, when each man would fain build to himself, and build for the little revolution of his own life only'.[33] By contrast to those 'gloomy rows of formalised minuteness' we should think when we build 'that we build for ever . . . let it be such work as our descendants will thank us for, and let us think, as we lay stone on stone, that a time is to come when those stones will be held sacred because our hands have touched them, and that men will say as they look upon the labour and wrought substance of them, "See! this our fathers did for us"'.[34]

This respect, for tradition, for what has been done by past generations, leads, paradoxically, to his condemnation of all attempts to restore old buildings, because restoration means destruction. Buildings should be preserved until they can last no longer and then they should be pulled down. It is not a 'question of expediency or feeling whether we shall preserve the buildings of past time or not. *We have no right to touch them.* They are not ours.'[35] Respect for ancestry and tradition of this order is usually associated with political conservatism. Ruskin's radical social concern was to take a singularly conservative, even authoritarian, form. The seventh principle, or lamp, of architecture is significantly called the Lamp of Obedience. It suggests that anti-libertarian, authoritarian character that we shall examine in the next chapter.

Architecture, the most political art, is an essential step in the transition from aesthetics to social criticism. It is an art that requires social organisation and, in terms foreign to Ruskin, the allocation of scarce resources, public or private, on a considerable scale. It

[32] *ibid.*, p. 218
[33] *ibid.*, p. 226
[34] *ibid.*, p. 233
[35] *ibid.*, p. 245

therefore incorporates public values, it demonstrates those values for which the society which created it believed were worth sacrifice. The implications clearly read by Ruskin were in the contrast between what Venice had been, what values it had esteemed, and what it had come to be and to value. The contrasts, visible in the decline of Venice, were as clear in the growth of London. The most savage and bitter denunciations of what we have since learned to call capitalist society belong to Ruskin's later work after he had given up 'pretty prose' and had arrived at a pessimistic view of the future.

In *Modern Painters*, Ruskin had concluded that the unique sin of the English was their hypocrisy. Other nations in other times had denied their gods bravely 'but we English have put the matter in an entirely new light: There *is* a Supreme Ruler, no question of it, only He cannot rule. His orders won't work. He will be quite satisfied with euphorious and respectful representation of them. Execution would be too dangerous under existing circumstances, which He certainly never contemplated.'[36]

Ruskin explains that he had no conception of the 'absolute darkness which has covered the national mind' until he first encountered economists:

The entire naivete and undisturbed imbecility with which I found them declare that the laws of the Devil were the only practicable ones, and that the laws of God were merely a form of poetical language, passed all that I had ever before heard or read of mortal infidelity. I knew the fool had often said in his heart, there was *no* God; but to hear him say clearly, out with his lips, 'There is a foolish God', was something which my art studies had not prepared me for.

This was a source of bewilderment to which Ruskin himself, naively perhaps, constantly returned throughout his life. It is an honest man's total failure to understand how men can profess a faith without being governed in their lives by its precepts, of how it is that they neither change their faith nor change their lives. To this extent it is a failure to understand human history but it explains, to some extent, the simplicity of Ruskin's expectation and the bitterness of his disappointment at its failure. In this respect (and fortunately, in this respect alone) there is a similarity to Robert Owen. It is only a simple thing that has to be done, a change in men's outlook that is not even inconsistent with their own best interests. Ruskin simply wants people to accept the practical consequences of their acknowledged faith. He

---

[36] Ruskin, *Modern Painters*, 7, pp. 447–8

points out the discontinuity between their lives and their faith and is distressed by their ultimate refusal to change either the one or the other. Any other consistent crime he could at least understand, but he never could come to terms with such inconsistency.

If this were all, it might go some way to explain Ruskin's tragedy but it would say nothing for his social philosophy. His work would be distinguished from the familiar material of weekly sermons only by the strength of its rhetoric and the polish of its prose. In this same passage in *Modern Painters*, however, he takes the matter further than an expression of religious despair or moral disapproval. This form of unbelief in God, he says:

is connected with, and necessarily productive of, a precisely equal unbelief in man.

Co-relative with the assertion, 'There is a foolish God', is the assertion, 'There is a brutish man'. 'As no laws but those of the Devil are practicable in the world, so no impulses but those of the brute' (says the modern political economist) 'are appealable to in the world. Faith, generosity, honesty, zeal, and self-sacrifice are poetical phrases. None of these things can in reality, be counted upon; there is no truth in man which can be used as a moving or productive power. All motive force in him is essentially brutish, covetous, or contentious. His power is only power of prey: otherwise than the spider, he cannot design; otherwise than the tiger, he cannot feed.'[37]

Ruskin does not instantly protest that this view of man is morally wrong, that he should be regarded as co-operative rather than competitive. In this particular sense there is always a singular absence of preaching in his writing, it is very rarely mere moralising. His care is constantly to stress that the contemporary view of human affairs is illogical, inconsistent with professed belief and, simply, untrue. It does not give an account of observable fact. It is not strange that this creed should have been adopted; if the Devil rules, men must be expected to be brutish. The strange thing is that there are no misgivings about its accuracy. As a matter of fact, men do good work quite independently of the rate at which they are hired. Whatever you pay them, some soldiers will fight well, some badly: 'Pay as you will, the entire goodness of the fighting depends always on its being done for nothing; or rather, less than nothing, in the expection of no pay but death.' For ten pounds history shows you can have *Paradise Lost*, for a plate of figs, a Dürer, Kepler will discover the laws of astronomy for nothing. 'Neither is good work ever done for hatred,

[37] *ibid.*, pp. 448–9

any more than hire – but only for love.'[38] Here are the suggestions which Ruskin was to elaborate later, that the science of economics was not simply immoral, but wrong, untruthful, incorrect in its account of human nature.

This is the essential unity of Ruskin's work in art criticism, architecture and social philosophy, that all relationships must be governed by truth. It is fidelity to truth that makes him the most rigorous of critics and makes his observations the most accurate. The relationship between art, architecture and society is established by moral principles, the most important of which is truth. Architecture provides the practical link to social criticism because it is art which requires social organisation. It is also the only art form which depends upon labour, upon a distinction between the conception by an artist and execution by the labourer. The analysis of architecture brought Ruskin to an analysis of work. Architecture not only exhibited the values of society, it expressed the labour of society, it was what men made with their lives. Architecture ultimately establishes the relationship between art and the life of men. Art itself is ultimately labour:

All art which is worth its room in the world, all art which is not a piece of blundering refuse, occupying the foot or two of earth which, if unencumbered by it, would have grown corn or violets, or some better thing, is art which precedes from an individual mind, working through instruments which assist, but do not supersede, the muscular action of the human mind, upon the materials which most tenderly receive, and most securely retain, the impressions of such human labour.[39]

The value of any work of art is exactly in the ratio of the quality of humanity which has been put into it.

But art does not parasitically feed upon the labour of men; architecture is not the conception of clever men carried out by labourers who are little better than slaves:

Your business as an architect, is to calculate only on the cooperation of inferior men, to think for them, and to indicate for some of them at least such expressions of your thoughts as the weakest capacity can comprehend and the feeblest hand can execute. This is the definition of the purest architectural abstractions. They are the deep and laborious thoughts of the greatest men, put into such easy letters that they can be written by the simplest. They are the expressions of the mind of manhood by the hands of childhood.[40]

[38] ibid., p. 450
[39] Ruskin, The Stones of Venice, 9, p. 456
[40] ibid., p. 290

So architecture is not so transcendental in its importance that it is to demand the sacrifice of labour. Architecture, the noblest architecture, demands the participation[41] of labour. The best architecture is of a kind that allows subordinate labour to contribute to its effect. Ruskin's examination of social questions and of work, once entailed by his study of architecture, went so far as to displace art from the position of primary concern for men. Despite the labour of 6,000 years the result of the chief occupations of farming, weaving and building is that people still starve, lack clothing and are unhoused. Therefore, our first duty is to live on as little as we can, to do as much wholesome work as we can, that we should first feed, clothe and house people and that then we should please them with art. The belief that there are two parts to Ruskin's life and to his work, the first aesthetic, the second social, is given some kind of credence by the way in which art comes to be displaced by the social question in his concern, so that it is an activity which must be postponed until men's primary needs have been met. But it is the study of art and architecture which leads to an examination of the social question and that question itself is raised by the recognition that art, or at least architecture, is built upon labour. We would say that the social question is arrived at by two paths, the first by the moral implications of art which entail an examination of social relationships, and the second by the need to examine labour upon which architecture rests.

The unitary view of art and society which seems to have been unacceptable to the Victorians has become by now almost a commonplace. It promises to become a commonplace vice. A recent analysis of the development of doctrines based on the close relationship of architecture and society links Pugin and Stalin in their consequences, if not in their intentions. The moulding of architectural doctrine to ideological and, ultimately, doctrinaire and indoctrinating purposes is a process which, if it did not begin with, at least was vigorously carried forward by the gothic revival. Ruskin is correctly associated with the gothic revival. So Ruskin has been associated with 'the extreme mechanistic and moral justifications of architectural form associated particularly with Viollet-le-Duc and with Pugin'.[42] Watkin's attack is impressive and important and it seems, to at least one reader who lacks knowledge of the subject

---

[41] This is a word now so devalued and corrupted that it is probably necessary to say that Ruskin did not advocate democracy in art, industrial or any other kind.

[42] David Watkin, *Morality and architecture* (Oxford, Clarendon Press, 1977), p. 1.

sufficient for a reliable judgment, to be an attack soundly directed against a deserving objective. For this reason alone it seems important to try to rescue Ruskin from associations which Watkin demonstrates to be contaminating in their influence. We must understand the attack before we can attempt the rescue.

Watkin begins by suggesting that Pugin's *Contrasts* published in 1836 and Pevsner's *Pioneers of the modern movement* published in 1936 are linked by a conviction that their preferred architectural style 'is not just a style but a rational way of building evolved inevitably in response to the needs of what society is or ought to be'.[43] Pugin's preferred style was medieval gothic, he, rather than Ruskin, was the pioneer of its re-introduction on a major scale. Pevsner is regarded as the most authoritative exponent and advocate of functionalism in architecture, of 'international modern'. The theories or attitudes which Watkin develops between these two unlikely partners, separated in time by a century and in style by apparent extremes of taste, rely upon seeing architecture as representing the spirit of the age. Architecture, when it is in a healthy state, possesses a unity of expression, it is in a state of harmony with the materials it uses (it avoids surface deceit, as Ruskin would put it), it is in harmony with its technical purpose (it fits the programme) and it is in harmony with the spirit of the times. This last assertion is the most important and the most pernicious. It ought to make sense only to a Hegelian philosopher, but it has become, unfortunately, a part of received contemporary architectural thinking. It also represents a wider conviction of a moral or social attitude which was criticised by Karl Popper as 'historicism'. The conviction is so widespread that the general public has by now been persuaded that current architectural modes 'whether it likes them or not, have an authority and inevitability which it would be improper to question'.[44] Architecture comes to be disassociated from any particular style; the very idea of style as representing the taste of an individual architect or the wishes of a particular client or the fashionable predilections of a class (unless it be the proletariat represented by the Party) comes to be seen as corrupt. The culmination is in functional international modern' which is styleless and from which any deviation comes to be seen as anti-social and immoral. Pugin's intention was to make England Christian (and Catholic) by re-introducing Christian (and Catholic) architecture. Bruno Taut wrote in 1929:

[43] *ibid.*, p. 1
[44] *ibid.*, p. 6

If everything is founded on sound efficiency, then efficiency itself, or rather its utility, will form its own aesthetic law. A building must be beautiful when seen from outside if it reflects all these qualities . . . The architect who achieves this task becomes a creator of an ethical and social character.[45]

Architecture, just as it was for Pugin, becomes a socially manipulative force. Watkin says we are not told about the kind of new society which the dominant, irresistible forms of architecture are going to engender. But Pugin told us, and the modern forms are readily discernible. The new society will be positivist, socialist, planned, materialist, subject to scientific calculation, rational, bureaucratically just and convinced that any major social problems which remain are the legacy of past mistakes and are shortly to succumb to expert attack. The new society is also, by now, sadly old-fashioned, our faith in it has not survived town planning and tower blocks. Ironically, architecture has proved remarkably representative of social values in being the field in which the fatuity of positivism was most vividly demonstrated to a wide public. It only remains for architecture to rediscover style for the wheel to have turned full circle.

If Ruskin is accurately linked with this doctrine his reputation is seriously damaged. There are similarities and it will not be sufficient to point to the well-known antipathy with which Ruskin regarded 'one of the smallest of conceivable architects'. The unfairness of that judgment exemplifies Ruskin's attitude to Pugin as one of the least creditable things about him. Lord Clark said that only once again, in the whole thirty-nine large volumes of his work, does Ruskin mention Pugin, in equally uncomplimentary terms. The reasons for Ruskin's dislike are not entirely reputable and his opinion should not be regarded as reliable on a remarkable man. Garrigan explains the 'savage, tasteless vehemence' of his attacks by Pugin's Catholicism and Ruskin's temptation to conversion; Ruskin 'never quite forgave Pugin for his alarming example'.[46] Ruskin's denial of Pugin's influence or of ever having had the smallest interest in his opinions was discredited by Patrick Conner who reproduced some careful and respectful notes by Ruskin in the care of Mr B. K. Bilton, curator of the Coniston Museum.[47] There are better reasons for making a distinction. Lord Clark said that one important difference between

---

[45] *ibid.*, p. 40
[46] Kristine Ottesen Garrigan, *Ruskin on architecture, his thought and influence* (Madison, University of Wisconsin Press, 1973), p. 20
[47] P. R. M. Conner, 'Pugin and Ruskin', *Journal of the Warburg and Courtald Institute*, XLI (1978), 344–50

the two men was that Pugin was an architect and Ruskin was not. 'Pugin believed that if the construction of a factory or railway station was strong, simple and bold, the building would, *ipso facto*, be beautiful: but Ruskin's conception of beauty, so complicated, so subtle, clouded with associations and resonant with overtones, could not allow so crude a theory.'[48] Ruskin insisted that architecture consisted of sculpture and painting, if not, the architect was a mere builder. Building was important, but it was less than architecture. The modern architect, says Clark, claims only to be a builder who constructs functional buildings, buildings that 'work'; he claims also that such building will eventually establish a new style of architecture. Lord Clark's judgment was published in 1928, almost at the same time as Mies van der Rohe was saying 'We reject all aesthetic speculation, all doctrine, all formalism. Architecture is the will of an epoch translated into space' and 'we refuse to recognise problems of form but only problems of building'.[49] It is interesting that Clark, independently of Watkin and fifty years before him, puts Pugin in this tradition of 'building' and concludes that the modern doctrine of functional building 'has shown an extraordinary power of survival, and still shelters men with such different ideals as Professor Lethaby and M. le Corbusier, and nearly all the young architects of the continent have made it their gospel'.[50]

It is the same gospel with the same disciples that is attacked by Watkin and it seems reasonable to claim that Ruskin was not part of it. What distinguishes this recent orthodoxy are two closely associated doctrines. The first is that architecture represents the character of society or, in more high-flown and Hegelian terms, the spirit of the times. Because of the intimate relationship of architecture and society, because a phenomenon found always in conjunction with another is often mistakenly believed to be its cause, architecture and society are next conceived to be in a reversible relationship. Society manifests itself in architecture; architecture influences society. The second doctrine is Pugin's, the belief that architecture can transform society. It is also the modern notion that functional architecture is right for the times, that it carries special ethical authority.

Ruskin did not take this view. He certainly sees society reflected in its architecture. A strong and moral society is mirrored in good architecture, a corrupt society in a lifeless and mechanical architec-

[48] Kenneth Clark, *The gothic revival* (London, John Murray, 1974; first published 1928), p. 200
[49] Watkin, *Morality and architecture*, p. 37
[50] Clark, *The gothic revival*, p. 200

ture. Ruskin identifies the good with the gothic and the corrupt with
the renaissance. The arguments he uses to press this distinction
beyond its limits are often prejudiced and doctrinaire. As Eastlake
said: 'Mr Ruskin was continually advancing propositions, often
excellent in themselves, which he as frequently failed to
maintain – not for want of argument, but because his arguments
proved too much.'[51] The preference for a style is a matter of taste,
itself a vastly complex matter, but Watkin is right to say that the
argument for a style on grounds of unrelated principle is a rationalisation which, as Eastlake demonstrates in Ruskin's case, is often self-
contradictory and 'exposed the author to criticism which is not only
severe, but, up to a certain point justifiable', particularly to be
regretted because it meant that 'the great moral of his teaching was
overlooked'.[52] Ruskin's wrongness in detailed defence of the gothic
cannot justify his classification with critics whose intentions and
arguments were entirely different from his, simply because he shared
some of the same methodological errors.

The strongest evidence is his own repeated effort to disassociate
himself from the Gothic Revival School. On this he is consistent
almost from the outset to the end. Regretting the aspect of a dead and
rigid architecture, in 1849, he wonders if we can return to the vigour
of youth and, in a reference to the Revival he says: 'The stirring which
has taken place in our architectural aims and interests within these
last few years is thought by many to be full of promise: I trust it is, but
it has a sickly look to me.'[53] In a footnote to this passage added in 1880
Ruskin said: 'I am glad to see I had so much sense, this early.' In 1865
he said 'the architecture we endeavoured to introduce is inconsistent
alike with the reckless luxury, the deforming mechanism, and the
squalid misery of modern cities; among the formative fashions of the
day, aided, especially in England, by ecclesiastical sentiment, it
indeed obtained notoriety'.[54] He frequently regretted the slavish
imitation of the style, often on his own recommendation, while the
reason for the recommendation, the ethic that it reflected, was
forgotten. He regretted 'the partial use of it which has mottled over
manufacturing chimneys with black and red brick, dignified our
banks and drapers' shops with Venetian tracery, and pitched our

---

[51] Charles Eastlake, *A history of the gothic revival* (New York, Leicester University Press, 1970; first
   published 1872), p. 370
[52] *ibid.*, p. 271
[53] Ruskin, *The Seven Lamps of Architecture*, 8, p. 194
[54] Ruskin, *Sesame and Lilies*, 18, p. 150

parish churches into dark and slippery arrangement for the advertise-
ment of cheap coloured glass and pantiles'.[55]

The fundamental error in the gothic revival that Ruskin regretted
was surely the belief that the reproduction of the architecture created
by a moral society could reproduce a moral society. Ruskin
constantly insisted, as he did to his audience at Bradford, that it was a
matter of indifference as to what style was chosen for their Exchange.
Nothing they did could improve their architecture if all they cared
about in their lives was business: 'if you will tell me what you
ultimately intend Bradford to be, perhaps I can tell you what
Bradford can ultimately produce. But you must have your minds
clearly made up . . .'[56] And if the decision is for an infinity of mills and
quarries then we should waste no more money on backing design.
Even the introduction of a Christian architecture would have a
formal and lifeless character if it was built by an un-Christian people.
It was the moral state of society, of which its architecture could be a
gauge or indication, that was crucial.

If Ruskin is rescued from this fashionable architectural fallacy it
may be merely a regressive argument in which the attack now shifts to
the moral character of society rather than its architectural facade. It
is just as likely that Ruskin turns out to be a historicist and a
determinist, a positivist or a tyrant in terms of his analysis of society
rather than of its architecture, in terms of his recommendations for
social change rather than for style. So we must now turn to a
discussion of the values he defended and exhibited in the social theory
to which his art work led him.

[55] Ruskin, *The Stones of Venice*, 9, p. 11
[56] Ruskin, *The Two Paths*, 16, p. 335

2

Justice and authority

'I am, and my father was before me', wrote Ruskin, 'a violent Tory of the old school; – Walter Scott's that is to say, and Homer's.'[1] His toryism implied 'a most sincere love of kings, and dislike of everybody who attempted to disobey them'.[2] This assertion or boast on Ruskin's part contrasts oddly with his reputation as a radical. He was no libertarian. The general submission of all things to the law of God meant that liberty was 'a treacherous phantom . . . there is no such thing in the universe. There can never be. The stars have it not; the earth has it not; the sea has it not; and we men have the mockery and semblance of it only for our heaviest punishment.'[3] Any revolutionary notion of freedom from authority was contradictory nonsense, a prescription for disaster and an explanation of current disorder in society. Ruskin was horrified by libertarian doctrine whether he found it among the sansculottes or the economists whose doctrine of let alone conceived 'the proper state of the world to be simply that of a vast and disorganized mob, scrambling each for what he can get, trampling down its children and old men in the mire'.[4] Either conception of liberty stemmed from an arrogant misconception of man as standing above God's dominion over nature.

If ideas of liberty were a delusion, ideas of equality were a mistake. Equality amongst men is impossible because of the obvious superiority that some men have over others in terms of strength (the original explanation of landowning, the exercise of that superiority in robbery) and ability. These more obvious differences are accompanied by differences in wisdom and moral quality. It is a matter of great importance that people superior in respect to these qualities should be appointed 'to guide, to lead, or on occasion even to compel

---

[1] Ruskin, *Praeterita*, 35, p. 13
[2] Ruskin, *Fors Clavigera*, 27, p. 168
[3] Ruskin, *The Seven Lamps of Architecture*, 8, p. 248
[4] Ruskin, *A Joy for Ever*, 16, p. 115

and subdue their inferiors according to their own better knowledge and wiser will'.[5] It was wrong to expect that any man could do any work, the result of that belief (lying as it does at the heart of the doctrine of self-help) could be tragic in its consequences for those who tried to act upon it. Great work would be done by men of great qualities and would be done by them with astonishing ease. It became a necessary and important part of Ruskin's social analysis that it was right to give men work suited to their abilities and to organise work and society so that those inequalities were recognised.

It follows that Ruskin was no democrat. 'I once saw democracy firmly illustrated by the beetles of North Switzerland, who by universal suffrage, and elytric acclamation, one May twilight, carried it, that they would fly over the Lake of Zug; and flew *short*, to the great disfigurement of the Lake Zug . . . and to the close of the cockchafer democracy for that year.'[6] He attacked the idea 'that everybody can be uppermost; or at least that a state of general scramble, in which everybody in his turn should come to the top, is a proper Utopian constitution'.[7] Ruskin's ideal state of affairs was far removed from such perpetual restlessness and was not too far from that state of settled agrarian stability which was believed to have been destroyed with the onset of industrialism.

Ruskin's critical attitude to democracy is very much that of Plato. The counting of heads is not likely to secure wisdom or justice in government. Ruskin would add that it is almost certain to bring about that banality in affairs which the doctrine of utilitarianism had contributed to Victorian society. The preferred alternative to seeking the opinion of a majority of the unwise and the ill-informed is also Plato's, to secure by what means can be found, the wisest and best of citizens and to educate them rigorously in principles of truth and justice. The programme has the attractive simplicity and the dangers of Plato's recommendations concerning the rule by philosopher kings. If our rulers are chosen because of their wisdom and are educated to respect truth and to accept responsibility then it will be a safe and a necessary duty for us to obey them. Justice, authority and obedience are essential ingredients in Ruskin's conception of government and leadership.

Ruskin's constant concern (just as it was to be Durkheim's) was the re-establishment of commercial activity within the moral order and

[5] Ruskin, *Unto this Last*, 17, p. 74
[6] Ruskin, *Munera Pulveris*, 17, p. 249
[7] Ruskin, *Time and Tide*, 17, p. 397

moral relationships of society; the establishment of just commercial relationships. Ruskin believed that competitive business activity had not only destroyed traditional Christian society but had overcome any remaining vestige of moral control. Contrary to some opinions, his concern was not to suppress commerce and industry but to control it within a re-established moral network of behaviour.

He quotes from a Jewish merchant who made an enormous fortune on the Gold Coast and who left business maxims which were, said Ruskin, deeply respected by the Venetians. In a discussion of these maxims and their translation, Ruskin dismisses the word 'justness' but he dismisses it because it is clumsy. The idea that is being conveyed is actually 'righteousness', he says, but that word has now become confused with godliness, even, we may say, with sanctity or self-righteousness. It used to refer, he says, to the justice of rule or of right. '"Righteousness" means, accurately and simply "justice".'[8] In *Unto this Last* he distinguishes between the justice of rule or right and 'equity' or the justice of balance; the former (righteousness) is king's justice, the latter (equity) is judge's justice. It seems that the former is absolute whereas the latter is measured and contingent, the former is universal, the latter specific. The implication of Ruskin's scattered discussion of this matter seems to be that judge's justice has come to replace king's justice. The distinction seems to relate to a difference which we often acknowledge, when we speak of the 'legitimate exercise of authority' or the 'legitimacy of rules'. Authority which is not legitimate will often be obeyed and rules which lack legitimacy will often be observed. This is partly because of the power exercised by the authority or available for the enforcement of the rules. But it may also result from a 'respect' for the authority or the rules. Thus the fact that we obey rules enforced by the police is not entirely explained by our fear of the power they exercise, we do not travel at 70 m.p.h. in a built-up area whenever we think we will not be caught. Our respect (approximate though it may be) for speed limits is a measure of legitimacy, of respect for equitable law, but it is not a recognition of a moral law. In certain circumstances, the equitable calculation will be broken without moral compunction. There are no circumstances in which moral rules ('king's law') may be broken, at least without compunction. A much more significant example of these distinctions is found in the rules of work where agreements and disciplinary rules will be accepted as legitimate without a recognition

---

[8] Ruskin, *Fors Clavigera*, 27, p. 145

of their moral authority. Leaving work early is an offence against 'judge's law'; blacklegging against 'king's law'.

Ruskin sees justice as a moral sentiment of what is owed to other men, 'such affection as one man *owes* to another'.[9] But it is quite clear that the debt is not the subject of careful calculation although the nature of the debt is, to some extent, determined by the action of other men in that it must reward virtue and be vindictive to vice:

> it is the national expression of deliberate anger, as of deliberate gratitude; it is not exemplary, or even corrective, but essentially retributive; it is the absolute art of measured response, giving honour where honour is due, and shame where shame is due and joy where joy is due and pain where pain is due. It is neither educational, for men are to be educated by wholesome habit, not by rewards and punishment, nor is it preventative, for it is to be executed without regard to any consequences; but only for righteousness' sake, a righteous nation does judgment and justice.[10]

It is not calculated, yet it is to be a measured response? The appearance of contradiction lies in the precise meaning of 'calculated'. Justice is not to be calculated in the sense that it must not look forward to a planned or expected response from others which is to be elicited by our own measured behaviour towards them:

> For no human actions ever were intended by the maker of men to be guided by balances of expediency, but by balances of justice. He has therefore rendered all endeavours to determine expediency futile for evermore. No man ever knew, or can know what will be the ultimate result to himself, or to others, of any given line of conduct. But every man may know, and most of us do know, what is a just and unjust act.[11]

The external mechanism of justice is based upon false principles, upon the assumption that what is incalculable is calculable, upon the erroneous belief that men are engines, the motive power of which is calculable. The motive force which drives men is affection and that force dries up in the face of any attempt at calculation. The result is that the tradition of mechanical, calculated justice leads to the opposite of its intention, to injustice. True justice 'consists mainly in the granting to every human being due aid in the development of such faculties as it possesses for action and enjoyment'.[12] More than once Ruskin says that just relationships are exemplified in employment and that the consequences of unjust relationships can also be best seen

[9] Ruskin, *Unto this Last*, 17, p. 28
[10] Ruskin, *Lectures on Art*, 20, p. 89
[11] Ruskin, *Unto this last*, 17, p. 28
[12] Ruskin, *Fors Clavigera*, 27, p. 147

in relationships between master and servant. Good work is done when affection is elicited by love. The mistaken view taken by the economist and by too many businessmen is that good work is a matter of careful calculation and control, of payment by results.

The difference in these views as they applied to employment was clearly shown in a correspondence between Ruskin and the editor of the *Pall Mall Gazette* in 1865 (the correspondence, incidentally, also illustrates Ruskin's awesome talent as a vituperative contro-versialist).[13]

The 'official view' taken by the *Gazette* was that 'justice' and 'right' are law terms implying the existence of fixed rules which confer powers and impose commands. Unless and until a contract has been made between employer and employee 'neither side has any rights nor can anything be said to be just between them', it all concerns the fulfilment of a compulsory agreement about 'the wages which you force the men to take, and they can force you to pay'. The view is remarkably similar to the common view today that justice has precious little to do with collective bargaining, which is largely a matter of the distribution of power, and that justice is a matter to be referred to only when there is an enforceable contract between the parties. Justice, for the *Pall Mall Gazette*, was the conformity of an action to any rules whatever, good or bad, and that good rules were those that promoted the general happiness of those whom they affect. So, says Ruskin, the relevance of force means that it will be just to get a man to give me £100 for throwing him a rope when he has fallen through the ice and, if justice is the conformity to any rule, 'justice . . . may as often as not promote the general misery of those who practise it'. Ruskin points out the 'ordinary distinction' between law and equity on the one hand, and Divine and human law on the other. He accuses the *Gazette* of regarding 'are' and 'ought to be' as alike in meaning. 'That wages *are* determined by supply and demand is no proof that under any circumstances they must be, – still less that under all circumstances they ought to be.' Ruskin asks whether notions of duty are entirely meaningless in relation to justice and whether, as far as the *Gazette* is concerned, it is an open question to be settled 'only upon evidence whether we will live as pirates, pedlars, or as gentlemen'.

Ruskin asserts that there is an absolute idea of a duty or 'devoir' in

[13] A typical barb is Ruskin's apology 'for having accused you of writing carelessly, I must hope your pardon; for the discourtesy, in my mind, would have been in imagining you to be writing with care' (*Time and Tide*, 17, p. 516).

the relations between one man and another and of any honourable man to himself. It is the Sinaitic equity of returning good for good, evil for evil: 'does a man take of your life, you take also of his'. We shall see later that Ruskin regarded labour as in some sense the giving up of life so that, in this sense, the calculation of wage was not a sufficient return from the employer. But there is a more ominous, chiliastic ring to the end of his last letter, a measure that was to beat more insistently as his optimism gave way to despair about the condition of society. If the law of careful retaliation was not replaced by the law of grace the consequence would be terrible. The latter is not to be calculated but if it is ignored it becomes the law of the wolf and the locust. 'The workmen of England – of the world, ask for the return – as of wrath, so of reward by law; and for blood resolutely spent, as for that recklessly shed; for life devoted through its duration, as for that untimely cast away; they require from you to determine in judgment, the equities of "Human Retribution".'[14]

Justice required the exercise of responsibility by authority or else it would be extracted from it. Ruskin's warnings on this account became more and more insistent. They were not untypical of the response of the Victorian intellectual to the social upheaval caused by the industrial revolution. The Church of England furnished several representatives who either denounced the morality of the times, like Southey in *Sir Thomas More*, or made a more or less unctuous appeal to the goodness of the upper classes, like Charles Kingsley in his Preface to *Alton Lock*. But the responsibility that Ruskin believed to be necessary was demanded not supplicated, its want was contrasted with the behaviour of true leaders in society of the past and the consequences of its continued withholding from social relationships was prophesied in apocalyptic terms.

Ruskin says that there are five great intellectual professions in a civilised nation, those of the soldiers who defend it, the pastors who teach it, the physicians who keep it in health, the lawyers who enforce its justice, and the merchants who provide for it. Each profession acquires status and respect because of the duty undertaken by its members and this means an acknowledgement that, on due occasion, each will die for it. The soldier will die rather than leave his post in battle, the physician rather than leave his post in plague, the pastor rather than teach falsehood, the lawyer rather than countenance injustice. And what is the due occasion of death for the merchant?

14 *ibid.*, p. 517

The absurdity of the question is the explanation of the greater respect that is paid to the professions than to trade; it has nothing to do with the intellectual demands of their work, of which Ruskin had no great opinion. Our estimate of the soldier 'is based on this ultimate fact . . . that put him in a fortress breach, with all the pleasures of the world behind him, and only death and his duty in front of him, he will keep his face to the front'. Whereas 'the merchant is presumed to act always selfishly. His work may be very necessary to the community; but the motive of it is understood to be wholly personal. The merchant's first object in all his dealings must be (the public believe) to get as much for himself and leave as little to his neighbour (or customer) as possible.'[15] The explanation of the high status of the professions and the low opinion of business remains, incidentally, valid in terms of the attitude of contemporary students, which is such a source of worry to representatives of business and for which they wrongly blame Marxist influence in universities. Business, despite its manifest utility, does nothing to satisfy the sense of duty in the young. The great advantage of Marxism over management in this respect, is that it seems to demand self-sacrifice rather than ambition.

Ruskin is certainly not sneering at trade as an occupation unworthy of a gentleman. His father, John James, whom he loved and respected and who acted as his literary agent and advisor, had spent his life in trade, successfully enough to ensure John Ruskin's independence. The epitaph he set upon his father's grave was: 'He was an entirely honest merchant.'

Ruskin's concern is that the understandable contempt for trade should cease, that we must find 'a kind of commerce which is not exclusively selfish', that will admit 'that sixpences have to be lost as well as lives under a sense of duty'.[16] The idea has to be established that it is no more the function of the merchant or the manufacturer to get profit than it is of the clergyman to work for his stipend. Both the merchant and the manufacturer provide services vital to society and bear a responsibility for the many lives with which they are involved. Ruskin argues that for the employer to re-establish that concern and responsibility for the employee would go far to repair the moral damage that had been done to society and the contempt in which the merchant was generally held.

There are two characteristic steps in this argument that are not

[15] Ruskin, *Unto this Last*, 17, p. 38
[16] *ibid.*, p. 39

confined to Ruskin. The first concerns damage, with the clear implication that what was once whole has been destroyed. The second concerns repair which is made contingent upon an infusion of moral responsibility into what have become self-interested and calculating relationships. Both these steps are representative of major pre-occupations in post-industrial social theory. Both are admirably summarised and equally well-exhibited by Alan Fox.

Pre-industrial society, says Fox, was characterised by status contract rather than by purposive contract (a distinction made by Max Weber), in which continuous and stable relationships are established upon diffuse commitments and obligations and in which expected behaviour is rarely specified. As markets and mobility develop 'relations become increasingly marked by specific short-term reciprocation – by economic as against social exchange'.[17] The individual's sense of responsibility for the discharge of his obligations is diminished as economic replace social relationships and become more depersonalised and more dependent upon restraint, definition and arms-length negotiation. Economic exchange becomes more typical and is accompanied by 'grudging concession and wary mutual inspection', it encourages the growth of doctrines which separate economics and ethics, utility and morality. These changes are reflected by legal changes in which the old legal analogy of employment to master-and-servant relationship, appropriate to the family enterprise and the engagement of apprentices, and redolent of status exchange, a besieged by industrialism and economic development and gives way to the contract of employment. Ultimately, 'the worker receives a defined... rate for the job whereas the employer receives an impalpable potentiality whose ultimate development and fruits it is largely for him to determine'.[18]

The first question is whether this account is accurate. There is an enormous weight of scholarship to suggest that it is. The destruction by capitalism (or by technology: the distinction comes to have great ideological significance) of the stable social relationships of the traditional (medieval) world by the establishment of paramount economic relationships which are transient, restless and revolutionary, is at the heart of received contemporary opinion, established there by authorities whose disagreements make their accord in this

[17] Alan Fox, *Beyond contract: work, power and trust relations* (London, Faber and Faber, 1974), p. 157
[18] *ibid.*, p. 190

account all the more impressive. When Marx, Weber and Durkheim agree it leaves little room for sociological contention.

There is some room for doubt, however, as to whether economic exchange and contract has entirely replaced social exchange and obligation. Historical evidence suggests that, in the fourteenth century, business was conducted in an entirely business-like fashion and that contract and calculation were not absent from men's affairs. The fact is that while economic exchange was not absent from the middle ages, social exchange is not absent from the nineteenth and twentieth centuries. Calculation and economic exchange may be more characteristic of modern than ancient times, but a statement of this sort is peculiarly difficult to endow with anything like precise meaning. What is more certainly true, by way of comparison between the two eras, is that economic exchange comes to be regarded as a model for all human relationships in modern times whereas, in former times, it was consigned to a subordinate and even a suspected area of activity. It may be that in both periods the employer and the businessmen have come to believe that contracts, agreements and work rules are a manifestation of purely economic exchange and that they can govern relationships and conduct in these terms. The belief reached its highest expression, perhaps in Herbert Spencer, who believed:

that mutual dependence of parts which we see in social organization, as in individual organization, is possible only on condition that while each other part does the particular kind of work it has become adjusted to, it receives its proportion of those materials required for repair and growth, which all the other parts have joined to produce; such proportion being settled by bargaining. Moreover, it is by fulfilment of contract that there is effected a balancing of all the various products to the various needs.[19]

It may equally have been the intention of work rules that they should precisely govern conduct in that golden age of stable social relationships, the middle ages. One belief is that they were no more successful then than now. Then, as now, the contest might have been between masters who were trying to convert social into economic relationships and men who would not let them. What may have distinguished the middle ages from modern times was not the intention or outlook of the employer but the moral constraints imposed upon him by a dominant religion and the material

[19] Donald Mácrae (ed.), *Herbert Spencer, the man versus the State* (Harmondsworth, Penguin Books, 1969), p. 176

constraints set by the size of markets. What may distinguish our own times is that the employer has been persuaded that the effort is worthwhile by the collapse of those constraints.

The transcendence established by economic relationships in modern society leads to a search for those steps that need to be taken in order to restore a measure of stability and harmony to social relationships. The consequences of the damage believed to be done in the modern world by the production of low-trust relationships are 'suspicion, jealousy, the misreading of men's motives . . . the inhibition to cooperation, the blockages created in the handling of differences and disagreements; the blight in fellowship and comparison; the withering of community'.[20] There are good grounds for believing that the consequences are as exaggerated as was the idealisation of pre-industrial society and the account of its destruction. The apocalyptic vision of a wholesome society destroyed but to be reborn seems to be inseparable from sociology, at least since Marx.

A society based purely on rational economic calculation has never been achieved. Fox gives several accounts of the preference for continued diffuse relationships which may accompany contractual relationships between businessmen, among members of a profession and between Japanese employees and employers. It seems at least possible to argue that the conception of a specified and calculative relationship is incompatible with the kind of co-operation that the employer normally requires from his employees. This is not to say that the model of the purposive contract is a figment or is unreal but that the model has been given an exaggerated significance and is taken, as Spencer took it, to be the type of all relationships in an industrial society. There are several reasons for this exaggeration. It is, in the first place, 'only' a theoretical abstraction which, in the hands of Max Weber, produces accurate insight into real developments and changes in society. It is not, solely on that account, a definitive statement of relationships to which there are no, or few exceptions. In the second place, it is our acknowledgement of the importance of calculation and control techniques as monitors of the performance of others in crucial situations. The 'others' may be parties to contractual obligations, trustees or employees. The techniques of control have certainly developed to an enormous extent with the growth of the world of economic activity, but it would be wrong to assume that

---

[20] Fox, *Beyond contract*, p. 317

these techniques are the only means of measuring or, worse still, of influencing performance.

To a certain extent industrial society is probably much as it was. One measure of guessing at its unchanging nature is to look at some of the features which anthropologists have found to be important in primitive societies and to attempt to evaluate their importance in our own. If we take Gouldner's account (based on evidence from anthropology) of what he calls the norm of reciprocity we see that reciprocity (the recognition that each party in a relationship has rights and duties) 'is a mutually gratifying pattern of exchanging goods and services' which entails mutual dependence.[21] The norm of reciprocity rests upon two minimal requirements: that people should help those who have helped them and that people should not injure those who have helped them. It imposes obligations in response to benefits conferred by others and Gouldner suggests that the obligations of repayments are contingent upon the imputed value of the benefit received. But the calculation takes into account moral as well as exchange elements; it varies with the intensity of the recipient's need ('a friend in need . . .'), the resources of the donor ('the widow's mite'), the motives imputed to the donor ('without thought of gain . . .') and the constraints present or absent ('he gave of his own free will . . .'). The norm of reciprocity serves to undermine or to mediate bureaucratic impersonality and it extends bonds and relationships over time. Gifts (or reciprocal debts of service or gratitude) are not returned immediately, the period can extend to a year and, in this time, 'men are morally constrained to manifest their gratitude toward, or at least to maintain peace with, their benefactors'. Because there is no precise calculation in reciprocity (indeed, evidence of precise calculation would destroy the 'value' of the reciprocal exchange), the requirement for only rough equivalence of repayment 'induces a certain amount of ambiguity as to whether indebtedness has been repaid and, over time, generates uncertainty about who is in whose debt'. This very indeterminacy generates stability.

Anyone with personal experience of life in a village or small community will recognise the complex web of relationships of obligation which are constructed in this way. They will also acknowledge the sanctions and feuds which accompany instances in which the obligation of repayment has not been met or has been deemed to be insufficient; all is not idyllic peace. But are these relationships confined to small and stable communities and, if there is an analogy with Ruskin's view of social relationships, are both irrelevant to relationships in large industrial communities? The answer is that there is no simple opposition of large and small communities. All communities are small, even a rolling mill or a motor car factory is composed of groups whose members are in face-to-face relationships and who will need to establish some stability in their relationships. The 'contract', negotiated between the union and the company, is an arrangement remote from the workplace and often ineffective in the control that it exercises over the behaviour of men or managers. The contract or negotiated agreement has important functions in providing minimum obligations for the employer (the payment of a minimum wage) and for the employee (attendance for a minimum number of hours at given times) but the actual performance of the parties is governed by a whole host of unwritten understandings and arrangements, some of which are summed up in the most evocative of all phrases in industrial relations, 'custom and practice'. It implies a considerable degree of stability built upon mutual understanding and obligation. The relationships between the representatives of work groups and managers are usually even more clearly marked by acknowledged reciprocity. Although the result is a degree of stability which could not be achieved by constant reference to the negotiated contract, the manner in which stability is achieved is ephemeral in the sense that it is not recorded and often not even articulated. It represents the unwritten sub-culture of work and, unlike the contracts and agreements, it leaves no record. For this reason it must be guesswork unsupported by evidence to suggest that work has always been controlled, as it is today, by unwritten understandings, informal arrangements and diffuse rather than specific relationships. But the contracts made between men have survived although their effect on those men's lives may have been small. All trace of the moral sentiment between them has vanished although it may have bound their lives.

Theorists who claim to bring the methods of science to bear on society are naturally prone to exaggerate the value of evidence, particularly when it seems to conform to their own valuation of the importance of measurement and calculation; scientists of society may be predisposed to see a calculative relationship between its members. Ruskin's contention is that moral reciprocity and affection are much more the normal characteristic of human relationships than the economist's theory or the *Pall Mall Gazette*'s ideology would acknowledge. His complaint is that the business version of human affairs actually sets out to pervert what is natural and normal in human conduct. Men normally display trust, affection and reciprocity in their affairs and where they do not they recognise that they should, to the extent that they impose retributive punishment upon each other (or, as Gouldner puts it, they resort to negative forms of reciprocity; Gouldner, like Ruskin, explains those sanctions by reference to the old Roman *lex talionis*). But the business ideology reverses this account, it says men behave in a selfish and calculating fashion towards each other and, even if they do not, they should. What essentially distinguishes Victorian England from the Christian Europe of the middle ages is not that men and social relations were much better earlier and got infinitely worse. It is, rather, that Christian doctrine was based on a more truthful account of their relationships which also set a pattern for its improvement. The doctrine of Victorian England was based upon a 'damned lie' and tended to reduce their relationship to the bestial. The people whose view of human conduct is 'bestial', says Ruskin, are those 'whose natural stupidity is enhanced always by their settled purpose of maintaining the interests of Fraud and Force', and he explains in a footnote to this passage that he means by those interests what is often referred to as 'the framework of society'.[22] The paradoxical result of the triumph of selfishness was that while business flourished and was regarded as the model of human affairs it was generally despised by the greater part of humanity. The paradox, too, was that it actually turned out to be bad business because it was based on a false view of humanity. The motive force of the worker is his soul or his affection which the economist's calculation is incapable of assessing or engaging. 'Treat the servant kindly, with the idea of turning his gratitude to account, and you will get, as you deserve, no gratitude, nor any value for your kindness; but treat him kindly without any economical purpose, and all economical purposes will be answered.'[23]

This is not only a good example of Ruskin's paradox, it is an admirably clear explanation of the error and the ineffectiveness of modern programmes of enlightened employment. They fail to motivate the employee because the motivation of the employer is

---

[22] Ruskin, *Fors Clavigera*, 29, p. 199
[23] Ruskin, *Unto this Last*, 17, p. 31

faulty. At least, the employer's motivation is not what it claims to be, an interest in the health, happiness and welfare of the employee; those are secondary and instrumental considerations to the achievement of the employee's greater productivity and the employer's greater profit. All hope of moral reciprocity is instantly destroyed; the employer gets, as he deserves, no value for his kindness. His policy can be readily identified as prudential and self-interested and it instantly loses its motivational power. Ruskin tells us that the employer's behaviour towards his employees must be just, it concerns duties which attach to the role of employer. Ruskin would agree, I think, that:

a moral practice is not a prudential act concerned with the success of the enterprises of agents; it is not instrumental to the achievement of any substantive purpose or to the satisfaction of any substantive want. No doubt there may be advantages to be enjoyed in subscribing to its conditions: perhaps honesty is the best policy; perhaps speaking the truth is a condition of all durable association for the satisfaction of wants. But a moral practice, unlike an instrumental practice, does not stand condemned if no such advantages were to accrue. Indeed, recognizing and subscribing to those conditions may be expected to add to the cost of those transactions.[24]

Ruskin insists that the activities of employers and businessmen must be subjected to moral regulation. The manner in which it is to be done is perilous. It requires the recognition that 'all human government is nothing else than the executive expression of . . . Divine authority . . . the executive fulfilment by formal human methods, of the will of the Father of mankind respecting His children'.[25]

The proposed practical expression of this authority was to be outlined by Ruskin in *Time and Tide* and, in more desultory fashion, in *Fors Clavigera*. It entailed the regulation of marriage to promote the physical and mental health of children, a programme of national education, a fairly rigid system of guild government in industry, salaried office for merchants and dealers, a measure of public ownership and control, and the moral oversight of the citizenry to be conducted by the bishops. We shall have later occasion to look at his practical proposals. Suffice it to say for the moment, that, with the exception of his stranger Episcopalian or eugenic proposals, Ruskin's foresight has been widely acknowledged and he has been frequently identified as one of the founders of welfare state socialism and as

---

[24] Michael Oakeshott, *On human conduct* (Oxford University Press, 1975), p. 60
[25] Ruskin, *A Joy for Ever*, 16, p. 105

recommending the provision of commonplace amenities such as the provision of free libraries, museums and art galleries. Ruskin's standing as a social reformer has always been high.

Recent concern about the benign but universal influence of government in the lives of its citizens, the more malevolent threat of governments engaging absolute power and great moral conviction and the nightmare political visions of George Orwell, have combined to re-establish a suspicion of state power which the work of Ruskin and others had largely overcome. It is not, by now, his practical proposals for change which are of great interest. The real concern is with his argument for a moral revolution and for the agent that will carry it through. Ruskin tells us that moral relationships must be re-established in a commercial society which has destroyed them. It is all very well for him to assure us that authority need not be placed in the hands of one person, one group or one class, as long as the nation establishes 'authority over itself, vested either in kings or councils or laws, which it must resolve to obey, even at times when the law or authority appears irksome to the body of the people, or injurious to certain masses of it'. The law must become positive as well as merely punitive, it must be a government which will become paternal as well as judicial, a government which will

direct us in our occupations, protect us against our follies, and visit us in our distresses: a government which shall repress dishonesty, as now it punishes theft; which shall show how the discipline of the masses may be brought to aid the toils of peace, as discipline of the masses has hitherto knit the sinews of battle; a government which shall have its soldiers of the ploughshare as well as the soldiers of the sword.[26]

These soldiers of the plough is a favourite idea of Ruskin's. It represents, in some way, that same nostalgia for a stable society united by legitimate authority and moral bonds in which all activities including those of the labourer were invested with moral feelings and a sense of duty. It is a vision perpetually vulgarised when politicians and businessmen appeal to dockers or motor car assembly workers to demonstrate what they call the spirit of Dunkirk. But the vision is not itself vulgar. The comparison of a trade dispute and the legend of Agincourt or Dunkirk is atrocious precisely because, as Ruskin says, the one is vulgar and the other is heroic. Ruskin wants to invest work with decency, even heroism.

But how is it to be done? A real attempt has been made by the

[26] *ibid.*, pp. 25–6

Soviet Union and the People's Republic of China. Russian expressionist art of the 1930s and Stackhanovite labour programmes were clearly concerned to establish the heroism of labour. George Bernard Shaw actually believed that the nearest practical application of Ruskin's ideal society was to be found in the Russian bolshevik regime of the 1920s.[27] The potential of totalitarian similarity is obvious. The intentions, however, are quite contradictory. The Soviet Union was (its present intention is more doubtful) concerned to bring about a classless society, or at least a society in which the proletariat would be dominant. Ruskin is convinced that the proletariat must be reconciled to the enjoyment of least power, least privilege and, by and large, the worst jobs. Social and political transformation to induce either greater liberty for the proletariat or greater power is illogical and wrong. But the continued subjugation and exploitation of workmen and their families in that subordinate social position is equally wrong. Ruskin's social proposals were largely concerned to right that wrong and to legitimate that position of subordination. One of the most serious criticisms of contemporary society was the almost universal restless striving of everyone to 'better themselves'. A healthy and stable society would at least exhibit a measure of content. To achieve it there had to be a great measure of social reform. Ruskin's social proposals were designed to achieve it. More important, there had to be a measure of moral reform.

In a sense, the least satisfactory aspect of Ruskin's social work consists of his proposals for practical reform and, in any case, the construction of the Welfare State since 1911 has consigned it to historical insignificance. The usual claim for Ruskin is that his proposals have been implemented. That claim must also acknowledge the danger which it carries of an insidious growth in state influence over all aspects of social life, a danger identified by Belloc in *The Servile State*. The moral reforms which he saw as of central importance and of which the social reform was a mere manifestation, has never been attempted and we are probably as far from its serious consideration now as we were in Ruskin's lifetime.

In the next chapter we will begin an examination of the distance that Ruskin saw separating a moral society from his own. The examination begins with that society which for Ruskin, as for Carlyle and William Morris, marked the extreme of comparison with nineteenth-century capitalist society and which was epitomised in the nature of gothic.

[27] George Bernard Shaw, *Ruskin's politics* (London, Christophers, 1921)

3

The nature of gothic

The sixth chapter of the second volume of *The Stones of Venice*, 'The nature of gothic', represents the fusion of Ruskin's aesthetic and social concern; just as neither element is separable from the other throughout his work, both are present in this chapter. Ruskin came to describe it as the most important in the whole book, as 'the creed, if it be not the origin, of a new industrial school of thought'. It made a profound and immediate impact on Burne-Jones and William Morris when they read it at Oxford. It was printed as an introduction to the men who attended the Working Men's College in London in 1854 when 400 copies were given free to the first attendants. Its most famous and influential separate publication was by William Morris with his own introduction at the Kelmscott Press in 1892.

'The nature of gothic' summarises and represents Ruskin's attitude to the historical past and to the contemporary condition of labour. The first, backward-looking characteristic is not Ruskin's alone. It is demonstrated in his 'master' Carlyle's *Past and Present*, in which present-day industrial squalor is contrasted with the settled and seemly administration of the Abbey of St Edmundsbury in Suffolk, and in Southey's account of the ghost of Sir Thomas More returning to harangue the age. It became almost a part of the intellectual tradition of the nineteenth century for every well-meaning critic or cleric, in revolt against the worship of Mammon, to look back affectionately to Old England. The type is gently lampooned by Peacock in the person of Mr Chainmail in *Crotchet Castle*. It probably reached its final and most exaggerated literary form in the work of William Morris. The contrast between Past and Present had been published by Carlyle in 1843. It had been given vivid illustration in A. W. Pugin's *Contrasts* in 1836. Shrimpton argues that the comparison of the medieval hierarchical social system to the disadvantage of modern competitive individualism had become an established technique of political analysis characterised by Carlyle in 1838 as

'Gotzism', after Goethe. It was because the genre had already become dated that Ruskin moved on, says Shrimpton, to a study of contemporary political issues conducted in a new poetic and visionary style.[1] But by then Ruskin had become associated and is now dismissed with a school believed to be concerned with the re-establishment of maypoles and Morris dancing and characterised by nostalgia for a medieval past that never was.

The association is unfair and the dismissal is unjust. Ruskin's admiration for gothic architecture is not imitative, it is based on the reasoned belief that it required forms of social organisation and forms of manual labour that are superior to those of contemporary society and that it reflected a social pattern based upon values which are essential to human development and happiness. Ruskin never says that medieval society is to be reconstructed in England and he specifically warned that such an intention was ill-founded. He had certainly advocated the gothic style for domestic and civic as well as ecclesiastical building but he quickly came to regret the impetus he had given to the gothic revival and his responsibility for a rash of meaningless gothic imitation in churches, shops and public houses.

Ruskin saw virtues in the constructional principles of gothic architecture and in the building methods which it employed. In particular, as we shall see, he believed that medieval architecture gave opportunities to the least talented to express themselves in magnificent creations which transcended the humble contributions of ordinary men. It must be acknowledged that, in several respects, his account of the gothic was either exaggerated or inaccurate. If Ruskin is not guilty of the romantic nostalgia of some of his contemporaries about the middle ages it may be because his admiration was concentrated and rationalised in his appreciation of gothic architec-ture. This appreciation is expressed in the most unsentimental terms. Every aspect of every feature of gothic building is subjected to intense scrutiny, meticulous measurement and exhaustive classification. The frequent contradictions which resulted were amicably observed by Eastlake and more severely commented upon by other architects. There is even some perversity in Ruskin's championship of Italian gothic, untypical as it is of the architecture of the European middle ages and 'permeated by the survival of Roman forms of antiquity'.[2] That characteristic of the gothic to which Ruskin attributed so much

[1] Nick Shrimpton, '"Rust and dust": Ruskin's pivotal work', in Robert Hewison (ed.), New approaches to Ruskin (London, Routledge and Kegan Paul, 1981), p. 52
[2] John Harvey, The master builders (London, Thames and Hudson, 1971), p. 54

importance, the discretion and inventiveness which it permitted
subordinate craftsmen and workmen, may well have been exaggerated. It seems that:

from at least as far back as the twelfth century the architect, or master mason
was accustomed to provide drawings of such details as the mouldings of
arches and tracery of windows. It follows that he was responsible not only for
the general plan of the building but also for a large proportion of its detail,
and that therefore the individual working mason did not have so free a hand
or so large a share in the development of the scheme as some writers have
imagined.[3]

And by the beginning of the fifteenth century it was becoming
customary, apparently, for the builders of churches to buy stock
mouldings from the quarries.[4] But by then, says Ruskin, the gothic is
in decay.

By reference to other fundamental principles of good workmanship, the gothic was never quite impeccable. Many medieval
buildings failed to pass the most elementary test of sound construction, they fell down. Workmanship was sometimes shoddy and
frequently the subject of complaint: 'it is refreshingly clear that bad
workmanship is not the monopoly of our own generation . . . if the
British workman of the present day is not as good as he used to be, he
probably never was'.[5] Gothic building was neither innocent of that
vice of large-scale organised work, the division of labour. A list of the
trades and occupations involved in gothic building is formidable,
each craft working with a particular material, like stone or wood, is
subdivided into specialist trades. The elite free-mason (so called,
perhaps, because he worked on free stone which could be carved) was
followed by layers, setters, wallers, rough-layers, hard hewers,
quarriers, marblers, polishers, and a host of associated trades like
plasterers, pargeters, daubers, whitewashers, paviours and, ultimately, bricklayers.

John Unrau adds a more serious criticism of Ruskin's treatment of
the gothic by attacking the social metaphor which it was intended to
provide. After making comic hay of some of Ruskin's exaggerations
(which 'amount in accumulated effect to demonstrable falsehood') he
concludes that 'the explanation lies in the "collaborative intro-
spection" which works upon writer and reader to make prejudice

---

[3] L. F. Salzman, *Building in England* (Oxford University Press, 1952), p. 22
[4] *ibid.*, p. 123
[5] *ibid.*, p. 29

seem like established truth, a process of self-hypnosis which provides a
sobering insight into Victorian class consciousness'.[6] The disabling
presence of 'class consciousness' is revealed in Ruskin's 'improper'
introduction of the Victorian labourer, 'a fallen creature, utterly
dependent upon his superiors for any morsel of spiritual sustenance
which may aid his regeneration'. The result is that Ruskin's accuracy
of observation and his commonsense is drowned in a 'deluge of social
conscience'.

There is some truth in this view although there is a suspicion that it
emerges from the current belief, true to the old tradition, of there
being two Ruskin's; that he was a sound aesthetic scholar spoilt by his
meddling in social affairs (it is sometimes even suggested that John
James was right to forbid his son's economic criticism and that the
younger Ruskin went to pieces after the old man's death). The
criticism is sound to the extent that Ruskin's purpose in using the
gothic for social criticism explained and probably demanded inaccuracy in its description. There is no doubt that his accuracy
suffered from his purpose, that is to say, that he was no mere academic
using a tape-measure to produce a thesis. If he had stuck to his thesis
his reputation might by now be safe but obscure.

A different judgment comes from Garrigan who also acknowledges
his occasional inaccuracy but explains that the contrasts he drew
'never consist of equal pairs, both quantities are frequently stated
extremely, and one side is clearly meant to be unattractive or
untenable. It is indicative that the contrast at the very heart of his
social criticism is Life/Death.'[7] She adds that the real value of
Ruskin's account of '"the Nature of Gothic" lies not in its moving, if
eccentric creation of Gothic as a style of architecture, but in its
interpretation of Gothic as a way of life'.[8] From the later volumes of
Modern Painters on, she says, Ruskin is always operating at two levels,
while his ostensible purpose is artistic analysis the principles he
enunciates are of symbolic significance. Ruskin is always talking
about the just distribution of resources, first in his work on art, last in
society. His work on art and architecture, she concludes, provides a
kind of 'metaphoric clothing' for more fundamental ideas about
human society.

We must defer discussions of Unrau's comments on Ruskin's

[6] John Unrau, 'Ruskin, the workmen and the savageness of gothic', in Hewison (ed.), *New
approaches to Ruskin*, pp. 43-4
[7] Garrigan, *Ruskin on architecture*, p. 41
[8] *ibid.*, p. 102

condescension to the Victorian worker but it would not do, mean-time, to dismiss Ruskin's architectural account of the gothic as worthless. If Ruskin is constructing a paradigm it has a basis in reality. If Ruskin exaggerates characteristics in gothic architecture and building methods those features were there to be exaggerated. The work of raising the great cathedrals was sometimes shared by the whole community, the master builders carrying out the design and organisation, the craftsmen the skilled work, and monks and inhabitants of the locality contributing unskilled labour. The master builder or architect, enjoying as much 'professional' prestige as his modern counterpart, possessed the distinction from the true pro-fessional of having come up through the trade, having worked on the tools of the craft: the master masons did no manual work but 'they were at least capable of doing it, having graduated usually as apprentices and always as working masons'.[9]

Ruskin was right also to suggest that gothic architecture was characterised by the vigour and freedom of its decoration and was markedly different from the regimental order of the renaissance style which superseded it. The contrast which Ruskin emphasised is put more judiciously by Harvey:

One of the profound changes which most clearly separates the quality of Gothic art from the Romanesque is an emphasis upon individuality. It is true that some degree of individual quality in design can be recognized at all periods, yet in certain cultures such as the Byzantine it was subordinated to strict adherence to rules and formulae. This implies that in the Byzantine world, or to a lesser degree in the Romanesque period in Western Europe, ancient tradition was recognised as something on a higher level than what could be attained by modern man on his own. A startling reversal of outlook comes in with the Gothic style: no canonical rules bound the new art within a straitjacket, and the masters exhibited their power of invention to the full, though borrowing ideas from each other.[10]

Ruskin's admiration for the gothic may have been exaggerated; he saw in it a compendium of virtues which may have been present in only limited degree, but there was a solid foundation for his own construction of gothic sublimity. This discussion has been by way of a necessary preface to an explanation of Ruskin's gothic edifice. Ruskin's exaggerations are partly endemic to his personality and his method of work. He was given to a very un-English way of arguing,

[9] Salzman, *Building in England*, p. 123
[10] Harvey, *The master builders*, p. 44

a priori, from given principles, exhaustively and rigorously to a series
of classifications and deduced conclusions. It is a method always
offensive to empiricists (and builders) and sometimes likely to end in
absurdity. But it can produce original insight and great understanding. Ruskin was not wrong so much as that he argued too much, as
Eastlake said. His discussion of the gothic is brilliant, illuminating
and not entirely reliable. Its significance lies largely in the fact that
Ruskin saw the gothic spirit as encompassing a view of work and of
social relationships which contrasted with the ethos of Victorian
England. In this context it matters little whether he was right or
wrong in detail, what is important is the contrast of values that he
presents to us rather than the accuracy of his historical and
architectural judgment. That judgment was not worthless because it
was imperfect: were it worthless the argument about social ethics
which rests on it would still be worth consideration.

Ruskin begins his discussion of the character of gothicness by
distinguishing between the external forms (like pointed arches) and
certain mental tendencies of its builders. These latter are the more
important, they comprise savageness, love of change, love of nature,
disturbed imagination, obstinacy and generosity. He returns to a
distinction he made earlier (in Chapter XXI) between three distinct
systems of architectural ornamentation: servile, constitutional and
revolutionary. In servile ornamentation the power of the subordinate
workman is entirely subjected to his superior, his work is entirely
ordered as in Greek and Egyptian building. In constitutional
ornamentation the subordinate workman is given a measure of
licensed or controlled freedom, he has an element of discretion. In
revolutionary ornamentation no 'executive inferiority' is admitted.
In the ornamentation of Christian gothic architecture the value of the
individual soul is recognised at the same time as its imperfection is
acknowledged.

This admission of imperfection into the ornamentation of building
is no grudging or reluctant coming to terms with reality. It is a
necessary feature of great work, a distinguishing feature of the
greatest because it is a frank affirmation of man's limitation and
therefore it tends to the glory of God. Ruskin says that 'no
architecture can be truly noble which is not imperfect'. No architect
can do everything himself, so 'he must either make slaves of his
workmen in the old Greek and present English fashion, and lend his
work to a slave's capacities, which is to degrade it; or else he must take
his workmen as he finds them, and let them show their weaknesses

together with their strength'.[11] We know, of course, the conclusion of this course, Ruskin will end with a preoccupation with the nature of work, with an analysis of the characteristics of good and valuable work. He will spend the latter part of his life almost entirely concerned in communication with workmen, in attempts, educational and practical, to change their outlook on their lives. His discussion of the gothic clearly leads him in this direction, but notice that the first steps are not taken out of social or sympathetic concern. The first step is that an acknowledgement of human frailty is a Christian requirement. The second is that the presence of human weakness is a characteristic of good art. The demand for perfection is the result of a misunderstanding of art. In nature, imperfection is a sign of life because nothing living is perfect, while a part of it is nascent another part is developed and another is in decay. Such naturalness is associated with the need for variety in art. 'Nothing is a great work of art, for the production of which either rules or models can be given. Exactly so far as architecture works on known rules, and from given models, it is not an art, but a manufacture.'[12] It is the effect of slavery (or manufacture) on art that Ruskin is first concerned about, not the effect of slavery on man; levelling work to a slave's capacity degrades the work, not the man. Just as Christianity recognises the individual value of every soul, the glory of gothic architecture is that it provides the opportunity for the individual imagination.

This is so because the great quality of the gothic is to 'receive the results of the labour of inferior minds; and out of fragments full of imperfection . . . indulgently raise up a stately and unaccusable whole'.[13] In every man employed in manual labour there are, even in the least able, some powers of 'tardy imagination, torpid capacity of emotion, tottering steps of thought'.[14] It is usually our fault that such powers are limited, but they can never be developed

unless we are content to take them in their feebleness, and unless we prize and honour them in their imperfection above the best and most perfect manual skill, And this is what we have to do with all our labourers; to look for the thoughtful part of them, and get that out of them, whatever we lose for it, whatever faults and errors we are obliged to take with it, For the best that is in them cannot manifest itself, but in company with much error.

It is an easy matter, says Ruskin, to get a man to draw straight lines

[11] Ruskin, *The Stones of Venice*, 10, p. 202
[12] *ibid.*, p. 207
[13] *ibid.*, p. 190
[14] *ibid.*, p. 191

and to copy forms with speed and absolute precision. Once you ask him to think about what he does, to consider whether he can improve it,

his execution becomes hesitating; he thinks, and ten to one he thinks wrong; ten to one he makes a mistake in the first touch he gives to his work as a thinking being. But you have made a man of him for all that. He was only a machine before, an animated tool.

And observe, you are put to stern choice in this matter. You must either make a tool of the creature, or a man of him. You cannot make both.[15]

Men were not intended for precise and perfect actions, they are not tools. To make them so requires great effort spent in dehumanising them,

all the energy of their spirits must be given to make cogs and compasses of themselves. All their attention and strength must go to the accomplishment of the mean act the eye of the soul must be bent upon the finger-point, and the soul's force must fill all the invisible nerves that guide it, ten hours a day, that it may not err from its steely precision, and so soul and sight be worn away, and so soul and sight be lost at last – a keg of sawdust, so far as its intellectual work in this world is concerned: saved only by its Heart, which cannot go into the form of cogs and compasses, but expands, after the ten hours are over, into fireside humanity.

Ruskin's descriptive powers in prose were not confined to sunsets and mountains. He gets off perfectly the jangling, continuing concentrated nightmare of some forms of repetitive work. He conveys in a line its emotional vacuity. In two words 'fireside humanity', he indicates much of what has subsequently been described in several volumes on the subject of alienation. He lays the ground for an attack on manufacture which rests upon its requirement for unmanning its labour, for the cancellation of human qualities. And he tells us with unique accuracy and candour that the reversal of this process will cost us money. To give men human work to do will reduce their productivity, increase waste and reduce profits, but it will produce better men. We are, indeed, put to stern choice in this matter as to whether we want better productivity or better men. Ruskin is almost unique in presenting the two courses as stark alternatives. Other critics of capitalist production have maintained that, if the right policies are pursued, we can have both better productivity and better men. Modern managerial literature is full of exhortations to the effect that if men are managed so as to engage them more thoroughly in

---

[15] *ibid.*, p. 192

their work they will become more fulfilled and will work more effectively. Ameliorative reformers from paternalist employers like Robert Owen to the early personnel managers and advocates of industrial welfare have insisted that happier employees are more productive employees. The Bullock Report on Industrial Democracy insisted that its radical sounding recommendations would, by achieving greater participation, achieve greater efficiency. Communists are just as consistent in their emphasis on a coincidence of objectives, they merely insist that the changes must be more thorough if men's cooperative potential is to be released; the Soviet government has consistently sought to establish that workers in a socialist society are more productive than capitalist employees.

Ruskin's discussion of the human element in work is unique and infinitely more radical than the agglomeration of rhetoric and piety with which we have become familiar from right and left, because Ruskin is concerned with the worker's condition in itself rather than as instrumental to the pursuit of profit, efficiency or socialist cooperation. But this is not merely the result of his greater sympathy or concern: it would be impossible to assert that Ruskin was better endowed in these respects than, say, Mr Tony Benn, because these qualities are not susceptible to qualitative measurement. Ruskin's premises are much more important in this respect than his sentiments (the reverse may be true of Mr Benn). The fact that Ruskin sets off from an axiom of Christian faith (the acknowledgement of human imperfection) and a principle of aesthetics (that great art is never perfect) enables him to escape from the confusion and contradictions which beset both reformist and revolutionary discussions of industrial work. Setting off, as they invariably do, from a concern with the improvement of human welfare they find it impossible to contemplate any change which will reduce human productivity because of its dire consequences for human welfare. The result of this constant dilemma seems to be a reluctance to free the workers of industrial Europe from their slavery out of a concern for the condition of the inhabitants of the non-industrial 'third world'. The contradiction is compounded, of course, when the whole conception of human welfare is conceived in economic terms and when progress towards improvement in the human condition is measured by economic indices. Ruskin, as we shall see, is ready with a consistent explanation of how the substitution of economic good for human good has been achieved. His general theme, apart from this passing attack on economic theory, is to plead that man's concern should be with God not Mammon. The

paradox is, he says, that if we devote ourselves to God and beauty we
will find that human welfare has been improved. If we devote
ourselves to a misguided conception of human good man's condition
will continue to deteriorate. Whether this is accurate or not, Ruskin is
certainly saved from the confusions of many other radical accounts
because he subordinates man's condition to other concerns.

Ruskin next suggests the consequences of this misdirection. The
perfection of finish achieved in much of the furniture of the middle-
class room has been achieved at great cost, it is the sign of

a slavery in our England a thousand times more bitter and more degrading
than that of the scourged African, or helot Greek. Men may be beaten,
chained, tormented, yoked like cattle, slaughtered like summer flies, and yet
remain in one sense, and the best sense, free. But to smother their souls with
them, to blight and hew into nothing the suckling branches of their human
intelligence . . . this is to be slave-masters indeed; and there might be more
freedom in England, though her feudal lords' lightest words were worth
men's lives, and though the blood of the vexed husbandman dropped in the
furrows of her fields, than there is while the animation of her multitudes is
sent like fuel to feed the factory smoke.[16]

This contrast between the comparative harmlessness of slavery and
the real servitude of industrial labour, between the real freedom of
decent work and the irrelevance of political liberty, was a theme to
which Ruskin was frequently to return. The great gothic cathedrals
show 'signs of the life and liberty of every workman who struck the
stone; a freedom of thought, and rank in scale of being, such as no
laws, no charters, no charities can secure; but which it must be the
first aim of all Europe at this day to regain for her children'.[17] Ruskin
explains and insists that he is not exaggerating the point. The
degradation of the factory operative into a machine does more than
anything else to lead

the men of the nations everywhere into vain, incoherent struggle for a
freedom of which they cannot explain the nature to themselves. Their
universal outcry against wealth and against nobility, is not forced from them
either by the promise of famine, or the sting of mortified pride. They do
much, and have done much in all ages; but the foundations of society were
never yet shaken as they are at this day. It is not that men are ill-fed, but that
they have no pleasure in the work by which they make their bread, and
therefore look to wealth as the only means of pleasure. It is not that men are
pained by the scorn of the upper classes, but they cannot endure their own;
for they feel that the kind of labour to which they are condemned is verily a

16 *ibid.*, p. 193
17 *ibid.*, pp. 193–4

degrading one, and makes them less than men. Never had the upper classes so much sympathy with the lower, or charity for them as they have at this day, and yet never were they so much hated by them; for, of old, the separation between the noble and the poor was merely a wall built by law: now it is a veritable difference in level of standing, a precipice between upper and lower grounds in the fields of humanity, and there is a pestilential air at the bottom of it.[18]

Ruskin follows this with a famous passage on the division of labour, one of the finest of its kind in the English language, marked by accuracy of observation and savagery of judgment. Its quality, once again, is hoped to be a sufficient excuse for such extended quotation:

We have much studied and much perfected, of late, the great civilized invention of the division of labour: only we give it a false name. It is not, truly speaking, the labour that is divided; but the men – Divided into mere segments of men – broken into small fragments and crumbs of life; so that all the little piece of intelligence that is left in a man is not enough to make a pin, or a nail, but exhausts itself in making the point of the pin or the head of the nail. . . And the great cry that rises from all over manufacturing cities, louder than their furnace blast is all in very deed for this – that we manufacture everything there except men; we blanch cotton, and strengthen steel, to refine, or to form a single living spirit, never enters into our estimate of advantages. And all the evil to which that cry is urging our myriads can be met only in one way: not by teaching nor preaching, for to teach them is but to show them their misery, and to preach to them, if we do nothing more than preach, is to mock at it. It can be met only by a right understanding, on the part of all classes, of what kinds of labour are good for men, raising them and making them happy; by a determined sacrifice of such convenience, or beauty, or cheapness as is to be got only by the degradation of the workman; and by equally determined demand for the products and results of healthy and ennobling labour.[19]

The priority which Ruskin gives to the nature of men's work and the consequences of the division of labour in explaining the social and political disorders of the day is significant; it explains some of the criticism to which his views have been subjected and it also explains their strength. The tendency to place him within that category of critics of capitalism called by Karl Marx 'utopian socialists' in *The Communist Manifesto* of 1848, is crude and incorrect. It is based on the untrue assertion that Ruskin, like Morris, was a nostalgic medievalist. But it is also associated with the much more formidable criticism that Ruskin's social analysis was irrelevant because it was not directed to the political basis of society, that his proposed reforms

---

[18] *ibid.*, p. 194
[19] *ibid.*, p. 196

were valueless because they took no account of the need for political means to accomplish them. Criticisms of this kind have been almost standard since they were expressed by Hobson.[20] They often took a somewhat patronising form, Ruskin's heart was in the right place and his sentiments were nobly expressed but he got nowhere at all with his attempt to improve the condition of the working men because he failed to understand the political nature of their exploitation or the need for their political organisation to end it.

The first difficulty with this view is to understand it. If politics and political activity means the deliberate attempt to win the support of others for one's views and the attempt to translate them into practical reality and application, then Ruskin was not politically inactive. When we come finally to attempt to assess his influence it will be my contention that his understandable conviction that he should do something practical to apply his principles to affairs was a disappointing disaster and wasted his time and energies in irrelevant activity, that he should have stayed in his study. In wider terms there is no shortage of testimony to establish that his practical influence on socialist politics was enormous, encompassing political leaders from Philip Snowden to Mahatma Gandhi, and political policies from the National Health Service to the provision of free libraries and museums. These, considerable though they be as memorials to his influence, are distinct from his purpose. In short, although it is untrue to say that Ruskin 'failed to understand politics', it is entirely irrelevant to his theme and intention. It is untrue because of a modern tendency to establish as axiomatic that a political analysis of a social problem is synonymous with a Marxist class analysis of society. Unless the problem is discussed in terms of the exploitation of one class by another then the discussion is certain to be deemed to be weak and irrelevant, to have missed or avoided the objective or concrete (both key indicative words) nature of political reality and thus unable to arrive at a definite proposal for action.

The reasons for the irrelevance of this account are more interesting. It is irrelevant to say that Ruskin ignored politics because, if Ruskin is right, politics do not matter (which is why his attempts to engage in political action and his undoubted political influence are, both of them, neither here nor there). Ruskin is saying that the fundamental cause of injustice and its highly probable consequence in social upheaval is *not* the inegalitarian advantage that one class enjoys over

[20] J. A. Hobson, *John Ruskin, social reformer* (London, James Nisbet, 1898).

another, it is not extreme states of political suppression, it is not slavery nor authoritarian government; it is the nature of the work that men have to spend their lives engaged upon. The quality of that work has for the first time in industrial societies added a new and entirely insupportable dimension to the familiar distinctions of birth, wealth and privilege, and it has led to an irrelevant demand that those distinctions should be abolished. Ruskin believed, as pessimism overtook him, that it was more than likely that egalitarian socialism would succeed in its objectives, that birth, wealth and privilege would come to be abolished. Now the man who gave away the whole of his inherited fortune and the better part of his considerable earnings and who constantly worried about whether he should not have given away the remainder is not likely to tremble at the triumph of egalitarianism for fear of his own skin. He believed that the political programmes which working men were being persuaded to adopt would have no effect whatsoever on the cause of their espousing them, on the degraded character of their own work and their own lives.

There is by now formidable evidence, increasingly acknowledged by socialist theorists, to suggest that he was right. The achievements of socialism in the advanced industrial countries have gone a great way to achieve its political objectives in terms of birth, wealth and privilege, but the condition of the working man seems somehow to be unchanged. Explanations of this fundamental failure range from attacks on the sectionalism and economism of the trade unions, on the corruption of leaders of the Labour Party, on the bureaucratic tendencies of all labour institutions, on the overpowering hegemonic control of capitalism, on the influence of the communication media on the working class, on 'consumerism', on social conditioning of the proletariat, on socialisation. The most likely explanation for the failure of the proletarian apocalypse lies in none of these; it is that the condition of the working man's life has, in many cases, not improved but has deteriorated, that its deterioration has been made acceptable to him by financial reward and by limitation of its duration, by the better provision of 'fireside humanity'.

But that is not sufficient, says Ruskin. We cannot set out to atrophy human qualities in men's working lives and expect them to flourish at night and at the week-ends. The conditions imposed upon men by their work have been ameliorated by changes outside it, by more cash, higher levels of consumption and more leisure. These changes have been achieved in large measure by socialism and the trade unions, they have made the worker's burden more tolerable by increasing the price paid for carrying it and by allowing him more rest; the burden itself has not greatly changed. The agencies that have won these improvements have, in fact, made changes in the work less likely.

Like Marx, Ruskin was wrong in his prediction that the burden would become intolerable. Socialism has helped to make it tolerable. Ruskin did not foresee that it would have that effect but, unlike Marx, he saw that socialism was irrelevant. Inhuman work is tolerated for the reward, just as dangerous work and unsafe surroundings are tolerated for the special allowances attached to them. Inhuman work may also be tolerated because those subjected to it are stupefied by it so as to be unaware of its inhumanity. If, as Ruskin tells us, the performance of degraded tasks demands that their performers should be prepared for degradation, should be de-educated and de-humanised, then it is no matter of surprise that they should find those tasks unexceptional and unobjectionable. This argument, in much more formalised language, is a very serious contention among contemporary Marxists who explain the absence of proletarian disturbance by the long process of social conditioning to which the proletariat is subjected in order to find its conditions 'normal'. So, in order to extend its challenge, socialism must assault and win the educational and communication media, must begin and then complete the lengthy process of replacing capitalist by socialist hegemony until a society, saturated with socialism as much as the present is by capitalism, is established. Socialism's victories are never sufficient for its purpose, there is always one more battle to be won before the fruits of victory can be taken. But Ruskin says that the final victories, although very likely, will be as arid as the first.

The most dangerous characteristic that Ruskin saw in manufacturing work was its tendency to separate all manual from all intellectual activity. Marx describes the same tendency in which intelligence itself becomes a specialist aspect of the capitalist and the work of his managerial functionaries. Marx gives a thoroughly coherent explanation of this as a part of the process by which the capitalist's drive for efficiency is directed at the production of greater surplus value in which the worker produces more for the capitalist. Marx clearly describes the extension and elaboration by which the drive is developed; one of its forms is the separation of intelligence from the worker. Marx takes the motive force behind the drive to be axiomatic, just as Adam Smith had done; it is the capitalist acting rationally in pursuit of his self-interest. Although Marx denounces the consequences of this process and predicts that the exploited proletariat will put an end to it, he does not condemn the process itself. Indeed, he regards capitalist production as a higher and more productive form of civilisation than that which preceded it. The division of labour and the specialisation of intelligence are both necessary measures by which man raises himself above a state of 'rural idiocy'. Ruskin, however, cannot accept as axiomatic that man must always behave rationally in pursuit of his own interest. The historical inevitability of capitalism is, for Ruskin, an aberration in human affairs caused by moral collapse and to be terminated by moral reform.

Other versions of socialism, less thorough and consistent in their analysis than Marxism, have stressed the inequity of the divisions in society by talent and by reward. Durkheim believed that deviant or pathological forms of the generally beneficent division of labour were the result of the too frequent interruption by changes in manufacturing processes or by the maldistribution of jobs and talent. It is by now a widely accepted principle of socialised industrial societies that opportunity should be given to talent. Ruskin, however, specifically refutes the notion that the evil of the separation of manual from intellectual work resides in the fact that talent is unjustly distributed leaving some stupid men in control (or thinking) and many clever men subordinated to them (or labouring). Why not, he asks, take the workman who has the ability to design, educate him, and then get his design carried out by other workmen of less ability? The proposal rests upon mistaken supposition, he says: 'the first, that one man's thoughts can be, or ought to be, executed by another man's hands; the second, that manual labour is a degradation, when it is governed by intellect'. The second is the more serious error

for it is no less fatal an error to despise it when thus regulated by intellect, than to value it for its own sake. We are always in these days endeavouring to separate the two: we want one man to be always thinking, and another to be always working, and we call one a gentleman, and the other an operative; whereas the workman ought often to be thinking, and the thinker often to be working, and both should be gentlemen in the best sense. As it is, we make both ungentle, the one envying, the other despising his brother; and the mass of society is made up of morbid thinkers, and miserable workers. Now it is only by labour that thought can be made healthy, and only by thought that labour can be made happy, and the two cannot be separated with impunity.[21]

[21] Ruskin, *The Stones of Venice*, 10, p. 201

If man was intended to work in this world he was certainly not intended to be made miserable by his work. Misery in men's work is a violation of divine law and 'a sign of some kind of folly or sin in their way of life'. For people to be happy in work it must possess three necessary characteristics: 'they must be fit for it; they must not do too much of it; and they must have a sense of success in it – not a doubtful sense, such as needs some testimony of other people for its confirmation, but a sure sense or rather knowledge, that so much work has been done well'.[22]

The doing of work that is 'fitting' requires more than the creation of a society open to talent or competitive examination, it needs the removal of contempt for 'humble employments'. In fact, says Ruskin, the creation of a more open society has made a settled humility in employment much more difficult to achieve: 'now that a man may make money, and rise in the world, and associate himself unreproached, with people once far above him, not only is the natural discontentedness of humanity developed to an unheard-of extent, whatever a man's position, but it becomes a veritable shame to him to remain in the state he was born in'. Every parent now wants his child to get on in the world, not out of any concern for the child's safety or moral welfare, but simply out of

a panic horror of the unexpressibly pitiable calamity of their living a ledge or two lower on the molehill of the world, – a calamity to be averted at any cost whatever, of struggle, anxiety, and shortening of life itself. I do not believe that any greater good could be achieved for the country, than the change in public feeling on this head, which might be brought about by a few benevolent men, undeniably in the class of 'gentlemen' who could, on principle, enter into some of our commonest trades, and make them honourable; showing that it was possible for a man to retain his dignity, and remain in the best sense, a gentleman, though part of his time was every day occupied in manual labour, or even in serving customers over a counter.[23]

A necessary part of the process of endowing subordinate jobs with a degree of respect is that they should demand some intelligence and skill. If the job of inspecting extruded plastic pellets for imperfections can be done better by trained pigeons than by people it is no surprise if pigeons and people are given equal status. If the union to which the inspectors belong prevent pigeons being substituted for people in such work, then the people deserve less respect than the pigeons. The fact that a trade union can show rather less concern about the de-

[22] Ruskin, *Pre-Raphaelitism*, 12, p. 341
[23] *ibid.*, p. 343

humanising results of such work than the Royal Society for the Prevention of Cruelty to Animals for the de-pigeonising results when the same jobs are given to birds suggests that Ruskin may have been right to suggest that socialism will do nothing to re-establish dignity and decency in work. Improving the wages for pigeon-work does nothing to make it honourable or honoured. The establishment of a democratic meritocracy makes matters a great deal worse because it establishes for all to see that pigeon-work is done by people whose talents (or at least, whose talents called for in their work) enable them to compete with pigeons, and, in a truly egalitarian society in which pigeons had the vote, to lose. Worst of all, the people doing such work will know how they are valued, however they are paid.

The destruction of the old world's values by the new has been described in different ways. Weber saw it as the overturning of traditionalistic norms and values by the Protestant ethic representing a spirit of worldly asceticism and a dominant sense of a calling, of a part to be played zealously in the world. Weber, while not arguing that this was a sufficient reason for the development of capitalism, said that it was necessary to overcome the dominance of traditional values over the minds of men before the spirit of capitalism could be released in the world. For other historians it has been the age of reason, the enlightenment, the encyclopaedists who changed the world, challenged the dominance of the medieval church and faith and laid open the way to rationalism and progress.

What is in common is the contradistinction between an old world and the new, between traditional values and modern. Ruskin is not, any more than Weber, giving an account of what happened in history. Ruskin takes as an ideal characterisation of the one, the gothic, and sets it against the renaissance. It is a metaphoric rather than a literal or historical confrontation of two ideal states of human society.

Ruskin recognised that there were two enemies of the gothic world, the reformation and the renaissance, usually thought of as allied but, in fact, independent, he says.[24] Earlier (1851), he had believed that there was a relationship between the two assaults, that 'the peculiar degradation of the Renasist superstition, and of the public in consequence',[25] brought about the reformation. Of these two adversaries of the corrupted papacy, Protestantism kept the religion but

---

[24] Ruskin, *The Flamboyant Architecture of the Valley of the Somme*, 19, p. 246
[25] Ruskin, *The Stones of Venice*, 9, p. 44

cast aside the arts of Rome while rationalism kept the arts and cast aside the religion. The result was catastrophy, 'instant degradation followed in every direction – a flood of folly and hypocrisy . . . Christianity and morality, courage and intellect, and art all crumbling together in one wreck, we are hurried on to the fall of Italy, the revolution in France, and the condition of art in England'.[26]

The third volume of *The Stones of Venice* entitled 'The Fall' is an analysis of the renaissance. Ruskin's account begins in comparative balance and good temper, the Casa Grimani is praised as the noblest example of Roman renaissance, a style represented in its newest form by Palladio's Town Hall at Vicenza, by St Peter's at Rome and by St Paul's and Whitehall in London – this is the true (presumably worthy) antagonist of the gothic school. It is not so much the form of renaissance architecture as its moral nature which is at fault. As he has already announced that painting is not as significant in its influence as architecture Ruskin can dismiss the poverty of renaissance painting with the contemptuous judgment that painters such as Claude and Poussin are of such slight significance that 'they may be left without grave indignation to their poor mission of furnishing drawing rooms and assisting stranded conversation'.[27]

Ruskin soon begins to lay aside his moderating qualifications and to prepare for the assault. Renaissance architecture is founded upon two principles: pride and infidelity. The first manifestation of pride is in science and knowledge, exemplified by the characteristic of carefully studied and accurately executed ornament. The trouble is that this perfectionism becomes the object of art, founded upon the error that science and art are the same. They are in fact opposites, both concerned with truth but art with the aspect of truth, science with its essence. Science deals with things as they are in themselves, 'art exclusively with things as they affect the human sense and human soul. Her work is to portray the appearances of things, and to deepen the natural impression they produce upon living creatures.'[28] The truth of art is in representing things as they appear, it studies the relationships of things to man rather than of things to each other and it asks of that with which it deals 'what it has to say to men, and what it can become to them: a field of question just as much vaster than that of science, as the soul is larger than the material creation'. Ruskin repeats the familiar romantic idea that 'the whole function of the

[26] *ibid.*, p. 45
[27] *ibid.*, p. 46
[28] Ruskin, *The Stones of Venice*, II, p. 48

artist in the world is to be a seeing and feeling creature', not to think, judge, argue or to know, he may think when he has nothing better to do but 'the work of life is to be two-fold only; to see, to feel'.[29] Knowledge and learning are not only unnecessary, they are likely to be inaccurate. Knowledge, in any case, is not an end in itself, it is not the object of life; we do not live to know but to contemplate, enjoy, act, adore. The evil of the renaissance is that knowledge is thought the one and only good. The renaissance veneration of knowledge in art stemmed in part from the great early renaissance artists, Leonardo, Raphael and Michael Angelo, all grown up in the old religious age and convincing the modern world that their greatness was due to their knowledge rather than their roots. And so the modern world tried and failed to produce new Leonardos by teaching them science. Pride in knowledge was the first characteristic of the renaissance mind and was sufficient in itself to 'cast it into swift decline'.

It was aided by pride of state. There is in the renaissance style an inherent expression of haughty aristocracy, 'coldness, perfection of training, incapability of emotion, want of sympathy with the weakness of lower men, blank, hopeless, haughty, self-sufficiency'.[30]

It was full of insult to the poor in its every line. It would not be built of the materials at the poor man's hand . . . It would be of hewn stone; it would have its windows and its doors, and its stairs and its pillars, in lordly order and stately size; it would have its wings and its corridors, and its halls and its gardens, as if all the earth were its own.

It was also luxurious, 'covered with the last luxuriousness of Paganism'. It made easiest and most direct appeal to a vulgar sense of superiority, an appeal which the dullest could appreciate, it was gigantic in scale. This titanic insanity, adopted in ecclesiastical building was aped by the luxurious aristocracies of Europe

now gathering themselves into that insolent and festering isolation against which the cry of the poor sounded hourly in more ominous unison, bursting at last into thunder (mark where, – first among the planted and plashing fountains of the palace wherein the Renaissance luxury attained its utmost height in Europe, Versailles).[31]

The danger of this pride in display was that it was socially insensitive and politically provocative. It rested too upon pride of system, a lower and formalised law quite inimical to art. The result was the

[29] *ibid.*, p. 49
[30] *ibid.*, pp. 74–5
[31] *ibid.*, p. 80

enslavement to the precise elaboration of the five orders of Vitruvius and the rules of proper proportions and the conclusion of this, of course, is that the architect is redundant, replaced by measurement and machines.

If luxury and pride were not enough, the renaissance style is founded also upon infidelity. Ruskin begins his account of this foundation with a lengthy description of the corruption of Christianity by the Roman Church (a series of sardonic footnotes added in 1881 denounces the bigotry of this attack and concludes that the passage is useless). Infidelity was deepened by a return to classical pagan imagery, as imagination became languid and divorced from reality and meaning so the manual skill of the artist increased and his object became simply a means for the demonstration of his skill until a point was reached 'when sacred, profane or sensual subjects were employed with absolute indifference, for the display of colour and execution; and gradually the mind of Europe congealed into . . . utter apathy'.[32] Infidelity deepened into the unscrupulous pursuit of pleasure and the renaissance sunk into its grotesque culmination, a 'perpetuation in stone of the ribaldries of drunkenness'.

Ruskin is led to a discussion of the grotesque as a spirit by no means confined to the renaissance period. The same perpetual jesting, frequently obscene, is often a characteristic of the best gothic work. But the renaissance grotesque is exemplified by the carved heads on Santa Maria Formosa and the Bridge of Sighs, which display bestial degradation and idiotic mockery. Ruskin presents engravings of two heads, one gothic, noble, grotesque, the other of sixteenth-century Venetian work.[33] The grotesque always combines two conditions of mind, two characteristics, playfulness and fearfulness. The proper function of play for man is a serious question because play is necessary to good work and because what we do in play is an exercise of our own choice while our work, for most of us, is dictated to us. The great value of playfulness for the man of no great talent and ability is that it can be expressed in his work far more readily than perfection of line or harmony of colour. Some degree of success will attend crude attempts to express humour while the endeavour to express solemnity or beauty will fail. Most of the architecture in the world is not noble, most of what we would now call vernacular architecture depends for its effect on some expression of the grotesque, 'precious as the fruits of

[32] *ibid.*, p. 131
[33] *ibid.*, p. 150, facing

a rejoicing energy in uncultivated minds'. Picturesque effects are usually produced by nature and time, but the grotesque is always produced by the imagination and the work of man. There are two principle 'passions' or characteristics in human imagination, the love of God and the fear of death.

Ruskin chides the contemporary religious fashion for stressing only goodness and peace 'by dwelling on the manifold appearances of God's kindness on the face of creation. Such kindness is indeed everywhere and always visible; but not alone. Wrath and threatening are invariably mingled with the love.'[34] The grotesque always contains an element of excitement produced by the inescapable human fear of death and sin. This 'terrible grotesque' always unites some expression of vice and danger. The two aspects of the grotesque are always combined because the grotesque itself represents the human mind 'playing with danger', concerned with images which would be awful were it not protected from them by its peculiar temper which protects it from acknowledging their true terror. This fear, inherent and inseparable from life itself, will force itself upon the workman engaged in trivial tasks, 'it is the world's work that he is doing, and world's work is not to be done without fear'.[35] 'He has seen these things; he wars with them daily; he cannot but give them their part in his work . . . He is but carving and gilding, and must not turn aside to weep but he knows that hell is burning on, for all that, and the smoke of it withers his oak-leaves.'[36]

In the true grotesque, fear and associated excitement intrude because they are a part of the workman's life, it is a 'terribleness taken from the life'. Because they are the subject of work done by ordinary men of ordinary talent and no spiritual distinction, the result is funny rather than noble. The grotesque is the only means of artistic expression open to undistinguished craftsmen and the effect they can attain is often ludicrous and sometimes obscene. It was not thought improper to include the most ribald humour in gothic cathedrals because sin was believed to be synonymous with folly and it was right that wickedness should be derided, 'so that the vices were permitted to be represented under the most ridiculous forms, and the coarsest wit of the workman to be exhausted in completing the degradation of the creatures supposed to be subjected to them'.[37] The 'noble'

[34] *ibid.*, p. 64
[35] *ibid.*, p. 167
[36] *ibid.*, p. 168
[37] *ibid.*, p. 173

grotesque of the gothic therefore has a spiritual function, it plays with what is fearful, reduces it to the comic, whereas the ignoble grotesque is sought out, deliberately evoked, elaborated by art, it is a manufactured terribleness. We should note that although Ruskin's account of the medieval gothic is plausible in its assimilation to the Christian religion of this most mysterious phenomenon, another explanation concerns its accommodation in Christian churches as the survival of popular forms of Celtic paganism. Sheridan and Ross confirm, however, the rich and infinite variety in which these basic themes, whatever their meaning, were elaborated.[38]

The workmen, allowed to express themselves freely, display a caustic humour ('more especially on the failings of their superiors') as a principle feature of their work. This independent humour of the workmen has been silenced by the manufacturers of modern times so that it passes into transient popular speech, finding expression in the working-class wit recorded by Dickens. The grotesque is still very much a part of the outlook of English workmen but they are now allowed to express it only in gesture and gibe, they are not allowed to express it where it would be useful. Ruskin goes on to claim that while the English are a more serious people than the French,

the habitual intercourse of our lower classes in London has a tone of humour in it which I believe is untraceable in that of the Parisian populace. It is one thing to indulge in playful rest, and another to be devoted to the pursuit of pleasure: and gaiety of heart during the reaction after hard labour, and quickened by satisfaction in the accomplished duty or perfected result, is altogether compatible with . . . a deep internal seriousness of disposition.[39]

Seriousness produces the richest form of the playful grotesque, the constant pursuit of pleasure leaves us incapable of happy jesting.

Ruskin's discussion of the grotesque illustrates a number of characteristic features of his philosophy. It inherits a marked sense of the medieval idea of the duality of good and evil, that both are present together in the universe and that each is dependent on, or relative to, the other. The merit of the grotesque is that it represents a recognition of this totality in the minds of ordinary men. Indeed, Ruskin comes close to acknowledging that the expression of the grotesque begins to disappear as men are educated and informed. 'Must all decoration be the work of the ignorant and the rude? Not so; but exactly in proportion as the ignorance and the rudeness diminish, must the

[38] Ronald Sheridan and Anne Ross, *Gargoyles and grotesques, paganism in the medieval church* (Boston, New York Graphic Society, 1975)
[39] Ruskin, *The Stones of Venice*, 11, p. 193

ornamentation become rational and the grotesqueness disappear.'[40]
The weakness of the repetitive pattern of renaissance decoration is in
the degree of skill and science which has gone to produce it, it is 'the
fruit of great minds degraded to base objects'.[41] At the same time as it
leaves great minds under-employed it leaves base minds with nothing
to do, with no opportunity of reflecting their own imperfect
understanding of the beauty and grandeur of their surroundings. The
grotesque also reflects Ruskin's understanding of the enormous
importance of humour, irony, a bitter and sardonic sense of
irrationality, even chaos, in the lives of working men. The pure
comedy of work and its importance, even in the comparatively
formalised world of industrial relations, has not been sufficiently
acknowledged in the work of industrial sociologists and the like. It is
recorded in the little notices displayed in engineering shops or stores,
'You don't have to be mad to work here, but it helps', or in that cliché
of working-class conversation, 'You've got to laugh, haven't you?'
with its tragic and unstated implication of the alternative. The
rebellious and sardonic reaction to authority in work which Ruskin
noted found expression in a rich tradition of workplace comedy and
was celebrated in some aspects of the Victorian music hall. As other
avenues for its expression have been closed one suspects that it retains
some importance in the unofficial industrial dispute, a small proportion of which are understandable only as jokes. The humour of
some instances of industrial action and a good deal of industrial
humour is the explicit mockery of pomposity and self-importance, or
the ironic contrast of values which it expresses.

Ruskin's comments on the grotesque might provide an opportunity
for returning to John Unrau's serious criticism of his 'disabling class
consciousness', his 'improper' introduction of the Victorian labourer
and his 'patronising condescension' toward him. By way of a
preliminary defence we can suggest that class consciousness, after
Marx, can surely not be regarded as a nugatory outlook, so that the
accusation of class consciousness must be presumed to imply a belief
in the superiority of one class over another. Ruskin certainly believed
in the superiority of some people over others, in the impossibility of
removing privilege and in the defensibility of a privileged class. But
his vilification of capitalists, industrialists, squires and clerics must
remove any suspicion of a belief in their natural superiority. His

---

[40] *ibid.*, p. 171
[41] *ibid.*, p. 170

attacks on them are directed against their lack of responsibility and failure in leadership, deficiencies which justify an end to their privilege, and this, of course, implies approval of a paternalist relationship between the 'upper' and the 'lower' classes. But that can hardly be held to demonstrate Victorian social conservatism in a writer who never ceased to argue for the moral responsibility to be exercised for the weak by the strong. If it is an improper intrusion of anything it is of Christian teaching.

The relevance to the gothic grotesque of this defence is in what it implies for the independence of 'the labourer'. The advantage of the gothic lay in its refusal to closely prescribe the subordinate's work, in its acceptance of his inadequacy from the perspective of his superordinate (the uglier word is preferred to 'superior' in order to avoid the 'class' overtones to which Unrau so sensitively objects). Ruskin goes far beyond a Victorian or many a contemporary preparedness to accept the importance of the rude or the vulgar. The extent of his implied acceptance of insubordination, scepticism of authority and resistance to efficient management would seem to make his anarchism a more justified target for criticism than his 'class consciousness'. If Ruskin condescends to the labourer it is to insist that he must be free to express his humanity in his work and that his work must be imperfect.

The closure of such forms of human expression in work, although never complete, has been largely accomplished by the extension of control, by Marx's filling up of the pores of the working day. The ritual traditions of apprentice initiation, intended to value maturity and to remind juveniles of their ignorance, have diminished with apprenticeship itself. The boisterous and sometimes often hazardous horse-play of the workplace has been tamed by safety committees and by the displacement of the demonstration of male pride and violence to the football terraces as work itself became less of a central activity than sport. These changes are in part the result of work study and scientific management; if people spend less time at work than their parents did, more of the time spent at work is subjected to strict control. It has been established since the 1950s that women workers find that factory work provides them with the opportunity of social relationships denied them in their homes. But the production control imposed in electrical assembly or textile work is so close that their social exchanges have to be achieved during temporary absences from the workplace. In their work, human relationships are confined to the lavatories. The working day is reduced only because each hour in it, as Marx said, is made more productive than were the more porous hours of the ten-hour day. The result is achieved by the extension of managerial control in the most precise and calculating fashion, by progressively reducing the intellectual capacity of the worker, by reducing his potential for taking intelligent (or stupid) decisions. And having enslaved the manufacturing worker by making him an appendage of the machine the process is extended to the clerical worker, the manager, and finally, to the professional.

It is capitalism or industrial bureaucracy that does this. What has it got to do with the renaissance, with that 'battle of the styles', the last exciting manifestation of which was to determine the monumental setting for the Foreign Office in its declining years? The answer depends on where one finds the motive force that drives industrial bureaucracy or capitalism, the energy, whatever one calls it, which Weber contended was necessary to destroy the old world. Ruskin believed that world was not so much destroyed by the renaissance but that its final assault of scientific calculation and rationalism was enough to topple a world based upon a decaying faith. Ruskin ends his discussion of the renaissance in a peroration which abandons the polite and balanced attempt at objectivity with which he began it. Any vestige of Greek or Roman or renaissance architecture must be cast out as

utterly devoid of all life, virtue, honourableness, or power of doing good. It is base, unnatural, unfruitful, unenjoyable, and impious. Pagan in its origin, proud and unholy in its revival, paralyzed in its old age . . . an architecture invented, as it seems, to make plagiarists of its architects in which intellect is idle, invention impossible, but in which all luxury is gratified, and all insolence fortified.[42]

It is powerful attack. It was left to Geoffrey Scott to make the most powerful reply acknowledging that 'an immense store of learning and research, of reason also, and sensitive analysis, far superior to that which Ruskin brought to painting, lay imbedded in these splendid admonitions'.[43] Scott conducted an admirable attack against the critics of the renaissance style in architecture and singled out Ruskin in particular for his responsibility for 'the ethical fallacy', for judging the style of architecture not intrinsically, but by its supposed effects, by the social and political consequences that are said to derive from it.

---

[42] *ibid.*, p. 227
[43] Geoffrey Scott, *The architecture of humanism* (London, Methuen, 1961; first published 1914), p. 132

This view is dismissed as the confusion of social consequences with aesthetic value, an error itself derived from what Scott calls the 'Romantic Fallacy'. Effective and enthusiastic though his defence of the renaissance is, it does seem to suffer from the same exaggerations which he correctly diagnoses in Ruskin. Having dismissed the error of establishing a relationship between aesthetics, morality and political consequences, Scott proceeds to argue persuasively that the renaissance did not enslave the workmen, was not guilty of moral atrocity, was enabled by its unparalleled knowledge of the aesthetics of architectural design to communicate a sense of exultant vigour and strength; he accuses, in short, its critics of having delivered an unsound moral judgment, which surely exonerates them from the accusation that their error was in making a moral judgment at all.

Ruskin's attack was certainly over-enthusiastic. It was justified, if at all, by what the renaissance style had become rather than by what it had been, by caryatids in tea rooms and, ultimately, cinemas and dance halls, rather than the balanced severity of the Mansion House. But it is the society that produced such massive, cold and repetitive monuments that Ruskin is attacking, it is, he says, an architecture which reflects meaninglessness, it is an architecture of inhumanism. It demonstrates changes in men's beliefs and values which will produce a society incapable of producing art or architecture. The features which demonstrate this decline are, in the first place, concerned with the decline of Christian faith. From that decline follow other consequences, the most important of which is the exclusion of workers of lower ability, talent and character, from a participation in the work of that society to the limit of their capabilities. It is dangerous to use a word already overburdened by polemical usage, but Ruskin is talking about the exclusion, if not the alienation of workers, from the social relationships made by work. Some vestige of 'fireside humanity' is to remain available to them, of course, but they are not going to be good enough as men, to do what they are capable of and they are, therefore, going to be only partially engaged, as hands, to do what cleverer men measure that they should do. Architecture is taken to represent the general enslavement of the worker to a precise and calculated routine. And this inhumanity is permitted and encouraged because man's place in the universe and his nature has been misunderstood, he has become subject to the pursuit of power, the victim of intellectual calculation, the instrument of accumulation.

Ruskin does not suggest that the renaissance style has brought this about but rather that a moral society with a Christian faith could not have produced the renaissance style. The measure of its destruction is to be seen in the extension of its calculating science to men themselves, to the reduction of human relationships to an expression in the principles of economies and to the establishment of the unchallengeable conviction that that science embodies all that is to be held of significance about the behaviour of men.

4

Economics, 'the damned lie'

For my own part, I feel the force of mechanism and the fury of avaricious commerce to be at present so irresistible that I have seceded from the study not only of architecture, but nearly of all art; and have given myself, as I would in a besieged city, to seek the best modes of getting bread and water for its multitudes, there remaining no question, it seems to me, of other than such grave business for the time.[1]

Thus, by 1865, Ruskin announced his engagement to a labour which had begun in lectures given in Manchester in 1857 (later published as *A Joy for Ever*), continued with *Unto this Last* (1862), *Munera Pulveris* (1862), *Time and Tide* (1867), and was to be a constant burden for the rest of his active life. He is said to have chosen the medium of lectures to deliver his first radical assaults in order to find some independence and protection from the critical attention of his father. When the first of the essays, to be known later as *Unto this Last*, was published by the new *Cornhill Magazine* in 1860, Ruskin's father confessed that he wished John would cease to meddle with political economy or 'they will mistake him for a Socialist – or Louis Blanc or Mr. Owen of Lanark'. The essays, as the elder Ruskin feared, provoked a great deal of abuse which was not diminished by the author's disclaiming the necessity of any acquaintanceship with economics as a preliminary to his attacks upon it. Thackeray, the editor of the new journal, and Smith, its publisher, were also subjected to hostile criticism so that, after three issues, the essays were discontinued. Ruskin was criticised for his ignorance of practical affairs and his presumptuous dismissal of the necessity of theoretical knowledge of the subject as a prior necessity for its attack. Hobson pointed out that this criticism was not justified: Ruskin had clearly observed the business activities of his father, accompanied him on his business journeys from an early age, and had profited from a more

---

[1] Ruskin, *The Study of Architecture*, 19, p. 38

direct observation of a successful man of affairs than many a theoretical economist.[2] As to his innocence of economic theory, Ruskin's analysis of the language of economics was justified by the fact that many of the technical terms of the 'science' were terms of art often used in the social sciences with considerable laxity. At the same time, the vulnerability of the vocabulary to a layman's logic was likely to incense the new academicians seeking to shelter behind their carefully constructed argot. Hobson further pointed out that many of the economist's claims to authority rested on an amalgam of other studies and were legitimately open to challenge. Ruskin's major criticism was, in any case, to be essentially moral, and this was not only a study of which the economists had no special knowledge, it was a study of which they advertised their incompetence.

Their reaction provoked by Ruskin was violent and it reflected and revealed the characteristic nature of his attack. It came from the press and from opinion formers rather than from economists and, although Ruskin did not release it, it was against ideologies rather than theorists that his own criticisms were more justly directed. Adam Smith, whom he frequently identified along with John Stuart Mill as one of the founding fathers of villainy, was inclined to much greater theoretical complexity and ethical reservation than he was allowed by Ruskin. Fain sums up this misdirection by saying that 'in so far as Ruskin's indictment applied to the work of the best exponents of nineteenth-century orthodox political economy, it is unsound. In so far as his indictment applied to the misuse of that doctrine by politicians and industrialists, it is sound.'[3] The reaction was also significant in its hostility, as though his critics saw more clearly than most of his friends had done, the truly radical nature of the attack that he directed. The essays 'raised a storm of indignant protest'. A leading article from the bastion of free-trade in the *Manchester Examiner* of 2 October 1860 warned its readers that, if Ruskin was not crushed, 'his wild words will touch the springs of action in some hearts, and ere we are aware a moral floodgate may fly open and drown us all'.[4]

There is no doubt that the violence of the reaction hurt this most violent of controversialists. Although Carlyle approved warmly, other friends objected to him or to his father at his lapse. He was accused of writing 'intolerable twaddle' of 'utter imbecility'. When

---

[2] Hobson, *John Ruskin*, p. 58

[3] John Tyree Fain, *Ruskin and the economists* (Nashville, Venderbilt University Press, 1956), p. 69

[4] Ruskin, editors' introduction, 17, p. xxxi

Unto this Last was put into a book in 1862 it was published in an edition of 1,000 copies; ten years later it had not been sold out. Worse, the damage to Ruskin's reputation appeared to have affected the sales of his other work. The concern coincided with a period of sickness and of some religious doubt, all of which seemed to combine in the painfulness of his social concern and in his determination to bring about improvement. He answered his parents' anxious enquiries by assuring them that his condition was not brought on by biliousness, but that his depression was 'for the sufferings and deaths of thousands, the follies and miseries of millions, the perishing of the greatest works and deeds of human intellect'. He could escape by shutting his ears and eyes but that 'is only as if I had buried myself in a tuft of grass on a battlefield wet with blood'.[5]

The publication of *Unto this Last*, whether as the result of the anger that prompted it or the hostility that received it, seems also to have marked the beginning of that bitter pessimism that was to recur throughout the rest of Ruskin's life.

However disorderly the outcome, at the outset, as always, Ruskin had a straightforward plan. He intended the book as a criticism of the prevailing orthodoxy of economics. His next object was to replace this received theory with a system of true political economy or social economy. This was to be set out in *Munera Pulveris* (1862). Finally, he would work out the practical applications of this system in terms of laws and social institutions in *Time and Tide* (1867). The structure was never accomplished in whole or in detail, but Ruskin laid down the lines of attack with sufficient clarity and considerable zest.

He distinguishes between political economy, which is the study of the economy of the State, and mercantile economy, which is the study of the acquisition of maximum inequalities of wealth.[6] The latter is concerned with injustice, the former with justice because the accumulation of wealth cannot be isolated from considerations of justice nor can wealth itself be divorced from morality. True wealth is 'the possession of useful articles which we can use' and value is 'that which avails towards life'. The science of political economy is 'the science of getting rich by just means'. The attempt of the economists to extract notions of justice and morality from their study has the

---

[5] *ibid.*, p. xl

[6] Discussions such as this can become confusing because of uncertainty as to whether Ruskin is considering economics in terms of the present state of the art or in terms of what it ought to be or of what it really is. We shall use the word 'economics' to signify the orthodox study (generally the subject of Ruskin's criticism) and 'political economy' to stand for his proposed alternative. This conforms to Ruskin's general but not always consistent usage.

effect of reducing it to a meaningless abstraction which is incapable of explaining relationships and behaviour in the real world. For this reason it is unable to deal with disputes between employers and labour about wages. On this particular score a very considerable body of learned opinion has subsequently lined up on Ruskin's side (although it almost certainly does not know it). A good deal of authority in the field of industrial relations has come to the view that economic considerations are neither exclusive nor paramount in the determination of wages which are more frequently drawn to reflect views concerning social status.[7] A further body of opinion argues that the institutions concerned in collective bargaining do not in fact engage in an economic process of bargaining so much as in a political process of pressure-group representation and negotiation.[8] And a third contribution has drawn attention to the feelings of justice which attend the determination of the individual wage.[9]

Ruskin quoted Adam Smith's conclusion that 'the effectual discipline which is exercised over a workman is not that of his corporation, but that of his customers. It is the fear of losing their employment which restrains his frauds, and corrects his negligence.' Ruskin comments in a note to the second edition 'what an entirely damned state of soul any human creature must have got into'[10] to have accepted such a statement. But there is surely a sense in which both Smith and Ruskin are right while neither is damned. Smith is laying down self-interest as the mainspring of the economic system, the minimum and essential individualism which can be assumed to be present in all men and which is sufficient to explain their economic collaboration in productive societies. Smith was aware, without benefit of Ruskin's advice, of the disastrous consequences of self-interest, when unchecked by co-operation or coercion. But Smith was not the first or the last to take self-interest as the lowest common denominator that could be assumed to be present in all in arriving at a rational explanation of economic behaviour. One of the first was Langland's Piers Plowman in sending for the help of Hunger to secure a necessary degree of work. One of the latest is Professor Milton Friedman.

Ruskin contrasts with this damnable calculation the words carved on the church of San Giacomo di Rialto in Venice: 'Around this

---

[7] Barbara Wootton, *The social foundations of wage policy* (London Allen and Unwin, 1955)
[8] A. Flanders, *Collective bargaining* (Harmondsworth, Penguin Books, 1969)
[9] Elliot Jaques, *Equitable payment* (London, Heinemann, 1961)
[10] Ruskin, *Unto this Last*, 17, pp. 20–1

temple, let the Merchant's law be just, his weights true, and his contracts guileless.' Smith and Ruskin are both right because the one is seeking descriptive accuracy, and the other prescriptive truth. Men always have behaved selfishly and can be relied on to do so in future. But that is the worst thing that can be said of them, says Ruskin, and to extract this unfortunate characteristic and to make it the fundamental principle of a so-called science of human behaviour is to make that science an unrealistic abstraction. The economists have created an ossified and unrealistic science because they have extracted all trace of social affection from mankind and discarded it as irrelevant to their explanation of its behaviour. The result is that economics not only fails to comprehend the most important aspects of man's affairs, is incapable of explaining the reasons for him doing his best work, and is mystified by his most noble manifestations; it actively contributes to making man worse than he is.

It is easy to imagine an enthusiastic affection existing among soldiers for the colonel. Not so easy to imagine an enthusiastic affection among cotton spinners for the mill proprietor. A body of men associated for purposes of robbery (as a Highland clan in ancient times) shall be animated by perfect affection, and every member of it be ready to lay down his life for the life of his chief. But a band of men associated for purposes of legal production and accumulation is usually animated, it appears, by no such emotions.[11]

Ruskin frequently returns to the negative aspect of economics. He points out the moral characteristics frequently found associated with the acquisition of wealth and with the endurance of poverty:

in a community regulated only by laws of demand and supply, but protected from open violence, the persons who become rich are, generally speaking, industrious, resolute, proud, covetous, prompt, methodical, sensible, un-imaginative, insensitive and ignorant. The persons who remain poor are the entirely foolish, the entirely wise, the idle, the reckless, the humble, the thoughtful, the dull, the imaginative, the sensitive, the well-informed, the improvident, the irregularly and impulsively wicked, the clumsy knave, the open thief, and the entirely merciful, just and goodly person.[12]

The acceptance of the science of economics is demoralising in its effect, not only because of its partial, crippled view of mankind, but because it entails systematic disobedience to the religion professed by the nation. 'The writings which we (verbally) esteem as divine, not only denounce the love of money as the source of all evil . . . but

[11] *ibid.*, p. 32
[12] *ibid.*, p. 89

declare mammon service to be the accurate and irreconcilable opposite of God's service.'[13] This inconsistency of professed faith and practice was to become a more and more frequent cause of Ruskin's disillusionment and despair. He saw the triumph of economic calculation as the abandonment by England of the Christian faith and making its decline into corruption when, like Venice, it would be incapable of the good work that had made it rich. Once again, there is the paradox, constantly drawn by Ruskin, that wealth will come to him who does not pursue it and will be denied to those who value it alone or, as Ruskin puts it, when discussing employment, 'in this, as in all other matters, whoever will save his life shall lose it, who loses it shall find'.[14]

It is, of course, the same paradox as that at the centre of the argument over the Protestant ethic, which makes Weber's transition from theological doctrine to the unfettered domination of capitalist enterprise impossible to accomplish. Enterprise directed at the manufacture of things for sale in markets to bring profits will not produce things of value and, ultimately, will not bring profits. Things of value are those that 'avail towards life'. The true science of political economy 'is that which teaches nations to desire and labour for the things that lead to life: and which teaches them to scorn and destroy the things that lead to destruction'.[15] In *Munera Pulveris* Ruskin returns to this doctrine; the aim of political economy is to produce, use or accumulate for use 'things which serve either to sustain and comfort the body or exercise rightly the affections and form the intelligence'.[16] Value signifies the quality of anything for sustaining life. Wealth means the accumulation of valuable things. The production of 'effectual value' requires the production of the useful thing and the production of the capacity to use it. Value appears to be both a primary or intrinsic quality and a secondary or derived quality. Value (what is literally implied in the term 'good' or 'goods') resides in the object, but it is acquired in the secondary sense when it is made available or produced and when it is desired or demanded. But it has nothing to do with cost or price. 'Cost is the quantity of labour taken to produce it; price the quantity of labour which the possessor will take in exchange for it. Cost and price are commercial conditions, to be studied under the head of money.'[17]

[13] *ibid.*, p. 76
[14] *ibid.*, p. 36
[15] *ibid.*, pp. 84–5
[16] Ruskin, *Munera Pulveris*, 17, p. 147
[17] *ibid.*, p. 153

Money is simply a convenience, says Ruskin, a documentary claim to the possession of valuble things, it is the agency by which choice is obtained. As such it is a useful and necessary instrument. But it easily comes to be desired in itself and this has dangerous consequences. In a description similar to Marx's account of fetishism Ruskin says that 'the less use people can make of things, the more they want them, and the sooner weary of them, and want to change them for something else; and all frequency of change increases the quantity and power of currency'. This power is increased further by the fact that the attraction of money is private, whereas 'in the enjoyment of real property, others must partly share'. And for unimaginative people it can be counted and compared in quantity with smaller hordes owned by others. Stupidity is no disadvantage in its enjoyment, 'everybody can understand money, everybody can count it and most will worship it'.[18]

There are wider dangers for society in this worship. As the habits of a nation become more complex and artificial the stock of its money must increase in proportion to the store of its goods or wealth. Money becomes the principle object of desire, 'the holding of it becomes the main object of life' and so the currency is enlarged still further. The tendency is to inevitable inflation and the constant demand for an increased quantity of money eventually becomes too burdensome and the ultimate result is that 'the popular voice is apt to be raised in a violent and irrational manner, leading to revolution rather than remedy'.[19]

Economics or mercantile economy is the art of acquiring riches or the accumulation of legal or moral claim by some individuals upon the labour of others and, for that reason, 'the art of making yourself rich, in the ordinary mercantile economist's sense, is therefore equally and necessarily the art of keeping your neighbour poor'.[20] So, the art of becoming rich is 'the art of establishing the maximum inequality in our own favour'. Money certainly gives those who possess it power over others but it is not the only source of power and, if it is divorced from justice, or if riches are too one-sidedly distributed, then it becomes a singularly fragile sort of power. A true science of wealth must concern usefulness, good, human capacities and human disposition. The economist, in ignoring these moral and psychological qualities, has concerned himself with a limited conception of men;

[18] *ibid.*, pp. 206–7
[19] *ibid.*, p. 192
[20] Ruskin, *Unto this Last*, 17, p. 44

having left out the soul, on the assumption that man is a collection of bones, the re-admission of anything but bones becomes an unnecessary and embarrassing complication. The science *will* work, based on the assumption from which it sets out, but it will work by constructing a grotesquely unrealistic model of man. This would be well enough if the results of such distortion were simply intellectual puzzles for the entertainment of scholars in their studies, but the game has acquired such a reputation that its popularity makes people conform to the model in order to play it. The economist has succeeded in getting into the heads of the English totally false notions of wealth, value and human character, and has thus transformed their behaviour so as to demonstrate the veracity of their misconceptions.

The social affections are accidental and disturbing elements in human nature; but avarice and the desire of progress are constant elements. Let us eliminate the inconstants, and, considering the human being merely as a covetous machine, examine by what laws of labour, purchase, and sale the greatest accumulative result in wealth is obtainable. Those laws once determined, it will be for each individual afterwards to introduce as much of the disturbing affectionate element as he chooses, and to determine for himself the result in the new conditions supposed.[21]

Ruskin's attack upon economics is based upon the observation by now familiar to us in the operation of all the social sciences, that the descriptive is indistinguishable from the prescriptive, that the claim to scientific objectivity conceals a normative element, that the study influences the behaviour of its subject. His argument about value is very similar to Marx's distinction between use value and exchange value, and so, in some respects, is his contention that the latter comes to displace the former. Marx argues that this degradation of social relationships into commercial relationships is an inevitable consequence of the capitalist's domination over society and his constant drive for profit. Ruskin sees the same process as anything but inevitable (although he became more and more pessimistic in the matter as he grew older), as the result of a reversible moral decline which, if not caused is encouraged by the economist's partial and distorting view of human nature. The economist barely avoids the conclusion that what the selfish man does is what the rational man ought to do. His account of the laws of supply and demand take no account of the conditions governing the supply and the circumstances which created the demand. The injunction to buy in the cheapest

21 *ibid.*, p. 25

market and sell in the dearest is wicked because it demands total unconcern with the conditions which made the one cheap and the other dear. And it encourages, as the old Catholic doctors noticed, an inevitable approval for disasters that produce cheap purchases and expensive sales, and a total incapacity to reverse those causal conditions unless they produce an interest. A limited modification of the consequences of economically advantageous disasters, like floods or famines, is, of course, acceptable if a general reaction to them demands their amelioration by a limited interference with market forces.

Commentators on Ruskin down the years have commonly agreed that this was one consequence to which he had an unchallengeable claim, he greatly encouraged the development of 'interventionist' policies which have resulted in a mixed economy and the perception of a need for welfare programmes. It is to be doubted whether Ruskin would have been satisfied with the result or grateful for the acknowledgement. The amelioration is broadly in conditions which are brought about by the market, the intervention is still in a process determined by the interaction of economic forces and the goods and services provided by way of improvement, extensive though they may be, are still regarded as costs rather than values. The economic process of calculation in the pursuit of interests determined by the meeting of demands rather than needs is still paramount and its domination is underlined by the number of exceptions it can afford to finance. Ruskin did not argue for its qualification so much as for its negation.

He was, of course, deeply critical of the philosophy of let-alone, of the doctrine of unrestricted competition. But this extreme version of the market economy was not his sole target or the reason for his most severe criticism of economics. Even if *laissez-faire* were to be finally abandoned as a practical programme or a theoretical model, even if a capitalist economic system could be demonstrated to be compatible with welfarist intervention, a measure of State control of industry together with free access to education, libraries and museums, Ruskin's criticisms of the economist's systems remains, that it is immoral, partial and ineffective.

He presses his criticism to the economist's defence of profit and to the great significance it has in business affairs. What is commonly thought of as profit is really an advantage gained in an exchange by one person over another.

If, in the exchange, one man is able to give what cost him little labour for what has cost the other much, he 'acquires' a certain quantity of the produce of the other's labour. And precisely what he acquires, the other loses. In mercantile language, the person who thus acquires is commonly said to have 'made a profit' . . . Wherever material gain follows exchange, for every *plus* there is a precisely equal *minus*.

While the pluses have made a great impression in the world, the minuses have 'a tendency to retire into back streets, and other places of shade, – or even to get themselves wholly and finally put out of sight in graves'.[22] Exchange should be mutually beneficial; where it is of advantage to only one of the parties it is dependent upon the ignorance or incapacity of the other. In this way Ruskin is contrasting the relationships involved in economic life with the reciprocal exchanges which bind members of a community together. He is pointing to the same deficiency in economic relationships which preoccupied Marx and Durkheim.

There can be no profit in exchange, only advantage, and the measure of advantage is the strength, cunning or duplicity which one party enjoys over the other. Profit arises only from labour. 'It is only in labour there can be profit . . . Thus one man by sowing and reaping, turns one measure of corn into two measures.'[23] This is probably the weakest point of Ruskin's criticism, whether it be directed against economic doctrine or business practice. J. A. Hobson, that most respectful of commentators on 'the master', pointed out that his attitude to exchange and the profit associated with it, is similar to and almost as limited as, the physiocrats who hold that value is truly produced only by agriculture. Even if the balance of advantage were enjoyed by one party over the other, the fact of exchange surely suggests that 'a residue of real gain or advantage must accrue to the weaker party, at any rate just such minimum advantage as is sufficient to induce him to be a party to the bargain'.[24] Hobson believed that Ruskin had attached himself to this mistaken view because of his conception of value as an intrinsic and unalterable quality attaching to forms of wealth. Hobson asks,

why should not an improved method of exchange, by merely putting the right things in the right hands, be held to make fortunes? for commodities, thus well disposed, are evidently worth more both in money and in real utility . . . The charge that bargaining distributes unfairly the advantage of exchange need not lead us to a virtual denial of the productivity of trade.[25]

There is no doubt that the weaker party is induced to engage in exchange because it offers him advantage, just sufficient to attract him, but Ruskin points out that his weakness is fastened upon in the process of exchange so as to exaggerate the disparity in the power of the parties, as in selling bread to a starving man. Exchange in the capitalist market is carried out for profit and that strengthens the control of the market over those who are driven to it by weakness while they are told that the process of exchange is neutral. It is neutral because it is blind to moral considerations and accepts differences in power. Ruskin did not wish to deny the utility of trade (its productivity is another matter) but he certainly wished to deny the justice of its speculative aspect and the disproportionate financial return which it sometimes attracted. The explanation for his hostility to exchange and the profit associated with it may lie in the business background of his own family and, additionally, in prejudice. Out of the tangled and acrimonious explanations and criticisms that followed the annulment of his marriage to Ephemia Gray emerged the charge that her father's business affairs had been unsound, and that his impending bankruptcy had been kept from the Ruskins. In the event, John James Ruskin settled £10,000 on his daughter-in-law, and his son came ultimately to believe that it had been a marriage of convenience from the point of view of his wife and her father. As far as his father was concerned, John James believed that this financial disaster was brought about by speculation. Shortly before the wedding he wrote to George Gray (Ephemia's father) 'I do not blame you individually for bold speculation – you are in a speculative society – and country – my miscalled cautious Countrymen are all speculative. They like amusement and getting rich without labour – but there is nothing like keeping to our *Shop* whatever it be.'[26] John James was horrified at the thought of speculation and believed its ultimate effects would be ruinous. His son respected his business probity and hard work; he was 'an honest tradesman'.

Ruskin believed that trade was a useful and necessary activity, that it would also be honourable if it were engaged in out of duty, for the service that it contributed rather than the profit it might bring. This is

[25] *ibid.*, p. 144
[26] Mary Lutyens, *The Ruskins and the Grays* (London, John Murray, 1972), p. 105

an attitude shared by many successful capitalist manufacturers. It was very much the outlook of Henry Ford, who believed that the only way profit can be made is through work. The lesson of the Wall Street crash was that 'everybody is the loser and no one the gainer by speculating in things already made . . . Prosperity and progress are in things yet to be made . . . the nation's recent experience will have taught the lesson that no money is to be made except out of service.'[27] Ruskin's critical attitude to the speculative, profit-seeking aspects of exchange is not necessarily a radical criticism of business behaviour, it is a criticism shared by many businessmen and it represents a division in capitalism between manufacturing or service-providing business and speculative or financial business.

The basis of Ruskin's criticism of economics is almost entirely traditional and it is therefore surprising that it took him so long to develop his own attack on the economist's idea of exchange into a full-scale assault upon interest. He came to this position under the influence of W. C. Sillar, the author of several pamphlets upon the subject of usury, who must have been one of the very few people to have entered into a critical correspondence with Ruskin which culminated in his recognition that his correspondent was right and that he was wrong.[28] He worked out his position, with the assistance of Mr Siller, in *Fors Clavigera*. The unusual character of that work enables the reader to see the debate unfolding for the three volumes are composed of monthly letters written mainly to the workmen of England although Hobson believed that Ruskin was led from a condemnation of extortionate levels of interest to the dismissal of the justice of any interest at all because he had

fallen a victim to a famous fallacy . . . The intellectual repudiation has nearly always arisen from the difficulty of conceiving that money could 'produce' anything, either more money or more wealth of any kind. Aristotle's famous dictum that 'money is barren' expresses concisely the point of view . . . held in common with Moses and Jesus, most of the fathers of the Church, Bacon, Luther, Bossuet, and many wise men of all ages.[29]

Such a lineage makes it the more surprising that Ruskin did not come to this view until 1872; it must also raise the question as to whether

[27] Henry Ford, *Moving forward* (London, Heinemann, 1931), p. 5

[28] Ruskin's 'confession' begins fairly tetchily (for he seems to have been bothered by Mr Sillar's persistence) in a letter dated 21 September 1872: 'Once for all, then, Mr Sillar is wholly right as to the abstract fact that lending for gain is sinful.' Ruskin goes on to qualify this agreement but, gradually, the qualifications are abandoned.

[29] Hobson, *John Ruskin*, p. 148

the view is so certainly fallacious; arguments from authority are never convincing but they always deserve consideration. The error, says Hobson, lies in abandoning the view taken of money in *Time and Tide*, that it is a sign of command over wealth in general, or as we have seen it in *Munera Pulveris*, that it is a documentary claim to the possession of valuable things. The clear implication of that view is

that a man who makes a loan of money is really handing over a general command of all forms of material or immaterial wealth, and that upon the productive use of this wealth, not upon the productivity of coins, depends the claim of interest . . . the substance is a loan of tools or goods and the receipt of tools or goods in return.[30]

But this very argument was brought to Ruskin's attention and he rejected it. If a spade is lent a spade should be returned in good order, but why should some part of the goods that the spade has enabled the labourer to produce be added to it? This is simply one of two forms of the 'Devil's law of Theft by the Rich from the Poor . . . either of buying men's tools, and making them pay for the loan of them – (Interest) – or buying men's lands, and making them pay for the produce of them – (Rent)'.[31]

Ruskin examined at various times the various reasons and defences that were given for the charging of interest. The dullest of all was that it did good. He acknowledged that it did

but the principle of Righteous dealing is, that if the good costs you nothing, you must not be paid for doing it. Your friend passes your door on an unexpectedly wet day, unprovided for the occasion. You have the choice of three benevolences to him, – lending him your umbrella, – lending him eighteen pence to pay for a cab, – or letting him stay in your parlour till the rain is over. If you charge him interest on the umbrella, it is profit on capital – if you charge him interest on the eighteen pence, it is ordinary usury – if you charge him interest on the parlour, it is rent. All three are equally forbidden by Christian law.[32]

Three other defences of interest are taken from Professor Fawcett's *Manual of Political Economy* published in 1869. The first is that interest is a return in the form of wages to the capitalist for the work of supervision of his business. Ruskin agrees that superintendence should be rewarded, like all other work, by the payment of a wage, but in this respect capitalists or investors who do not superintend

---

[30] *ibid.*, p. 149
[31] Ruskin, *Fors Clavigera*, 29, p. 136
[32] *ibid.*, p. 179

anything should not be paid for doing nothing. The second is that interest is the reward or compensation for risk taking. Ruskin acknowledges that every business involves some risk which the prudent businessman allows for and guards against (here speaks the son of John James) but if he fails to do so and is improvident he should not expect to be compensated by his customers. Finally, Ruskin dismisses the argument that interest is a reward for the abstinence of the investor.

It strikes me, upon this, that if I had not my £15,000 of Bank Stock I should be a good deal more abstinent than I am, and that nobody would then talk of rewarding me for it. It might be possible to find even cases of very prolonged and painful abstinence, for which no reward has yet been adjudged by less abstinent England . . . 'You cannot have your cake and eat it'. Of course not; and if you don't eat it you have your cake; but not a cake and a half![33]

It is an illustration, if not a measure, of the extent to which Ruskin's criticism of economic orthodoxy has been misunderstood, even by his admirers and sympathisers, like Hobson, that his criticism of interest is invariably regarded as error and unfortunate. Ruskin maintains that interest is unjustified in terms of justice and morality; his critics say that it is a part of the way the world works, an ingredient in the economic system. Ruskin says that it should not be so and has not always been so. His objections are not so much those of the radical enemy of business as the criticism of the prudent man of business anxious not to over-reach himself and to keep out of the hands of the bankers. Interest is, of course, necessary to speculative development as it was to the vast investment involved in canal and railway development. But Ruskin was sceptical of the value of speculative development and convinced that the extent of investment in railways was disastrous, that railways should be built that could pay their way, that the elaboration of railway architecture was an indulgence to provide builders with profit on unnecessary decoration. The present dependence of capitalist society on a minimum lending rate which, at any previous time would have been regarded as outrageously usurious, and the ability of established business enterprise to finance its own affairs must raise a question as to the technical importance of interest to sound economic activity. And Ruskin would surely add that it is a mistake to look to economics for technical explanations of some mechanical system that works its inexorable way with us. 'Political Economy is neither an art nor a science; but a system of

[33] Ruskin, *Fors Clavigera*, 27, p. 318

conduct and legislature founded on the sciences, directing the arts, and impossible, except under certain conditions of moral life.'[34] The object of this study is, or should be, the extension of life as it is signified by the power and happiness of human beings in an indivisible and harmonious relationship with nature. Real wealth is to be found in the people themselves, 'the final outcome and consumption of all wealth is in the producing as many as possible full-breathed, brighteyed, and happy-hearted human creatures'.[35]

Production is never an end in itself, it is engaged in for consumption; 'consumption is the crown of production and the wealth of a nation is only to be estimated by what it consumes';[36] consumption is the end and aim of production. Sherburne argues that this stress on consumption marks a change in emphasis from the bias of the classical economists.

While Mill's formula allows him to focus on production and neglect consumption in the belief that it will take care of itself, Ruskin places consumption at the center of the economy. This difference . . . leads to the distinction between a quantitative and qualitative view of economics. Ruskin's approach brings home to each consumer that he is responsible for *what* he consumes and the type of labor he instigates. Mill's emphasis on production could lead to a concern for quality. Historically, it has not. Production has imaginative tones of infinite utility – the piling up of valuable quantities, the addition of ciphers.

The real question, says Sherburne, is what *can* be supplied and *ought* to be demanded.[37]

Ruskin constantly asks us what ought to be demanded. If a labour theory of value were correct, he says, then the lithographic stones used to produce coloured prints of dancers would be more valuable, because more labour went into each one of them, than a painting by Tintoretto.[38] Each stone can produce many impressions and, as there is a demand for them, the economist would conclude that Paris was richer because of its dancer prints than Venice with its Tintorettos. This is not true because the prints ought not to be demanded, they are false riches or, as he called them in *Unto this Last*, illth rather than wealth. When we spend money we buy labour and it is a moral

[34] Ruskin, *Munera Pulveris*, 17, p. 147
[35] *ibid.*, p. 56
[36] Ruskin, *Unto this Last*, 17, p. 10
[37] J. S. Sherburne, *John Ruskin or the ambiguities of abundance* (Cambridge, Mass., Harvard University Press, 1972), p. 179
[38] Ruskin, *Munera Pulveris*, 17, p. 131

question as to how we direct that labour and what we require it to produce for us.

The alternative to the determination of these questions by blind chance, or by the 'laws' of supply and demand or by the invisible hand at work, must be a deliberate attempt to make justice a pre-eminent requirement of relationships in society. Ruskin is not saying the economic system will not work but he is saying that it will work pre-eminently to the satisfaction of some people and grossly to the dissatisfaction of most of the others. He is vigorously denying the claim that the system will both 'work' and, coincidentally, will produce a decent and just society which is not blind to moral considerations. It will accumulate riches which are likely to turn out to be poisons, will condemn labourers to servitude in their manufacture, and will grossly mismanage distribution of the proceeds of their sale. If social relationships are left to the chance determination of the market then they will reflect the worst and most selfish of human qualities because these are the traits that uncontrolled market place behaviour encourages and develops. For this reason Ruskin inverts biblical teaching in a diabolical litany 'Thou shalt hate the Lord thy God, damn His laws and covet thy neighbour's goods.'[39] A society which has itself become a monster is founded on 'the New Commandment, Let him that hateth God, hate his brother also'.[40]

The alternative demands intervention. In so far as Ruskin's social criticism has left any widespread impression it amounts to an acknowledgement that his criticism of capitalism and his advocacy of intervention distinguishes him as a socialist, a pioneer of the Welfare State. Ruskin was no socialist. He said that his intention was to examine the moral results and the possible rectification of the laws of the distribution of wealth:

Laws which ordinary economists assume to be insoluble, and which ordinary socialists imagine to be on the eve of total abrogation. But they are both alike deceived. The laws which at present regulate the possession of wealth are unjust, because the motives which provoke to its attainment are impure, but no socialism can affect their abrogation, unless it can abrogate also covetousness and pride, which it is by no means yet in the way of doing.

In any case, socialism will effect no great change in the state of things because 'the utmost efforts of socialism will not hinder the fulfilment of (nature's) intuition, that a provident person shall always be richer

[39] Ruskin, *Fors Clavigera*, 29, p. 64
[40] *ibid.*, p. 146

than a spendthrift; and an ingenious one more comfortable than a fool'.[41]

The purpose of intervention in the operation of market forces is anything but egalitarian. 'The first necessity of all economical government is to secure the unquestioned and unquestionable working of the great law of Property – that a man who works for a thing shall be allowed to get it, keep it, and consume it, in peace.' This first law of all equities must be enforced 'by law and police truncheon . . . that the cupboard door may have a firm lock to it, and no man's dinner be carried off by the mob, on its way home from the baker's'.[42]

Social economics must succeed in re-directing men's activities to valuable ends. It is never quite certain whether Ruskin is accusing the economists of having caused, by their misconceptions of wealth and sound business activity, a general abandonment of honesty and sense among businessmen, or whether they have simply described accurately the worst aspects of business behaviour. He may have meant that each has learned from the other but he never clearly worked out the relationship between practice and preaching. What is clear is that there must be a total transformation, almost as though Ruskin were asking for a re-definition, or even an inversion of every economic concept. What looks like earnest, purposeful effort is, in fact, worthless, because the goals at which it is directed are without worth. The City of London, for example, 'a ghostly heap of fermenting brickwork, pouring out poison at every pore, – you fancy it is a city of work? Not a bit of it! It is a great city of play; very nasty play, and very hard play, but still play.'[43] This is so because real work is 'a thing done because it ought to be done, and with a determined end'.

Social economics requires the re-definition of every economic term to incorporate some conception of 'ought'. The first task is to rescue the poor by introducing an element of justice into relationships with them. Poverty is always the result of indolence or the misapplication of labour:

it is not accident, it is not Heaven-commanded calamity, it is not the original and inevitable evil of man's nature which fill your streets with lamentation, and your graves with prey. It is only that, when there should have been providence, there has been waste, when there should have been labour there

[41] Ruskin, *Munera Pulveris,* 17, p. 144
[42] *ibid.,* p. 193
[43] Ruskin, *The Crown of Wild Olive,* 18, p. 406

has been luxuriousness, and wilfulness when there should have been subordination.[44]

True economy must be concerned with the wise management of labour, in applying it rationally, in preserving its produce carefully and in distributing it sensibly and according to need. The present economy was so untrue that a great deal of activity concerned with the production of luxuries should be abandoned as, in the present state of need, criminal. Addressing women (as he frequently did, believing them to be both more receptive to moral arguments and far more influential on the conduct of men) he appealed to them to remember the reality of the decorations that 'crown your fair heads, and glow on your wreathed hair, you would see that one weed was always twisted which no one thought of – the grass that grows on graves'.

We do not expect to see strong men take food from children and yet we tolerate and applaud while a clever man beats his competitors so as 'to gather some branch of the commerce of the country into one great cobweb, of which he is himself to be the central spider'.[45] This is injustice of which honourable men should be ashamed to be guilty. It is proper that ability should have wider influence than ineffectiveness, energy should surpass idleness and that wisdom should be better off than folly but is the fool therefore to be utterly crushed?

What do you suppose fools were made for? That you might tread upon them, and starve them, and get the better of them in every possible way? By no means. They were made that wise people might take care of them. That is the true and plain fact concerning the relations of every strong and wise man to the world about him. He has his strength given to him, not that he may crush the weak but that he may support and guide them . . . not merely . . . the meritoriously weak and perishably poor.[46]

Nothing could better illustrate the literally revolutionary nature of the change that Ruskin requires in business behaviour and economic relationship. The possession and the exercise of personal advantage is, in a real sense, to be justified by the acceptance of greater responsibilities. The strong will protect rather than exploit the weak and will use their advantage for greater work and greater sacrifice than that of which those less powerful than themselves are capable. The established order, in which weakness is expertly exploited

[44] *A Joy for Ever*, 16, p. 51
[45] *ibid.*, p. 100
[46] *ibid.*, p. 10

requires men to behave worse than animals whose ferocity is at last dulled when their appetites are sated. But capitalist appetite is never sated and its brutal gluttony is set up for admiration and emulation as the model of the most civilised behaviour. Ruskin denies that his criticisms are based on naivety or ignorance of the real world. The 'real world' as it is described by economists is a perversion of reality and the point of his frequent historical and literary homilies is to demonstrate that the values common to all civilised ages have to be inverted in order to allow for the primacy of economic man. In this way, Ruskin suggests that it is the world of nineteenth-century capitalism that is unreal and that it is the prevailing lunacy of the times that make his own appeal to human values seem insane.

The force and the extent of this critical standpoint is still, after more than a hundred years, difficult to grasp, and the difficulty explains the limited, partial understanding achieved even by Ruskin's admirers. That difficulty may be a measure of the remarkable success achieved by the nineteenth-century ideologies of capitalist economic theory in entrenching it as beyond possibility of question.

Among the more recent and persuasive accounts of the way in which economics came to be established as a science dealing in infrangible laws, Maxine Berg has described how the doubts and anxieties of the 1820s over the process of industrialisation were quelled by a mixture of economic theory and popular science which produced a vulgar faith in economic growth and technical progress.[47] The march of economics succeeded in routing the established and traditional tory protest against the mechanism and unsettlement of industrialisation until it achieved for itself a position of unchallengeable ideological supremacy. The ultimate achievement was when economics, with its attendant sciences of statistics and social administration could acknowledge, with a candour and confidence denied to earlier apologists like Andrew Ure, that there were real problems of social unrest and dislocation to be dealt with, but that their solution lay in the hands of the very science that had exposed, if not produced them. As Berg puts it, 'by setting aside the consideration of social problems as a sphere separate from political economy, the social reformers actually acted to protect political economy from the criticisms of its methodology and its doctrines on industrialization'.[48] Problems of poverty or unemployment came to be regarded as social,

---

[47] Maxine Berg, *The machinery question and the making of political economy, 1815–1848* (Cambridge University Press, 1980), p. 145
[48] *ibid.*, p. 296

or moral, or technical issues which were independent of the influence of political economy. Berg quoted J. P. Kay, writing on the condition of the working classes in Manchester in 1832: 'The evils here unreservedly exposed, so far from being the necessary consequences of the manufacturing system, have a remote and accidental origin, and might by judicious management, be entirely removed.'[49]

That view, or something very like it, came to seem natural and unchallengeable so that the old hostility to economics was quite forgotten. The merit of Ruskin's criticisms of economics lies not in their originality but in their faithfulness to the old tradition. He was, indeed, an old tory. It is a mark of the remoteness of that tradition and of the hegemony achieved by economics that the full extent of his hostility is so often missed and he is claimed as a forebear of welfare state socialism. He is not. He simply reminds us that the calculation of self-interest promoted to an inviolable law of behaviour (whether proposed as the motivation of an individual, a group, or a class) is the foundation of a perverse and demoralised society. Economics is not science, it is no-science. Ruskin's criticisms cannot be incorporated within the framework of economic science, whatever other startling success is claimed for it in turning its geese into swans.

There remains the question as to whether economics has been transformed to any extent by the nature of the criticisms he launched against it. In one sense they can be expected to have little influence for the reasons of impracticability that were originally given by economists for their rejection. A study purporting to be a science can hardly be impressed by an injunction that it should regard one of its central terms, 'value', as that which avails to life. 'Mr Ruskin', as Hobson noted, 'has substituted for the objective commercial standard of money a subjective human standard.'[50] While economists have become more ready to acknowledge the subjective element in value and the subjectivity of choice there is a point beyond which these considerations must be abandoned by economics and ceded to psychology. In this other sense Ruskin's criticisms have come to matter less as the place of economics in the social sciences has been supplemented by psychology and sociology. While these developments have exempted economics from accusations of unreality and ignorance of the effect of moral sentiments in motivating men they have also enabled the science to proceed as though those develop-

---

[49] *ibid.*, p. 305
[50] Hobson, *John Ruskin*, p. 78

ments were none of its business; there is not much evidence of fruitful interchange between economists on the one hand and sociologists and psychologists on the other.

The division within the social sciences cannot be said to have solved the problems created by the unreal abstraction of economics because, as Myrdal says, 'the isolation of one part of social reality by demarcating it as "economic" is logically not feasible. In reality there are no "economic", "sociological", or "psychological" problems, but just problems, and they are all complex.'[51] Nowhere is the truth of this comment better illustrated than in the application of economics to industrial relations and trade union behaviour. A famous controversy between Dunlop and Ross turned on the latter's criticism of the unreality of regarding unions as entirely subject to economic laws. Ruskin, too, contended that economics had virtually nothing to say about relations between employers and workers. The contemporary vision of that criticism is to say that economists misunderstand the field in two respects. The first is in their determination to ignore power, prestige, status and the psychological and social factors concerned in association and in relative pay comparisons. The second is the perversions that their addiction to the market model impose. The economist encompasses trade unions only to blame them to a degree 'ranging from the monetarists' interpretation of trade unions being an irritant through to the contemporary neo-classicists who feel paying wages above subsistence to be a crime against society itself'. And, 'finally by using the neutral notion of the market the economist legitimates the existing distribution of power and this is perhaps one of the greatest criticisms of the economic approach. At the extremes this inequality is reflected in management having the authority to manage, direct and control while the workers work.'[52]

Other evidence suggests that in some respects little has changed since Ruskin's polemical assault upon the Bishop of Manchester's defence of the ruling theology of that noble city. On the count of abstraction, a modern critical economist acknowledges that economic theory has always suffered from this vice and that it still does, that the assumptions entailed are unreal and unexplicit and that 'the very concepts used are defined in relation to those implicit assumptions' so that serious questions can be raised about the adequacy and

[51] Gunnar Myrdal, *Against the stream, critical essays on economics* (London, Macmillan, 1974), p. 142
[52] D. H. Simpson, 'Is there an economics of industrial relations?' (paper presented to University of Wales Colloquium, Duffryn House, July 1980)

usefulness of such economic theory.[53] While some historians suggest
that *laissez-faire* ideology never was characteristic or influential in
nineteenth-century economic doctrine, Professor Milton Friedman
has achieved considerable fame and influence as a defender of
something very like the original dogma. One of the current consequences sometimes attributed to that influence is an unemployed
population in Britain of over three million people and a conviction
that to attempt to do anything about it would be a sentimental breach
of the unalterable laws of economic reality. In a perverse way Ruskin
would have agreed, not with the law of 'do-nothing' but with the
truly unalterable law that we cannot become richer by paying each
other more money but only by producing and providing things of
value. To suggest that the current state of the older economies justifies
Ruskin's worst forebodings for the results of economic insanity is to
fall into the Marxist trap of gleefully predicting that, once again, the
capitalist world is to end on Monday, but much of his criticism is more
convincing now than it has ever been.

In any case, Ruskin's attack on economics was not new, its impact
being in its directness and its return to a classical and tory tradition
that had virtually been silenced by the time he launched it.
Sherburne dismisses any claims to originality on behalf of his criticism
of competition ('it is difficult to find a critic of the *status quo* who does
not oppose competition or wish to restrict its sphere of action')[54] or of
his alternative version of social economics leading to a co-operative
and integrated society. While this acknowledgement is undoubtedly
correct, Sherburne's claim that his one original idea is the notion of
'social abundance', of a provident nature squandered by wasteful and
unnecessary competition, is not entirely well-founded on two grounds:
the first that it was not original, and the second that it was not
Ruskin's. Sherburne argues that the most important of his 'principles
of social criticism' is his pioneering perception of the possibility of an
abundance of good things for all men and his rejection of the usual
Victorian belief that life is a struggle in which scarcity is the expected
condition, that his 'awareness of the possibility of social abundance' is
his most important and original principle.[55] The 'possibility of
abundance' was present, if not pioneered, in the Bible, argued by
Wynstanley, a familiar theme in the English debates following the
Civil War, popularised by Defoe and Cobbett and must have lost all

[53] Myrdal, *Against the stream*, p. 142
[54] Sherburne, *Ambiguities of abundance*, p. 80
[55] *ibid.*, pp. 69 and 84

claim to originality by the mid nineteenth century. It was, in fact, taken up in a new form by the very economists and industrialists against whom Ruskin launched his assault. Berg suggests that the unfavourable attitude taken to economics and industrialisation was attributed to the unfortunate and pessimistic doctrines of Malthus and that something very like the 'abundance' argument was pressed into its defence; she quotes Richard Jones, 'the produce of the earth, so far from experiencing a gradual diminution, is capable of being indefinitely augmented, in proportion to the increase of skill and assistance it receives from capital'.[56] Such a view was very much a part of nineteenth-century capitalist optimism; science and labour (as long as it remained frugal and temperate) would together promote continuous progress and harmony. Ruskin cannot be said to share this optimism. While he agreed that nature was sufficiently beneficent to provide the means of life for all, he acknowledged that life for many would be lived in somewhat straitened circumstances. He was at the same time appalled at the waste of natural resources, which, he was amongst the first to point out, were the basis of real wealth, were finite and exhaustible. For this reason he deplored the waste of materials involved in the decoration of railway stations (the railway station 'is the very temple of discomfort, and the only charity that the builder can extend to us is to show us plainly as may be, how soonest to escape from it'). Railways should work efficiently, 'give large salaries to efficient servants, large prices to good manufacturers, large wages to able workmen; let the iron be tough, and the brickwork solid . . . The time is perhaps not distant when these first necessities may not easily be met . . .'[57] How can the man whose dominant interest was in art be said to believe in abundance when he concluded that art itself would have to be abandoned while we attended to the primary problems of starvation and disease? And in the most precious of all resources, artistic talent, Sherburne acknowledges (without acknowledging the contradiction) that Ruskin sees that here 'there is no surfeit of artistic talent' and that each instance of it must be nurtured with the greatest care.

These minor misunderstandings of Ruskin are largely the result of attributing him, probably falsely and certainly unusefully, to the 'romantic movement'. This is a frequent impediment to his understanding to which we must return, but in the essential feature

[56] Berg, *The machinery question*, p. 119
[57] Ruskin, *The Seven Lamps of Architecture*, 8, pp. 159–60

Sherburne is right to conclude, when all other influences have been catalogued, that Ruskin's criticism 'is an attempt to infuse the ethics of the Gospels into capitalist society',[58] although he seems to be puzzled as to 'what is one to make of Ruskin's infusion of Christian morals into economic analysis. An ethical approach and Biblical rhetoric are, perhaps, the proper medium for an audience inculcated so thoroughly with Christian attitudes as the Victorian.' And he concludes that Ruskin's ethical concern contributes to the stiffening and calcifying of his opinion. The conclusion about Ruskin's economics must be a matter of personal judgment just as the taste for his 'rhetoric' must be left to the individual. It seems to me that the application of ethical standards to economic analysis and behaviour, together with the thunderous language in which that application is conducted, make Ruskin's criticism unique and important.

[58] Sherburne, *Ambiguities of abundance*, p. 163

5

The division of society

We come now to the results of the massive misunderstanding of which Ruskin accuses the economists. The consequence is a succession of splits in society so severe as to threaten its continued existence. The first of these divisions is between rich and poor brought about by capitalism. Ruskin does not complain of the fact of the distinction between rich and poor, he was a consistent defender of inequality, but he insists that capitalism has robbed that distinction of all reason and justice. It is not that the poor are poor, it is that they are poor because they have been robbed and that they are constantly reminded of this wrong by the extravagant display of the rich. A second fatal division which has been brought about by mechanisation is the division between manual and intellectual labour. A third division in society has not so much been created as irritated by capitalism; relationships between classes which should, in a just and moral society, serve to repair damage done to the weak and unfortunate, have been changed by capitalism and the pursuit of wealth so as to intensify such damage and to defend it, as natural or inevitable, even as 'good'. A fourth division is described in terms of a general social decay and demoralisation often set out in metaphorical or even metaphysical terms. Finally, Ruskin sees these divisions as leading to revolutionary breakdown. To begin with, Ruskin warns of this outcome as a nightmare possibility unless the world mends its ways. As he became more and more pessimistic about the possibility of reform he came almost to take a savage pleasure in the prospect of inevitable revolution. In a very qualified sense he was, by the end of his productive life, a revolutionary.

The scale of Ruskin's account of the destruction wrought by capitalism easily compares with Marx. In both, the story begins with robbery and ends with vengeance and violence. Robbery takes several forms. It follows from the economic injunction to buy cheap and sell dear. Whenever we buy cheap goods 'remember we are stealing somebody's labour . . . taking from him the proper reward of his work, and putting it in our own pocket'[1] so that 'the definite result of all our modern haste to be rich is assuredly, and constantly, the murder of a certain number of persons by our hands every year'.[2] This would be unsupportable enough, but the rich add insult to injury by requiring of the poor the moral character of saints in order to make them put up with it.

'Be assured, my good man', – you say to him – 'that if you work steadily for ten hours a day all your life long, and if you drink nothing but water, or the very mildest beer, and live on very plain food, and never lose your temper, and go to church every Sunday, and always remain content in the position in which Providence has placed you, and never grumble, nor swear, and always keep your clothes decent, and rise early, and use every opportunity of improving yourself, you will get on very well, and never come to the parish'.[3]

In this way the poor are doubly oppressed: made poor by the rich, set standards too high for either rich or poor, and despised for their inability to attain them.

Robbery is also carried out by more direct means. The entire business of the world 'turns on the clear necessity of getting on table, hot or cold, if possible meat – but, at least, vegetables, – at some hour of the day'. Turnips can be taken to stand for all food ('since mutton is a transformed state of turnips'). Humanity is divided into two groups, 'the peasant paymasters – spade in hand, original and empirical producers of turnips; and, waiting on them all round, a crowd of polite persons, modestly expectant of turnips, for some, too often theoretical service'.[4] This crowd includes the priests who expect payment for their moral advice, the lawyer, the courtly person, the literary persons 'whom the peasant pays in turnips for talking daintily to him, and there is, lastly, the military person, whom the peasant pays in turnips for standing, with a cocked hat on, in the middle of the field, and exercising a moral influence upon the neighbours'.[5] All of which is perfectly right and proper as long as all those consumers of the peasant's turnips do their jobs well, but those arrangements begin to get out of hand when they don't and they are subject to severe strain if these 'polite persons' get hold of the peasant's land or his tools and begin to charge him an annual rent for what he produces and for

---

[1] Ruskin, *The Two Paths*, 16, p. 401
[2] *ibid.*, p. 405
[3] *ibid.*, p. 400
[4] Ruskin, *Fors Clavigera*, 27, p. 184
[5] *ibid.*, p. 185

using the tools to produce it. The peasant then finds himself paying twice for what has become a service of questionable value to him.

This 'arrangement' in society is defended by economists on the ground that a return to land in the form of rent, to capital in the form of profit and to labour in the form of wages is perfectly natural. It is certainly the way things are in the world but it is not to be supposed that it is natural, says Ruskin. It was not always held to be so:

to receive either a 'remuneration' or a 'portion', or a 'share' for the loan of anything, without personally working, was held by Dante and other such simple persons in the Middle Ages to be one of the worst sins that could be committed *against* nature, and the receivers of such interest were put in the circle of Hell with the people of Sodom and Gomorrah.[6]

Later, defending his own social experiments against the charge of novelty, Ruskin was to say that it was political cowardice that was new 'and your public rascality, and your blasphemy, and your equality, and your science of Dirt'.[7]

The result of this 'arrangement' is that the rich have an ideal of a civilised, cultivated and leisured life which is dependent upon something quite alien to it, on the factory which contains 'in constant employment from eight hundred to a thousand workers, who never drink, never strike, always go to Church on Sunday and always express themselves in respectful language'.[8] But, the defenders of the 'arrangement' say, those people in the factory have a chance to get out of it. They do, just as in a lottery, but the proportions are always fixed and it makes no difference whether they are settled by chance, by ability or by power.

The next defence of the 'arrangement' is that work has to be done and that someone must direct it and someone must do it, some must be at the top and some at the bottom. Quite right, says Ruskin, 'but I beg you to observe that there is a wide difference between being captains or governors of work, and taking the profits of it'. There can be no objection to hard work which is purposeful and useful but hard work which comes to nothing is cruelty. The riches which are based upon the labour of others have the effect of making labour worthless in two senses. In the first, it means that labour is not justly rewarded, the hard working man remains poor. In the second, the labour is wasted: 'of all wastes, the greatest waste that you can commit is the waste of

[6] *ibid.*, p. 189
[7] Ruskin, *Fors Clavigera*, 29, p. 133
[8] Ruskin, *The Crown of Wild Olive*, 18, p. 453

labour'.[9] It can be wasted when workers are employed in the painstaking, life-consuming, production of frivolous luxuries for the rich (in this sense Ruskin was often to admonish young women for their devotion to luxury in dress). It can be wasted also in the condition of life which the type of work imposed upon the worker, worse than death because base labour stultifies thought, deadens the senses and removes hope from life. In the last analysis, then, the irresponsible employment of labour wastes life itself.

The fundamental explanation of such a division in society is not that control of the means of production has fallen into the hands of the few who exploit the many to their advantage. It is, rather, that the few have begun to want to control the means of production, or at least the means of consumption, and have come to see it as a measure of their superiority over the many. Ruskin quotes a passage from Plato's *Critias* to illustrate his conclusion, that every conception of God held by man has consistently warned against succumbing to 'the coarseness of fortune' and has stressed the need to bear 'lightly the burden of gold and possessions'. The current tendency is to displace God by Mammon but the effect of worshipping this new deity will be that

soon no more art, no more science, no more pleasure will be possible. Catastrophe will come; or worse than catastrophe, slow mouldering and withering into Hades. But if you can fix some conception of a true human state of life to be striven for – life, good for all men, as for yourselves; if you determine some honest and simple order of existence ... so sanctifying wealth with 'commonwealth', all your art, your literature, your daily honour ... will join and increase into one magnificent harmony.[10]

So the crippling weakness of the present division in society is not that it perpetuates inequality or even that it is unjust. It is that it corrupts moral judgment, defines vices as virtues, encourages behaviour that is inimical to social good and demands the emulation of selfishness, the most ignoble of human characteristics. When the rich address the poor and catalogue the various virtues and forms of abstinence required of them, they are acknowledging the extent of the real division between them. While the rich deify success, they are horrified at any real prospect of the poor joining the congregation of the same church, for the poor are consistently expected to worship the 'goddess of not-getting on'. The principles, economic rather than moral, on which capitalist society is said to be founded cannot rest upon

[9] *ibid.*, p. 426
[10] *ibid.*, p. 458

leadership or example; it is required that they should rest upon hypocrisy.

Ruskin attributes this inversion of values to capitalism. Fumbling towards the analysis which Marx articulated, he insisted that the struggle between wealth and pauperism had nothing to do with the struggle between rising democracy and receding feudalism. Despite contrary appearances and beliefs no two quarrels could be more different: 'the causes of wealth and nobility are opposite and the causes of anarchy and of the poor are opposite'.[11] He insists time and time again that it is not the sheer inequality of wealth that matters nor even the fact that it may have been acquired by means not far short of robbery. 'Honest' robbery at least suggests the greater strength and purpose of the robber over his victim and hence has the ultimate justification of superior wealth founded upon superior force. The contrast between wealth and poverty under capitalism is explained by guile and deceit, by the contradiction of officially accepted values, by a contradiction of the values upon which society is said to be founded. For this reason, capitalism produces the opposite of good. After a description of the destruction of the South of England and the pollution of its rivers brought about by industrialisation, Ruskin says

that a little good work could put this right but the work that is being done adds to the problem. Why is it that useful work will not be done and useless work will be done, that the strength and life of the English operatives were spent in defiling ground, instead of redeeming it?

Because 'the capitalist can charge percentage on the work in the one case, and cannot in the other'.[12]

The most serious disadvantage of capitalism is rarely considered.

Even by the labourers themselves the operation of capital is regarded only in its effect on their immediate interests, never in the far more terrific power of its appointment of the kind and the object of labour. It matters little, ultimately, how much a labourer is paid for making anything; but it matters fearfully what the thing is, which he is compelled to make.[13]

This is capitalism's weakness, that it cannot produce what is needed and will produce what is either unnecessary or harmful. This is not merely bad for society in a general way, it wastes and distorts the labour of the men and women condemned to produce what it dictates. Ultimately, it may not matter that they should be poor, but

[11] *ibid.*, p. 498
[12] *ibid.*, p. 388
[13] *ibid.*, p. 390

it must matter greatly that they need never have been born for all the good they have done, or worse, that it would have been better that they had not be born for all the bad they have done. Capitalism ill-uses its labour and corrupts it at the same time. And it robs it of any vestige of control. This may be a necessary aspect of the power of capitalism over labour but Ruskin seems to see that the removal of capitalism is not a step sufficient in itself to give labourers control over the means of production. For this to be accomplished, we must ensure that the means of production should never become so complex that they cannot be controlled (or even understood) by the labourers. This is the ultimate explanation for Ruskin's insistence that the motive power of machinery must be provided by hand, wind or water. This is, of course, one of the least acceptable aspects of his outlook, one which influenced William Morris (although Morris has been praised for being much more equivocal or uncertain upon the matter of machinery) and which got them both the reputation of being romantic recidivists in the matter of industry. Ruskin's extremism on this point, however, avoids the difficulties of those modern radical critics of capitalism who abhor its control of the means of production while having no alternative to the manner in which that control is exercised. Critics of 'the technocracy' have reminded us, by reference to the example of the Soviet Union, that belief in a practical utopia to be ushered in, as Kropotkin argued, with productive, scientifically based factories, is likely to founder upon the entrenchment of industrial authority and division that those factories entail. Ruskin asserts that the productivity is likely to be ill-directed (under capitalism) and that complexity is likely to entail servitude (under socialism).

While having no fundamental objection to inequality (apart from frequently warning that its maintenance and defence in extreme form is stupid and likely to be unsuccessful) Ruskin maintains that the inequalities produced by capitalism are irrational.

Generally, good, useful work, whether of the hand or head, is either ill-paid, or not paid at all ... People, as a rule only pay for being amused or being cheated, not for being served. Five thousand a year to your talker, and a shilling a day to your fighter, digger, and thinker is the rule ... Some day assuredly, we shall pay people not quite so much for talking in Parliament and doing nothing, as for holding their tongues out of it and doing something; we shall pay our ploughmen a little more and our lawyers a little less.[14]

[14] *ibid.*, pp. 423–4

These irrationalities of pay differentials, as we might describe them today, are no mere matter of market determination settled by laws of supply and demand. Neither can they be settled by the application of the various techniques of job evaluation. In fact, job evaluation techniques demonstrate, once they are examined, the extent to which culturally determined values play a part in the differences between salaries and wages. However the various aspects of a job are weighed or counted, there is usually a requirement to give a weighting to particular factors. I have never encountered a job evaluation method in which 'education', 'responsibility', 'supervision', or 'mental effort' have not been highly valued in terms of the weighting to be applied to it, while physical effort, discomfort, or repetitive routine have not been valued relatively low. The result is that, with few exceptions, lawyers, managers and salesmen do relatively well, farm labourers, nurses and lorry drivers do relatively badly. Nurses do more important work than hairdressers or journalists and, as it happens, there is usually a shortage of them; what depresses their income is the values of the society that pays them.

Ruskin identifies the difference in terms of a distinction between intellectual and manual work: the one is commonly valued highly, the other not. In itself, he says, the distinction is worthless:

we usually fall into much error by considering the intellectual powers as having dignity in themselves . . . the truth is that the intellect becomes noble or ignoble according to the food we give it, and the kind of subjects with which it is conversant. It is not the reasoning power which, of itself, is noble, but the reasoning power occupied with its proper objects . . . the intellect, going through the same processes, is yet mean or noble according to the matter it deals with, and wastes itself in mere rotatory motion, if it be set to grind straws and dust.[15]

So whether intellectual work is valuable or not depends upon its object and its purpose, it is not by definition valuable in itself. But there must be a distinction between brain work and manual work. In the first place, if manual work is not done we cannot live; but if brain work is not done life will not be worth living. Rough work has to be done by rough men and gentle work by gentle men. Ruskin's understanding of the distinction was probably deeper and more realistic than any other 'gentlemen' and we shall return to his account later. But he is distinguishing between two kinds of work, not between work and idleness and certainly not between working poverty and

[15] Ruskin, *The Stones of Venice*, II, p. 203

idle luxury. The first necessity of social life is 'that he should keep who has justly earned' as this is the proper basis of division between rich and poor but 'the power held over those who are earning wealth by those who already possess it, and only use it to gain more' is an improper basis of division in society.

It is physically impossible for a well-educated, intellectual, or brave man to make money the chief object of his thoughts; just as it is for him to make his dinner the principal object of them. All healthy people like their dinners, but their dinner is not the main object of their lives. So all healthy-minded people like making money – ought to like it, and to enjoy the sensation of winning it; but the main object of their life is not money, it is something better than money.[16]

Ruskin seems to have particularly despised the man who took up artistic or literary work simply as a means of making money; it would be better for him to have been maintained by honourable beggary.[17]

Ruskin was not always entirely consistent in his attitude to the division between intellectual and manual labour. On the one hand he believed that the division was inevitable and that nothing could or should be done to disguise it or to patronise the labourer with fine words about the honourableness and dignity of manual work. But he also maintained (particularly in relation to the gothic) that the separation of the two was dangerous. Labour should be illuminated by thought and thought made healthy by labour. In each profession,

no master should be too proud to do its hardest work; the painter should grind his own colours; the architect work in the mason's yard with his men; the master-manufacturer be himself a more skilled operative than any man in his mills; and the distinction between one man and another be only in experience and skill, and the authority and wealth which these must naturally and justly obtain.[18]

Ruskin's later experiments in community work in the Guild of Saint George were unsuccessful and his recruitment of an intellectual and aesthetic work force to rebuild the Hincksey road was deservedly the subject of great mirth, but both at least demonstrate the seriousness of his belief that the division of society between clever and stupid work was to be overcome. A good deal of the reason for his energetic contribution to workers' education arose from his conviction that workmen needed the stimulus of intellectual activity, not so that they

[16] Ruskin, *The Crown of Wild Olive*, 18, p. 412
[17] Ruskin, *Fors Clavigera*, 28, p. 646
[18] Ruskin, *The Stones of Venice*, 10, p. 201

could work better or work at better paid jobs, but so that they could be compensated or atoned for the dull and unrewarding nature of their work. The evidence of his convictions and a good deal of the activity of his life suggests that he believed the overriding distinction between manual and intellectual labour to be the most dangerous fissure in society and we shall see that his educational proposals are built upon the need for a unity to be established between the two.

But he was far from maintaining that 'rough men' could be turned into intellectuals and 'gentle men' turned into labourers. His conclusion was amongst the most radical that have ever been reached, that an element of thoughtfulness appropriate to the level of the work was so morally and socially necessary that the work itself should be kept within the technical limits which facilitated its inclusion. Ruskin's example of the gothic is held up to us largely to make this point, that at whatever cost in productivity or profit the engagement of the workmen's mind in what they do in work must be achieved to prevent their decay and the decay of their society. We are familiar with the discussion of the consequences of not doing this in terms of the discussion of conceptions of alienation and anomy. Many of these discussions entail the steps that are to be taken in order to repair the consequences of industrialisation and the extension of the division of labour. Durkheim, in particular, seems to acknowledge that some damage to the workmen is inevitable and must be faced in the process of coming to terms with industrial processes. Much of the positivist social science tradition established since Saint-Simon regards the development of industrialisation as inevitable, or progressive, or both, and requiring some kind of deliberate human adjustment so as to reduce the evident threat. Ruskin incurs the hostility of criticism of his 'romanticism',[19] or of his lack of realism, medievalism, or reactionary character.

In fact, and in one respect, Ruskin is more realistic than most of his critics and most of the optimistic radicals who believe that the forces of industrialisation can somehow be won over, or managed, or humanised; the possible exception among sociologists is Max Weber. Marx quite clearly saw that capitalism would be driven, in the pursuit of efficiency, to draw off intelligence from the production process in order to make it a special function of management. The development of this special function has become the central feature of

[19] This has become a standard epithet or starting point in the critical appreciation of Ruskin, particularly in relationship to his aesthetics. We will attempt to give it some attention in the final chapter.

advanced capitalism (or, as it is variously described, 'post-capitalism', or 'the technocracy') to the extent that it is seen as the crucial area in production and its control as therefore representing a much more critical and revolutionary area than the territory once believed to be so hopefully occupied by the proletariat. This preoccupation with the role of the intelligentsia in the productive and social relationships of capitalism is expressed clearly by Gramsci who notes, in passing, that although all men are intellectuals not all men have in society the function of intellectuals. He goes on to suggest that 'in the modern world, technical education, closely bound to industrial labour even at the most primitive and unqualified level, must form the basis of the new type of intellectual' and he concludes

the mode of being of the new intellectual can no longer exist in eloquence, which is an exterior and monetary mover of feelings and passions, but in active participation in practical life . . . from technique-as-work one proceeds to technique-as-science and to the humanistic conception of history, without which one remains 'specialised' and does not become 'directive'.[20]

The special relationship of intelligence to production and the special role of the intelligentsia leads to special problems within the Marxist perspective on capitalism. The problems are of two kinds. Intelligence is so closely related to the production process that its influence is extended to the wider areas of science and general historical thought; thought becomes the generalised expression of capitalist production as it is more and more closely related to the direction of capitalist production. In this way, productive relationships and requirements influence the whole of intellectual and cultural life. The second feature is that the proletariat, against whom intelligence is directed as a controlling agency, is itself progressively deprived of any intellectual activity in its work. Outside it, as Gramsci says, workers may remain intellectuals in their private or non-productive capacity but the 'private' area is itself subject to capitalist control by way of consumerism and the exploitation of leisure. Thus, there is little intelligence left in work and less opportunity for its exercise outside it. The consequence is the cretinisation of the proletariat which Marx sometimes alluded to but the consequences of which, in terms of his own theory, were too bleakly pessimistic to examine. The Marxist analysis of the completeness and efficiency of capitalist control subsuming, as it finally does, intelligence itself,

[20] Quinton Hoare and Geoffrey Nowell Smith (eds.), *Selections from the prison notebooks of Antonio Gramsci* (London, Lawrence and Wishart, 1971), pp. 9–10

leaves no room for any voluntary, willed or intelligent reaction. The result must be despair at the ultimate triumph of rational bureaucracy and capitalist control.

It is as though Ruskin sees or intuitively grasps this trap laid by the immense power of the capitalist industrial process. He certainly argues that, to break free from that trap, the process must be challenged and controlled or, as the critics of his 'unrealism' might have put it, that he demanded that the clock must be put back. In one sense the conclusion from within the Marxist analysis may be that he was right.

Ruskin's discussion of class divisions in society is relatively simple and rather archaic in that he focuses on a class which had come to be regarded, even in the nineteenth century, as anachronistic. But Ruskin's explanation of the foundation of the power of the landed squirearchy is anything but irrelevant.

In January 1877, addressing his first letter to working men after a break of two years of illness, Ruskin explains that wealth is finite, limited by the natural resources of the earth, and that the ownership of land was first established by force and is now maintained by force.

Some day, I do not doubt you will yourselves seize it by force. Land never has been, nor can be, got, nor kept, otherwise when the population on it was as large as it could maintain. The establishment of laws respecting its possession merely defines and directs the force by which it is held : and fraud, so far from being an unimportant mode of acquiring wealth, is now the only possible one.[21]

Three years earlier Ruskin had been equally clear in explaining to the landowners that their title had been established in force and could be maintained only by force. If the land was to be kept out of the hands of the mob ('deaf and blind as you') the squires would have to fight for it as their ancestors had fought, 'this is your only sound and divine right'.[22] And Ruskin disabuses them of the fallacy of relying on the laws of political economy or of the British constitution. The natural laws of political economy will be no defence, 'the vast natural law of carnivorous rapine . . . will be in *equitable* operation then; and not, as they fondly hoped, all on their own side'.

The important characteristic of this and similar passages is that it demonstrates Ruskin's clear understanding of the basis of ownership

[21] Ruskin, *Fors Clavigera*, 29, p. 16
[22] Ruskin, *Fors Clavigera*, 28, p. 152

in power, his refusal to consider any cant about constitutional rights
as anything but a legitimatory mask for power. The unusual extent of
his respect for power in ownership leads him to dismiss, not only
constitutional or legal titles, but almost to refuse to engage in any
discussion of morality and ownership, as though he acknowledged
that power was the basis of morality itself. This is a position of unusual
rigour, similar to that taken up, with great success, by Thrasymachus
in his debate with Socrates in the *Republic*. The possession of land
(achieved by force) is justified only by the will and the ability to
defend it. 'If a man is not ready to fight for his land, and for his wife,
no legal forms can secure them to him. They can offer him possession;
but neither grant sanction nor protect it. To his own love, to his own
resolution, the lordship is granted; and to those only.' Possession is
justified only by the will to defend it. The first respect in which the
landowners have been irresponsible, have abandoned their role, is
demonstrated in the failure of the will to defend themselves. Without
that will they have lost all right to acquire obedience of others. But
this failure of will turns out to be a moral failure after all. The 'right'
to exercise force, or the readiness to exercise it in defence of property,
is one that the landowners have withdrawn from themselves. Ruskin
asks the titled landowners are they 'Lords of What? . . . Do you mean
merely when you go to the root of the matter, what you sponge on the
British farmer for your living and are strong bodied paupers
compelling your dole?' It is not from cowardice but shame that they
will not be ready to fight for their dole and their shame is brought
about because they transgressed, claimed God's heritage as their own,
abandoned their responsibilities and, as a result, have abdicated all
moral responsibility.

Ruskin's prophecy of an apocalyptic judgment for the landed
gentry of England (a false prophecy as it turned out to be) is based on
his conclusion that its members had failed to live up to the
responsibility of leadership and privilege in a society knit together by
mutual dependence. Some of his most violently polemical passages are
devoted to a description of that failure. In 1873 in *The Bible of Amiens*
he returned to his description of the English upper classes in order to
defend it. They were, he said, 'the scurviest louts that ever fouled
God's earth with their carcasses'. He went on with typical care to
classify louts into three groups: the third, 'the Ducal or Marquisian
lout has no knowledge of anything under the sun, except what sort of
horse's quarters will carry his own . . . and no faculty under the sun of

doing anything except cutting down the trees his fathers planted for him, and selling the lands his fathers won'.[23] The explanation for Ruskin's venom lies in his account of the trees and the land. Aristocracy and kingship play a vital part in his outlook, he was, as he maintained 'an old tory'. Society could not be held together without a responsible, self-sacrificing leadership. His despair was largely the result of what he saw as the behaviour and the corruption of this vital class. While Charles Kingsley and others were somewhat unctuously telling the aristocracy that it was the finest in Europe and had only to set an example of propriety for the masses to follow, Ruskin was enraged at its failure. His despair was proportionate to his expectations:

you will see your father the Devil's will done on earth, as it is in hell.

I call him your father, for you have denied your mortal fathers, and the Heavenly One. You have declared, in act and thought, the ways and laws of your sires – obsolete, and of your God – ridiculous; above all, the habits of obedience, and the elements of justice. You were made lords over God's heritage. You thought to make it your own heritage; to be lords of your own land not of God's land. And to the issue of ownership you are come.

And what a heritage it was, you had the lordship over . . . the earth with its fair fruits . . . the men, souls and bodies, your fathers' true servants for a thousand years, – their lives and their children's lives given into your hands, to save or destroy; their food yours . . . their thought yours, – the priest and tutor chosen for them by you; their hearts yours, – if you would but so much as know them by sight and name, and give them the passing grace of your own glance, as you dwelt among them, their King. And all this monarchy and glory, all this power and love, all this land and its people, you pitifulest, foulest of Iscariots, sopped to choking with the best of the feast from Christ's own fingers, you have deliberately sold to the highest bidder.[24]

This passage represents perfectly Ruskin's rage at the wasted opportunity and the consequences of the aristocracy's stupidity and selfishness. He went on to tell the squires what they had to do to survive if they were not to give way to small peasant proprietorship in which they would discover whether they could survive as peasant proprietors. They should fix their tenants' rents and diminish them as they improved the land. They should fix the income necessary for their own lives and spend the rest on estate management and improvement, and on the education of their tenants' children.

It is very doubtful whether the importance attached to the landowners by Ruskin is justified and whether it does not open him to

[23] Ruskin, *Love's Meinie*, 25, p. 129
[24] Ruskin, *Fors Clavigera*, 28, pp. 153–4

the charge of preoccupation with an agricultural condition in an industrial and commercial age. In Marx's terms he is returning to an aspect of class conflict long since settled, he is trying to resurrect a dead class. But Ruskin would say that all wealth comes from the land so that who owns the land and how he administers it is a crucial question. Further, the aristocracy were vital factors in the capital formation of the nineteenth century and were transforming themselves from a land-owning aristocracy into a share-owning bourgeoisie. In this respect the comment of an historian serves both to confirm Ruskin's account of the aristocracy's profligacy and to explain why his prediction of their fate turned out to be wrong. Checkland says that a number of landed estates were saved from general collapse only by sales but that 'by means of windfalls and retrenchment the aristocratic families redeemed a situation which by Victoria's accession in 1837 had become dangerous, and were thus to continue their hold upon government and the affairs of the nation'.[25] It is for this very reason that Ruskin accuses them of sacrificing their heritage and their leadership. But what of the class they join? Is it not possible for the entrepreneurs to demonstrate the same qualities of leadership and responsibility that have been quit by the aristocracy, all the more so as their own ranks are intermingled with the gentry? This raises the interesting question as to the possibility of paternalism as a social policy in an industrial society. Again, we must defer its examination until we come to a final attempt to measure the significance and importance of his views. Ruskin certainly does not confine his examination of class relationships to the single case of landowners and arcadian peasants.

He produces a four-fold classification based, not on ownership, but on modes of activity. He distinguishes between those who work and those who play, those who produce the means of life and those who consume it, between those who work with their head and those who work with their hands, and between those who work wisely and those who work foolishly. In order to establish the first division he defines play as 'an exertion of body or mind, made to please ourselves and with no determined end; and work [as] a thing done because it ought to be done, and with a determined end'.[26] He goes on to catalogue the games engaged in by the 'playing classes'. 'The first of all English games is making money.' It is a game of no practical purpose done to

[25] S. G. Checkland, *The rise of industrial society in England, 1815–1885* (London, Longmans, 1971), p. 283
[26] Ruskin, *The Crown of Wild Olive*, 18, p. 404

please those engaged in it and without any determined or useful end.
It has the appearance of being unlike other games because they are
costly while this one appears to produce money. The difference is
deceptive and rests upon the difference between making money and
winning it. The other games include hunting and shooting, the ladies'
game of fashion, playing at literature, playing at art, but 'the play of
play, the great gentleman's game', is war.

All these games are paid for in real work and, says Ruskin, a
distinction between classes in which the play of one is sustained by the
blood of the other cannot be tolerated. But this is not to deny wealth
to those who have 'lawfully' (that is, with moral justification)
acquired it. The proper basis of wealth is that a man should be paid
the fair value of his work which, if he chooses not to spend it today he
should be free to spend tomorrow. If the idle person (and that
category, of course, will include the financial speculator) 'is then
allowed to attack the other, and rob him of his well-earned wealth,
there is no more any motive for saving, or any reward for good
conduct; and all society is thereupon dissolved, or exists only in
systems of rapine'.[27]

In *Fors Clavigera*, Ruskin sets out to examine 'the complex modes of
injustice' which govern the relationship between the industrious
classes. These are basically of three kinds: clergy (who live by
teaching), soliders (who live by fighting, 'either by robbing wise
peasants, or getting themselves paid by foolish ones'), and peasants
(who are the producers of food). He is clearly using these terms in the
broadest sense, the manufacturer and artist are, he says, developed
states of the peasant. The unjust relationships between these three
groups are constant in all advanced societies, and are full of mystery
and beauty in their inequity. The relationship between peasant and
soldier depends in part upon the acceptance of the continual risk of
death in order to escape the 'injury of servile toil'. The distinction
between clergy and peasant depends upon greater intelligence which
prefers to learn and to teach in return for the smallest pay as long as it
can remain so occupied. Both soldiers and clergy become tyrannical
when they cease to be satisfied with their maintenance in order to
carry on their preferred tasks and when the one uses his strength and
the other his sanctity in order to gain elevation over other men.

The clergy, in the narrower sense of priests, came to be the object of
references that were consistently contemptuous in Ruskin's later life.

[27] *ibid.*, p. 412

Their case paralleled his attitude to the aristocracy; his expectation of
their duty and importance was great and his rage at their performance was proportionate. In 1871 an aggrieved clergyman's wife
wrote to complain of Ruskin's treatment and to remind him that the
clergyman was the poor man's only friend. Ruskin replied that it was
the worst thing that could be said of them.

Have they, then, so betrayed their Master's charge and mind, in their
preaching to the rich; so smoothed their words, and so sold their authority,
that, after twelve hundred years' entrusting of the gospel to them, there is no
man in England (this is their chief plea for themselves forsooth) who will
have mercy on the poor, but they . . .?[28]

Since the greatest cause of current decay was the abandonment of
Christian practice in a society still devoted to the forms of Christian
preaching, Ruskin believed that a heavy responsibility lay upon the
preachers whose effort seemed to have contributed only to their own
comfort and the maintenance of a corrupted order. He accused the
clergy of taking the name of God in vain every Sunday, and when
they objected that they had nothing to do with the condition of
society he replied: 'You have everything to do with it. Were you not
told to come out and be separate from all evil? You take whatever
advantage you can of the evil work and gain of this world, and yet
expect the people you share with to be damned out of your way, in the
next.'[29] A relatively minor aspect of his clerical criticism turned on the
extent to which the clergy's lives represented the division in society
between those at work and those at play. He reported the views of a
clerical friend who had been much affected by the degenerate nature
of brickmakers. 'Let him go and make, and burn, a pile or two with
his own hands; he will thereby receive apocalyptic visions of a nature
novel to his soul.'[30]

Ruskin seems constantly to be amazed at the patience, fortitude or
stupidity of the poor in putting up with their position in a divided
society. He compares it to the divisions of a theatre, and asks, why do
the people in the pit allow us to keep our places in the stalls and the
boxes: 'here we sit at our ease, the dressed dolls of the place, with little
more in our heads, most of us, than wax; stuck up by those poor little
prentices, clerks and orange-sucking mobility . . . What for?'[31]

The purposelessness and injustice of these divisions in society

[28] Ruskin, *Fors Clavigera*, 27, p. 173
[29] *ibid.*, p. 204
[30] Ruskin, *Fors Clavigera*, 28, p. 567
[31] *ibid.*, p. 490

seemed to be reflected in a general social decay which goes beyond poverty. Ruskin sees its material form in the City of London, absorbing food produced by agricultural land in order to feed a variety of unproductive trades engaged in a life so vile that 'they are compelled to seek some pastime in a vile literature, the demand for which again occupies another enormous class, who do nothing to feed or dress themselves'.[32] In this way the country is impoverished so as to feed 'this fermenting mass of unhappy human beings, – news-mongers, novel-mongers, picture-mongers, poison-drink-mongers, lust and death-mongers; the whole smoking mass of it one vast dead-marine storeshop ... with every activity in it, a form of putrefaction'.[33] The spreading suburbs of Sydenham and Penge were just as depressing, full of men with 'no faculty beyond that of cheating in business; no pleasures but in smoking or eating; and no ideas, nor any capacity of forming any ideas, of anything that has yet been done of great, or seen of good in this world'.[34] The suburbs were composed of damp shells of brick, packing cases to temporarily store the rising middle classes, trying to live like the Duke of Devonshire on the salaries of railroad clerks.[35]

The utter demoralisation of urban society is symbolished in the descriptions of polluted scenes in which Ruskin seemed to take a perverse (even perverted) pleasure. After such a description of the destruction of the once beautiful Croxted Lane he speculates about the consequences of such calamities. What will be the effect on children brought up with Croxted Lane as the only alternative to their front street? Because it is natural for children to take pleasure in their surroundings what kind of pleasure will derive from such unnatural surroundings? They may require the finding of pleasure in physical corruption, evidence of which Ruskin finds in signs of moral disease in modern fiction (the novels of George Eliot were amongst his favourite objects of criticism in this respect). This argument takes a further turn when he says that great natural beauty is often very difficult to describe but human language can always 'make a shift, somehow, to give account of it' because beauty has been in the world

---

[32] ibid., p. 135
[33] ibid., p. 137
[34] Ruskin, Fors Clavigera, 27, p. 530
[35] The irony of this bitter account is that the Ruskin family itself, as representatives of successful tradesmen, was amongst the forerunners of this suburban extension, moving from Hunter Street to Herne Hill in 1823, to Denmark Hill in 1843, and finally, in the person of John, retiring to a comfortable retreat in the English Lakes near Coniston at Brantwood in 1872 (James S. Dearden, Facets of Ruskin (London, Charles Skilton, 1970))

since the world began and man has lived with it and fashioned his language to express it, 'whereas the peculiar forms of devastation induced by modern city life have only entered the world lately; and no existing terms of language known to me are enough to describe the forms of filth, and modes of ruin'.[36] He then suggests an orderly and established cohabitation of man, nature and language which has been grossly disturbed by industrial urbanisation. 'Ordinary' language and forms of literature will be inappropriate even to the description of the new environment, much less to its analysis. The consequence of the development of new forms must be their corruption. Thus the ultimate effect of the development of an industrial civilisation will be the destruction of language itself.

Ruskin suggests that the causes of this corruption include the overcrowding and isolation, or what he significantly calls the 'secrecy' of city-dwellers, the 'trampling pressure and electric friction of town life', and monotony, the prevention of any emotion derived from nature so that, deprived of the natural excitements of the seasons' changes and the seasons' discipline, the town-dweller turns to more morbid sources of excitement. Confronted with such oppressive surroundings the inhabitants of towns sink under them, 'the incapacity of their own minds to refuse the pollution, and of their own wills to oppose the weight of the staggering mass that chokes and crushes them into perdition, brings every law of healthy existence into question ... and every alleged method of help and hope into doubt'.[37]

This sense of the unavoidable interaction between the mind and its environment, human perceptions and the language used to express them, is very much part of Ruskin's conception of the unity of all things. There is, he says, a 'practical connection' between physical and spiritual light, 'you cannot love the real sun, that is to say physical light and colour rightly, unless you love the spiritual sun, that is to say justice and truth rightly'.[38] It was a connection he had made before and it was consistent in him to develop the opposite comparison, between moral pollution and darkness.

This is the theme of the lectures he gave in 1884 under the title *The Storm Cloud of the Nineteenth Century*. For once, he tells us, he means his title to be taken literally: he wishes to draw to our notice 'a series of cloud phenomena, which so far as I can weigh existing evidence, are

---

[36] Ruskin, *Fiction, Fair and Foul*, 34, p. 266
[37] *ibid.*, p. 269
[38] Ruskin, *Fors Clavigera*, 28, p. 614

peculiar to our own times' which are given no description in classical or modern literature and which have not been noticed by meteorologists. After an analysis of different kinds of cloud formations he quotes from his diary an entry on 4 July 1875 which noted, after a clear calm sky at 5.30 a.m.

a gradually rising wind, of which the tremulous action scarcely permits the direction to be defined . . . This wind is the plague-wind of the eighth decade of years in the nineteenth century; a period which will assuredly be recognised in future meteorological history as one of phenomena hitherto unrecorded in the courses of nature, and characterized pre-eminently by the almost ceaseless action of this calamitous wind.[39]

Ruskin says he first noticed the phenomenon in 1871 and described it in the August issue of *Fors Clavigera*, adding that the cloud looked partly as if it were made of poisonous smoke, but more 'as if it were made of dead men's souls – such of them as are not gone yet where they have to go'.[40] Ruskin gives several extracts from his diaries: 'raining in foul drizzle, slow and steady; sky pitchdark . . . diabolic clouds over everything', 'south plague-wind of the bitterest nastiest, poisonous blight, and fretful flutter', a pale sun 'like a half-crown seen through soap suds'. After many such descriptions he concludes that he cannot explain the new weather 'but I can tell you what meaning it would have borne to the men of old time . . . Of states in such moral gloom every seer of old predicted the physical gloom.'

Ruskin's account of the Storm Cloud was received with ridicule. He quoted an extract from the *Daily News* of 6 February 1884 which suggested that the most plausible explanation was that 'Mr Ruskin, as he gets on in years, is more sensitive to disagreeable weather.' Mr H. L. Lees, a substantial citizen of Oldham and the original owner of my own Library Edition set (and whose annotations are almost as enjoyable as the printed text) noted the Storm Cloud as an example of Ruskin's 'eccentricity'. Ruskin seems to have anticipated this reaction, hoping that the extracts from his diary of perfect weather would serve 'to guard you against the absurdity of supposing that it all only means that I am myself soured, or doting, in my old age, and always in an ill humour'.[41] His loyal editors assure us that it was not so because as they point out, in the matter of the close observation of weather, Ruskin was an expert: 'few men have ever studied so many

[39] Ruskin, *The Storm Cloud of the Nineteenth Century*, 34, p. 31
[40] *ibid.*, p. 33
[41] *ibid.*, p. 36

sunsets, and perhaps no man has ever studied so many sunrises, as Ruskin'.[42] They also quote evidence and argument to suggest that a significant climatic change had indeed been brought about by industrial pollution and smoke but that Ruskin chose not to advance this solid material explanation. It seems more likely to be the case that Ruskin did not want to suggest this simple cause. At the very least, he was deliberately exploring the metaphor of nature as a reflection of the state of society. There is little doubt that the language he uses to describe this phenomenon goes far beyond the description of an effect attributable to material causes; some of the passages produce a frisson of realisation of a gradually unfolding natural catastrophy. Ruskin seems to be deliberately seeking the same nightmare effect as is produced in biblical prophecy or in the parallel between human and elemental violence in Shakespearian tragedy.

The tragedy which Ruskin is attempting to prophecy is total social and moral collapse. Ruskin begins by warning of its imminence unless the employers and landlords begin to exercise a real responsibility for their dependants, unless they begin to exercise guardianship rather than exploitation. It is certain that, by the end, he sees catastrophy as unavoidable, the world as irredeemable except through some cleansing cataclysm. It is not at all certain whether he is prepared to welcome this conclusion. He describes the situation of a Glasgow clerk who cannot afford books:

Only a day and a half in the week on which one can get a walk in the country (and how few have as much or anything like it!), just bread enough earned to keep me alive, on those terms – one's daily work asking not so much as a lucifer match's worth of human intelligence; unwholesome besides – one's chest, shoulders and stomach getting hourly more useless. Smoke above for sky, mud beneath for water; and the pleasant consciousness of spending one's weary life in the pure service of the devil!

And then follows a passage of rare ambiguity in the writer who, above all else, prided himself (when once accused of 'hedging') on being 'pretty well known to be precisely the one who cares least either for hedge or ditch, when he chooses to go across country'. This is what he says to the poor clerk:

Very solemnly, my good clerk-friend, there is something to be *done* in this matter; not merely to be read. Do you know any honest men who have a will of their own, among your neighbours? If none, set yourself to seek for such; if any, commune with them on this one subject, how a man may have sight of

[42] Ruskin, editor's introduction, 34, p. xxiv

the Earth he was made of, and his bread out of the dust of it – and peace! And find out what it is that hinders you now from having these, and resolve that you will fight it, and put end to it.[43]

The language has a conspiratorial, muffled tone. Ruskin may be an uncertain revolutionary in that his enthusiasm was less than complete, but he was totally convinced of the inevitability of some kind of revolutionary finale to the capitalist tragedy, of the immanence of 'mercantile catastrophe, and political revolution which will end the "amusement" of managers and leave the ground (too fatally) free'.[44]

In his earlier and more optimistic days he had wagged an admonitory finger at the upper classes, warning them of the need to mend their ways, but showing no great sympathy for their radical chastisement. The extravagance of the upper classes is hastening the advance of republicanism, 'no agitators, no clubs, no epidemical errors, ever were, or will be fatal to social order in any nation. Nothing but the guilt of the upper classes, wanton, accumulated, reckless, and merciless, ever overthrows them'.[45] Ruskin sees this situation coming about because 'the people' will come to suspect that they have been exploited, and will be right. But Ruskin is none too clear about the consequences of this exploitation. If it is to be a socialist demand for fair shares, or for a 'radical' re-distribution of wealth, for robbing the rich to pay the poor, he sees that the cure will be no better than the disease that prompted it; the people will simply adopt the same corrupting catechism of economic greed that caused the downfall of their masters. He does not blame them for this reaction, he simply believes it to be no improvement on the present situation and that it provides anything but a radical alternative to it. In this sense he seems to arrive at a state of considerable doubt about the possibility of any improvement at all. He rarely voices this doubt with any great clarity, but its existence may explain the greater pessimism into which he sank.

One reason for its development is the suspicion that 'the people' come to share the corruption of their masters. The past system of misgovernment, he says, has produced a class which is by now very difficult to govern because it has lost the habit and faculty of reverence or respect. There is by now a large sector of the population which

---

[43] Ruskin, *Fors Clavigera*, 27, p. 291
[44] *ibid.*, p. 661
[45] Ruskin, *The Oxford Museum*, 16, pp. 343–4

worships only itself, 'which can neither see anything beautiful around it, nor conceive anything virtuous above it'.[46] He sees the people as an understandably vengeful mob, a gypsy hunt, 'deaf and blind as you – frantic for the spoiling of you'.[47] They will rise because of their distress and because they will understand the extent to which they have been deceived.

Not all the lying lips of commercial Europe can much longer deceive the people in their rapidly increasing distress, nor arrest their straight battle with the cause of it . . . with what burning and fuel of fire they will work out their victory, – God only knows, nor what they will do to Barabbas, when they have found out that he is a Robber, and not a King. But that discovery of his character and capacity draws very near; and no less change in the world's ways than the former fall of Feudalism itself.[48]

The revolution impending will make all previous insurrections seem like trifles because this time the division is between informed men seeking redress by honourable and lawful means on the one side and, on the other, 'men capable of compassion and open to reason, but with personal interests at stake so vast, and with all the gear and mechanism of their acts so involved in the web of past iniquity, that the best of them are helpless, and the wisest blind'.[49] The suggestion is here of innocent exploiters, swept along in a materially determined tide, acting out their part as though they were in control of economic forces of Marxian proportions. But the wider implication of the people, able to revolt because they are corrupted by their masters to the extent of sharing their masters' values, is the more usual of Ruskin's predictions for society. The people have been misgoverned and will try the system of no government and, as they are an extensive class, the experiment is likely to be widespread and conducted to the delight of all foolish persons and the profit of all wicked ones. Ruskin takes a savage, almost nihilistic delight in the prospect of this revolution without hope. It will not be prevented by the landowners protesting that their divided lands will

not give much more than the length and breadth of his grave to each mob-proprietor. They will answer, 'we will have what we can get; – at all events, *you* shall keep it no longer'. And what will you do? Send for the Life Guards and clear the House, and then with all the respectable members of society as special constables, guard the streets?[50]

[46] Ruskin, *The Crown of Wild Olive*, 18, p. 497
[47] Ruskin, *Fors Clavigera*, 28, p. 151
[48] *ibid.*, p. 671
[49] Ruskin, *Fors Clavigera*, 29, p. 258
[50] Ruskin, *Fors Clavigera*, 28, p. 153

In contemplation of this ultimate crisis, Ruskin did not stop short of examining the ultimate question: what should be the duty of the army? The soldier's position is closely comparable to that of a slave, bound to do the work he is directed to do. The kind of work that they are to be put to ought to be an important question for society. The soldiers of society are likely to be its best men, most suited to be the masters; in present society those who are the masters are most naturally suited to be its slaves. He asks of the soldiers who were 'too proud to become shop-keepers: are you satisfied, then, to become the servants of shop-keepers?' And Ruskin proceeds to a series of questions so severe that they were, had the conditions he predicted come about and had his questions been given wide circulation in the army, of the kind that are followed by prosecution for sedition:

You imagine yourselves to be the army of England: how, if you should find yourselves at last only the police of her manufacturing towns, and the beadles of her Little Bethels?

A soldier's vow to his country is that he will die for the guardianship of her domestic virtue, of her righteous laws, and of her anyway challenged or endangered honour. A state without virtue, without laws, and without honour, he is bound *not* to defend; nay, bound to redress by his own right hand that which he sees to be base in her.[51]

Although Ruskin often doubts whether the moral conviction of the rich will be sufficient to enable them to defend their property by force (force being the only ultimate title) he suggests that for a number of logistical reasons the force will not be sufficient even if the will is there. Sending for the Life Guards answered well enough against the Chartists on Kennington Common in 1848 but in 1880 it will not be the Chartists who have to be dealt with.

Are you prepared to clear the streets with the Woolwich infant – thinking that out of the mouth of that suckling, God would perfect your praise, and ordain your strength? Be it so; but every grocer's and chandler's shop in the thoroughfare of London is a magazine of petroleum and percussion power; and there are those who will use both among the Republicans. And you will see your father the Devil's will done on earth, as it is in hell.[52]

The most obvious and necessary comment on Ruskin's dire predictions is that they were wrong. There was to be no civil disturbance on anything like the Chartist scale for the next thirty to forty years and even then, the engineering strikes of 1917 and the later

[51] Ruskin, *The Crown of Wild Olive*, 18, pp. 483–4
[52] Ruskin, *Fors Clavigera*, 28, p. 153

general strike of 1926 showed no real sign of producing general revolutionary ferment. Ruskin was not only wrong about the revolutionary potential (or danger, the choice depends upon which side of the barricade you are likely to stand) of England; social and economic conditions were better than they had been throughout the nineteenth century and were destined for further improvement apart from the depression of the 1870s (and even then it was raw material prices that went up while food prices rose less or actually declined).[53] There is a real sense in which Ruskin seems to have joined his voice to the debate about the 'condition of England' when the debate was over and the condition had improved. Professor Gash concludes that 'all the indications suggest in fact that from the mid-1840's conditions improved for the working classes as a whole and from 1850 it is indisputable that there was a rise in real wages'.[54] If that is true for the general condition, he adds that 'in the industrial areas the aristocrats of labour lived on a scale unknown to the Southern rural labourer and beyond the dreams of the half-starved London seamstress'. While conditions were generally improving more and more employers were turning to philanthropy and to enlightened paternalism in the treatment of their employees while charitable organisation was developed to an unprecedented degree to the extent that 'it has been estimated that the annual expenditure by private charitable organisations in London alone in the early 1860s may have been between £5m. and £7m., or as much as the entire official poor relief expenditure for the whole country'.[55] Education and municipal amenities began to be provided and the workers themselves began to set about the establishment of the conditions for their own improvement with the growth in the Co-operative movement and, more particularly, the expansion of trade unionism and its extension to the unskilled labourers. By the time the first of Ruskin's letters to working men in *Fors Clavigera* was published in 1871, he could be accused of addressing himself to a problem that had already been solved.

Ruskin knew it. That same first letter said, 'I have listened to many ingenious persons, who say we are better off than ever we were before. I do not know how well off we were before; but I know positively that many very discerning persons of my acquaintance have great difficulty in living under these improved circumstances.' And, he continued, while so many are living 'in honest or in villainous

[53] John Burnett, *A history of the cost of living* (Harmondsworth, Penguin Books, 1969)
[54] Norman Gash, *Aristocracy and people* (London, Edward Arnold, 1979), pp. 324–6
[55] *ibid.*, p. 332

beggary' they cannot be considered well off: 'I simply cannot paint,
nor read, nor look at minerals, nor do anything else that I like, and
the very light of the sky, when there is any . . . has become hateful to
me, because of the misery that I know of, and see signs of, where I
knew it not, which no imagination can interpret too bitterly.'[56]

Two comments seem to be appropriate to this passage, the first on
the objective conditions which occasioned Ruskin's real distress and
the second on the subjective from which its expression took.
Acknowledging the improvement in living standards after the 1850s
and 1860s, Hobsbawm puts it in perspective when he says 'the
stagnant mass of poverty at the bottom of the social pyramid
remained nearly as stagnant as before'.[57] We are too near to the
sanguine belief of the 1960s that poverty had been eradicated to
assume that the general improvement of the mid nineteenth century
left Ruskin with no real cause for concern. As to the expression of that
concern, the reference to the light of the sky reminds us of the
complexity of his 'storm clouds' references. There may have been,
over and above the metaphorical harmony between nature and
man's moral condition and beyond the resonant biblical reference
('did the sun really stand still at Ajalon?'), a real truth for Ruskin in
the relationship between physical and spiritual light. The most
insensitive of people experience exhilaration in good weather and
depression in storms; it is possible that the most aesthetically
perceptive of men suffered a real change in perception and that this
change was reciprocal, that is, both that a darkened sky caused moral
depression and that moral depression caused, if not the perception of
a darkened sky, then that its light should 'become hateful'. His later
work gives every evidence both of real pain caused by signs of misery
which 'no imagination can interpret too bitterly' and of an almost
blind indignation at the apparent failure of 'Christian' men and
women either to attain the same degree of sympathetic understanding
of suffering or to do anything about it. This hypersensitive reciprocity
is also likely to have been related to Ruskin's recurrent periods of
mental illness. Wilenski suggests that the 'storm cloud' was one of
several obsessions and delusions which grew upon his mind in the
1870s and that the 'storm cloud' in particular was a rationalisation
and transfer caused by his lost delight in nature which he had
reported ten years earlier. Wilenski's persuasive explanation for

---

[56] Ruskin, *Fors Clavigera*, 27, p. 13
[57] E. J. Hobsbawm, *Industry and empire* (Harmondsworth, Penguin Books, 1969), p. 162

Ruskin's deteriorating mental condition is that he was or became a chronic manic depressive exhibiting the typical symptoms of 'extreme mobility of interest, manic projection of grandiose schemes and moods of depression'.[58]

The strength of his subjective reaction to the social conditions of the day seemed almost to have isolated him and it is this isolation which may explain the dreadful warnings of revolution that he issued. On this count there is no doubt that events have proved him wrong. But there are several possible explanations as to why he was wrong.

The condition of England may have improved but it had certainly undergone a dramatic change. 'It was increasingly an urban phenomenon, or perhaps, so far as its middle layers were concerned, a suburban one, for the migration of the non-proletarians to the outskirts of the cities gathered speed, particularly in the 1850's and later in the 1880's. Townsmen outnumbered countrymen for the first time in 1851.'[59] Hobsbawm adds that by 1881 approximately two out of every five Englishmen lived in six giant conurbations; by 1881 only 1.6 million out of 12.8 million working people were engaged in agriculture. It is this fundamental change in the character of the nation, accompanied by a conviction bordering on hysteria that the change would lead to social and political collapse, which explains the concern of many observers apart from Ruskin. Gash tells us that the frequent expressions of anxiety have given us a distorted view of the social consequences of the industrial revolution in the nineteenth century. 'The fashion for "social protest" from about 1840 is a sign of social conscience; it reflected an interest, it did not create it.'[60] If, as he adds, Disraeli, in *Sybil*, was following fashion rather than leading it, how much more is this true of Ruskin twenty years later? Gash's verdict on the industrial revolution is, even now, unfamiliar: 'The times were difficult enough; without industrialization there might have been a social catastrophe. For all its harshness and crudities the industrial revolution was the saviour of British society in the conditions which prevailed between 1815 and 1865.'[61]

But it could not have seemed so at the time. William Maginn could write in *Fraser's Magazine* in 1834:

All the alarms of our situation in 1830 – quieted for a short period

[58] R. H. Wilenski, *John Ruskin: an introduction to further study of his life and work* (London, Faber and Faber, 1933), p. 120
[59] Hobsbawm, *Industry and empire*, p. 157
[60] Gash, *Aristocracy and people*, p. 1
[61] *ibid.*, p. 3

only – now revive in full force. Incendiarism reigns through half our counties – combination disorganizes our large towns – all is perplexity, alarm and fearful foreboding. Nor is there hope behind, for the old Tory principles are banished, and the economists bear sway.[62]

Professor Gash agrees that 'the age of the Luddites and Chartists, of Peterloo, the Nottingham and Bristol riots, rural machine breaking and incendiarism, was the most prolonged period of recurrent social disorder in modern British history'.[63] But that period was over when Ruskin came to address his letters 'to a working man of Sunderland' in 1867, or began the publication of *Fors Clavigera* in 1871. Not only was there no revolutionary outcome to prove the accuracy of his predictions, but there was very little evidence for his analysis to rest upon.

The best explanation for his error is the one that, in a variety of forms, is used to explain why Marx was wrong: he ought to have been right. One popular version of this story concerns the treason of the proletariat in abandoning its revolutionary role. One must, of course, be careful about using strong and slanderous language about one's hero, particularly if the plot still holds out some hope of his returning to the central role. And so the explanation becomes more subtle and complicated. The proletariat, wronged though it has been, is subverted, the victim of false consciousness, dazzled or drugged by the fetishism of commodities, entangled in a web of bourgeois hegemony, and so on.

Ruskin did not get that far, partly because his analysis transcended the crudities of class warfare and partly because it contains a contradiction. The contradiction is between physical deterioration in the conditions of workers and the moral deterioration in the whole of society. While the former is neither certain in its extent or beyond the capacity of capitalist amelioration it is, to a large extent, the reason for Ruskin's prophecies of doom. His preoccupation with the physical suffering caused by business and industrialisation is in the tradition of concern over the 'condition of England' and it was a part of that tradition to predict the most woeful consequences. It was also a part of the tradition to be wrong. Berg has cogently argued that the whole nineteenth-century debate about poverty, about economics and about social reform, was redirected away from a concern with problems in the economic system. The separation of social problems,

[62] Berg, *The machinery question*, p. 260
[63] Gash, *Aristocracy and people*, p. 5

as matters of moral reform, statistical study and administrative improvement, from political economy 'acted to protect political economy from the criticisms of its methodology and its doctrines on industrialization'.[64]

Ruskin is a rare embodiment of that contradiction between material improvement and root and branch opposition to the prevailing economic system. His concern with poverty and material conditions actually helped, as it always does once it is articulated, to redress those conditions and hence to make less likely the revolutionary outcome which he foresaw. It is in this sense that Ruskin is often hailed as a forerunner of socialism, a founder of the Welfare State, and it is in this sense that Ruskin represents the poverty of socialism and its irrelevance to the removal of the problem with which it is concerned. Berg explains the 'fundamental intellectual irresolution' of radical criticisms of the machinery issue by their failure to maintain a fundamental attack on political economy. Ruskin goes beyond radical criticism of social questions by maintaining a most resolute intellectual criticism of political economy. He was well aware, as he repeatedly pointed out, that radical criticisms did nothing to touch the fundamental wrongness of a society based upon selfishness and profit; that socialism, if successful, would simply spread wider the disease inherent in capitalist society. Yet his concern with material conditions and the need for their improvement led him to engage in social experiments and in the advocacy of social programmes which demonstrate the contradiction in attempts at reform in a society held to be morally corrupt. The 'practical' side of Ruskin is often banal and always ineffective. The moral assault which he delivered against capitalism is, on the other hand, radical in the truest sense. While the attempts at improvement weaken the force of that assault and make it more likely that the defences will stand against it, the moral analysis of society also serves to explain that the material condition of the poor will not, in itself, bring them to the point of revolution.

Ruskin's account of the moral division in society brought about by industrialism stands on a level with Marx's 'alienation' and Durkheim's 'anomy'. He demonstrates that the moral corruption consequent upon the inversion of all the values that have ever held civilised societies together leaves the strong without the will to defend themselves and the weak incapable of anything but the general

[64] Berg, *The machinery question*, p. 296

imitation of their masters' worst acts. The result of industrialisation was the establishment of fundamental disunity in society and the destruction of any basis for moral intercourse. Ruskin's commentary on the social consequences of the different techniques and styles of building are a paradigm for the effects of the extension of rational control and measurement. Berg points out that a great deal of the enthusiasm for technical progress and economic advance in the nineteenth century was aimed at the creation of labour hierarchies, the separation of the skilled from the unskilled and at the extension of labour discipline. The introduction of the power loom, she says, was not simply introduced to make bigger profits; it was often clear 'that the productivity of the power loom was not its greatest asset. Consistent production time and control and supervision over manufacturing process in the factory were rather its more powerful attractions to the manufacturer.'[65] Ruskin saw this remorseless extension of control (which he symbolised in the form of renaissance architecture) as creating the worst kind of slavery in which the slaves were bound to their tasks but not to their taskmasters, except by feelings of mutual avarice and hatred.

The severity of his account of the moral squalor to which capitalism had reduced England serves to explain the failure of his prediction of social upheaval. There is no bastion left from which an attack upon capitalism can be launched. Neither Marx nor Durkheim were prepared to face the bleak conclusion to which their analysis pointed. Marx, like the writer of the weekly thriller instalments whose hero was faced with impending disaster in several inexorable forms, appears to say 'with one bound our hero was free'. Durkheim makes scholastic distinctions between forms of the division of labour in order to demonstrate that the very instrument of man's torture can somehow save him. There is no such optimism available for Ruskin. Even the bleak hope of revolution, in every sense unwelcome and abhorrent to his nature, is denied because the moral vacuity of capitalism is concealed by the very materialist mask which it constructs. The only possible outcome that Ruskin can hint at is a moral collapse so total as to be unimaginable when, in prophetic terms, the world will be destroyed in order to be remade. The desolation of this conclusion explains the rage of his later prose and the silence that more or less shrouded the last eleven years of his life.

[65] *ibid.*, p. 241

6

Education

Education is always the refuge of the radical who is too timid to contemplate more revolutionary change. It seems to offer the prospect, to the individual with a determined view of the best way of ordering the world, of achieving his purpose with the minimum of trouble and cost. Its subjects are usually children who seem ideal instruments for altering the world. They are inexperienced and ignorant and, therefore, deemed unlikely to have strong views about alternative versions of an ideal world. They are compliant because they have no interest and are unorganised. The one supreme advantage which they are believed to possess is, fortunately, the greatest weakness in the theory of change through schooling; they are regarded as *tabula rasa* upon which the reformer can engrave what he wants at will.

The earliest and most influential version of reform through school is to be found in Plato, who, in books 2 and 3 of the *Republic*, has Socrates convince a compliant discussant as to the necessary changes to be made in education if the ideal State is to be achieved and maintained: 'the most important part of every task is the beginning of it, especially when we are dealing with anything young and tender. For then it can be most easily moulded, and whatever impression anyone cares to stamp upon it sinks in.'[1] With such malleable material the question of who does the stamping is most important. Nurses and mothers must be 'persuaded' to tell selected stories and to reject most of the tales in common currency and to substitute for them stories, if we can find them, 'to persuade them that no citizen has ever hated another, and that such a thing is impious'.[2] This censorship must be exercised by the guardians who are to have the sole power of determining what is to be an obviously false version of human behaviour in which citizens

[1] A. D. Lindsay, *The Republic of Plato* (London, J. M. Dent, 1950), pp. 57–8
[2] *ibid.*, p. 59

125

never hate each other and heroes are never afraid of death. It is for the guardians 'and them alone, to tell falsehoods, to deceive either enemies or citizens for the city's welfare. To all other persons such conduct is forbidden.'[3] Socrates concludes that 'we must speak to our poets and compel them to impress upon their poems only the image of the good, or not to make poetry in our city. And we must speak to the other craftsmen and forbid them to leave the impress of that which is evil in character.'[4] And, of course, once such proscriptions begin to be laid down, one thing leads to another and we end up with injunctions to avoid Syracusan living, Sicilian food and Corinthian women.

The very same tradition of precise advice to the young came to seem absurd when it was delivered by earnest and successful employers to their apprentices, even when it was more elegantly put. 'Fly the excesses of that enchantress Pleasure. Pleasure, when it becomes our business, makes business a torment.' 'Frolic at night is followed with pains and sickness in the morning; and then, what was before the poison is administered as the cure; so that a whole life is often wasted in this expensive frenzy.' There is advice to 'be officiously serviceable to your master' to avoid music as 'totally superfluous in such a station as yours', to visit theatres but rarely and the inevitable word of warning about Corinthian women or of the dubious advantages of marriage. 'As a duty to Nature and the common wealth, I cannot help recommending it; but, with regard to your own easy passage through life, I am half inclined to the contrary.' As to the particular choice to be made, avoid deformity and hereditary disease, 'neither fix your eye on a celebrated beauty. It is a property hard to possess and harder to secure . . . But do not wholly despise harmony of shape or elegance of feature. Women are called the fair sex, and, therefore some degree of beauty is supposed almost indispensable.'[5]

Between Plato and a Lord Mayor of London there is a succession of diets, disciplines and proscriptions intended to set the feet of the young unerringly upon the path, whichever it might be that was chosen for them. The belief in moulding and forming took its severest form when puritanical zeal in finding the influence of the devil was accompanied by a new and 'scientific' conviction of the absolute

---

[3] *ibid.*, p. 70
[4] *ibid.*, p. 84
[5] From 'A present for an Apprentice or A Sure Guide to gain both Esteem and an Estate', by a late Lord Mayor of London (undated). The particular copy was shown me by Mr Richard Herbert and is inscribed 'The Gift of Mr. and Mrs. Potter to George Harding 1805 and now presented by the above G. H. to George Jenkins upon the day of his apprenticeship in 1849'

importance of the environment in shaping character. The only weakness in the theory of education as the former of character and behaviour (apart from the great good fortune that it does not work) is that it takes some time, perhaps even more than a generation, before the beneficent influence of the school can be seen to work, and by then, of course, the received view as to the direction of the chosen path is likely to have been changed or even reversed. The singular problem of industrialising England in the nineteenth century was that the great changes deemed to be necessary were needed to be brought about with speed. The problem was exacerbated by a general absence of organised or extensive education except for the upper classes which itself had to wait for the attention of Arnold and the extension of university education, largely directed at the production of Anglican clerics and colonial administrators.

A further difficulty was that education serves best as a panacea when the goals at which it is directed are simple; it has its greatest perceived utility when they can be stated in simple catch-words. But the requirements of industrial England were complex. Flinn suggests that while 'the Charity and Sunday Schools were the principal channels through which the middle and upper classes sought to impose their social ideas upon the working class' by reinforcing class barriers and emphasising the importance of hard work and submission, the mechanics' institute movement of the 1820s emphasised independence, self-help, knowledge and social mobility.[6]

It would be much too crude to distinguish between the two processes by describing one (the long-term social process) as education and the other (the short-term technical process) as training, because the one tends to get confused with the other and because process and purpose become blurred. One of the objectives of an educational process is to pass on the characteristics of a culture to the next generation, to maintain cultural identity and a tradition. But the aim is associated with an almost opposite tendency to limit rather than open the process of transmission so that

the culture that imparts separates those receiving it from the rest of society by a whole series of systematic differences. Those whose 'culture' . . . is the academic culture conveyed by the school have a system of categories of perception, language, thought and appreciation that sets them apart from

---

[6] M. W. Flinn, 'Social theory and the industrial revolution', in T. Burns and S. B. Saul (eds), *Social theory and economic change* (London, Tavistock, 1967), p. 14

those whose only training has been their work and their social contacts with people of their own kind.[7]

Education is also directed at the preparation for generalised roles within society, or at least at the provision of a foundation upon which deferred, specialised and usually professional training can be provided later. Thus the general posture and outlook provided on the playing fields of Eton may be sufficient, with or without subsequent professional training, to assure victory on the battlefield of Waterloo, or competent and honest administration of the colonies or command of the parishioners from the pulpit. But as war, administration and theology become more complex, the professional specialisation begins to erode the general and education begins to create specialist orders and groups who find it difficult both to relate to each other and to exclude those defined as culturally deprived. So education, contributing to the spread of technical specialisation, begins to undermine the cultural exclusiveness at which it is directed; anyone can join who has acquired the necessary certification of competence; membership of the bourgeoisie is open to competitive examination. The process is extended to all social castes of society and the ultimate accomplishment of the process is the achievement of the classless society.

The end is never quite achieved, however, because education never gives up its generalised role of stressing a residuum of value possessed by the insiders and which has yet to be acquired by the outsiders. Hence the complaints of the spokesmen of the disadvantaged groups (the groups themselves are by definition incapable of voicing their concern in terms intelligible to those who have excluded them) who have failed to gain the advantage offered by comprehensive education or the extension of universities. If culture has any relationship to occupations and social roles it cannot be otherwise. Those meritocrats who pass the examinations and have acquired the necessary competence to occupy leadership roles will necessarily have been provided, in passing, as it were, with the language and values necessary to facilitate communication with their near peers. But the control of the curricula, the values and the standards of success and failure remain with the examining group rather than with the aspirants whose influence is confined to reinforcing the values which they must acquire.

It is more than a process of the provision of specialist competence,

---

[7] Pierre Bourdieu, 'Systems of education and systems of thought', in M. F. D. Young (ed.), *Knowledge and control* (London, Collier-Macmillan, 1971), p. 200

although that is an important part of it. The elaboration of technical groups, each commanding a degree of specialist expertise, is accompanied, according to Gramsci, by an elite among the entrepreneurs whose members 'have the capacity to be an organiser of society in general, including all its complex organism of services, right up to the state organism, because of the need to create the condition most favourable to the expansion of their own class'.[8] Two educational processes proceed, the first can attempt to deepen and broaden the functions of the intellectual, the second can attempt to multiply and narrow the various specialisations.

It is difficult to see how any relationship between the two can continue. The conflict between them is summed up in C. P. Snow's well-known interpretation of the two cultures and in F. R. Leavis's bitter and hostile response to the proposal that the gulf between the two must be bridged. The split, in Gramsci's terms, concerns the production of an intellectual caste who function as 'dominant group's "deputies" exercising the subaltern functions of social hegemony and political government' who produce 'the "spontaneous" consent given by the great masses of the population to the general direction imposed on social life by the dominant fundamental group'.[9] But the broad consensus that must be the object of this group can only be threatened by the accompanying requirement of increasing specialisation and technical narrowness, by the constant 'Taylorising' of intellectual work. The outcome is likely to be the end of any kind of universal culture, the erosion of general values and the end of scholarship in any traditional sense. It represents a contradiction in the intentions of the ruling class which makes the view that education is simply one of the processes by which the ruling class exercises social control over the proletariat in its own interests seem a little crude and over-simplified. Who are the ruling class? Who was the ruling class when tory radicals and Anglicans were fighting off the rising tide of nineteenth-century industrialism? One answer is to suggest that the industrialists ruled because they won. But Johnson, describing the influence of the educational experts whose emphasis was 'laid on transforming working-class belief and behaviour' (in the direction of Gramsci's ruling hegemony) acknowledges that their campaign failed and explains the failure of a movement in the interests of the ruling class by the severity of the blow that it would have dealt to 'the Established

---

[8] Hoare and Smith (eds.), *Gramsci's prison notebooks*, p. 5
[9] *ibid.*, p. 12

Church and the whole of the conservative end of the ruling-class repertoire'.[10] The outcome, he says, was a compromise between factions of the ruling class. When factions can be so much at odds one must wonder about the hegemony that binds them. Our point is that the existence of such 'contradictions' reflect society's complexity and make the effectiveness of the direction of education at the achievement of desired goals unlikely.

Even the goals are not always clear. Johnson acknowledged that 'Brougham's early schemes, especially the mechanics' institute movement, do represent an attempt to create an educational alliance with working-class adults. Workers were called upon to educate themselves, with middle-class aid to be sure, but without the stifling patronage of the past.'[11] The alliance failed (although, he says, it 'prefigured the 1860's') and so 'the lines between working-class counter education and middle-class liberals were drawn more finely'.[12] It is always a comfort to have one's lines drawn finely because it helps one to know on which side of them one should stand. Unfortunately, unless one is committed to a particular perspective in line drawing or line standing, it seems that in education the lines between the working and the middle classes, between labour and capital, between radical and conservative, have never been clearly drawn. The complexity of the attitude to mass education in the 1820s, most of them in favour of its extension, is clearly set out in Marilyn Butler's biography of Thomas Love Peacock.[13]

The mechanics' institute movement well illustrates the confusions which obfuscate a clear vision of the class war (unless, that is, one can see nothing else). It grew out of a class begun in Glasgow in 1800 by Birkbeck, for the artisans who made his laboratory equipment. By the fourth lecture the class had grown to five hundred. The class was continued by Birkbeck's successor, Andrew Ure, and it became the Glasgow Mechanics' Institute in 1823. The London Mechanics' Institute was established the same year. After set-backs caused by depressions in trade and unemployment, about 500 mechanics' institutes had been established by 1851.

Tylecote attributes three influences to the mechanics' institute

---

[10] Richard Johnson, 'Educating the educators: "experts" and the State 1833–9', in A. P. Donajgrodski (ed.), *Social control in nineteenth century Britain* (London, Croom Helm, 1977), p. 100
[11] *ibid.*, p. 97
[12] *ibid.*, p. 98
[13] Marilyn Butler, *Peacock displayed* (London, Routledge and Kegan Paul, 1979), pp. 190–4

movement: educational, industrial and social.[14] The first concerned an Owenite enthusiasm for progress and faith in the potential for human improvement. The second was represented by a more specifically scientific faith in the future. This faith can be related to the plethora of literary and scientific societies, the most famous record of which is to be found in the minutes of the Pickwick Club for 12 May 1827, which recorded approval for a paper entitled: 'Speculations on the source of the Hampstead ponds, with some observations on the theory of tittlebats'. It is also reflected in the universality of Ruskin's interests and in a more general and practical belief that the teaching of science to working men would promote invention and industrial development which would, in turn, serve to repulse foreign competition. The social purpose was understandably more confused and was concerned with a benevolent wish to improve and reform and partly stemmed from reports designed to alarm a middle-class readership with descriptions of 'nightly scenes of drunkenness and riot', of 'animal gratifications' and licentiousness in the streets, of mechanics 'besotting themselves with the fumes of tobacco and draughts of porter, stupefying their minds and bringing disease on their bodies'.[15] Such accounts of almost prurient attention, of which several can be found in Ruskin, are common in middle-class tales of proletarian life. They always signify the shock of the civilised observer's encounter with barbarism and they always, as in Ruskin, suggest that barbarism has been produced by the factories and mills. It is in fact more likely that the uninhibited, licentious, and often uncivilised behaviour of the poor, had not changed for many centuries and was in an undisturbed tradition of 'rural idiocy'. It was not created but revealed by industrialism, becoming visible and unavoidable when both the poor and the refined and educated middle classes jointly occupied, however briefly, the same new industrial towns. The ancient lineage of lewdness is well illustrated in *The collier's rant*.[16] Far from being a phenomenon produced by industrialisation, drunken licentiousness was a problem which industry encountered and endeavoured to overcome, as Owen demonstrated. The 'making of the English working class' could be presented, in other terms, as a process of cleaning its members up so

[14] M. Tylecote, *The mechanics' institutes of Lancashire and Yorkshire before 1851* (Manchester University Press, 1957)
[15] *ibid.*, p. 40
[16] Robert Colls, *The collier's rant: song and culture in the industrial village* (London, Croom Helm, 1977)

that they could decently cohabit with the bourgeoisie in the new industrial world.

The mechanics' institutes' early preoccupation with science did not long survive. Harrison says it took about five years after the foundation of an institute before the failure of science to prove relevant and advantageous to the artisans became apparent and that when it did 'a remedy was sought in the introduction of literary and cultural subjects. Science was not abandoned but the emphasis of the Mechanics' Institute entirely changed.'[17] The clientele also began to change from artisans to members of the lower middle class. In a course of lectures at Wakefield in 1846, the average attendance was 200 of whom the majority were women. Berg does not see a clear distinction between science and the social aspects of their programmes; they were intended to produce a more adaptable labour force and were based upon the view that 'moral virtue was an intrinsic part of the ideology of science for the working man. Industry and temperance were the virtues of the good mechanic.'[18]

But science began to take a new form with the confident assertion of the dogma of economics. It explained the unparalleled prosperity of Britain and it was conducive to a disciplined acceptance of the prevailing (or ascending) order. Thomas Chalmers said that he 'was not aware of a likelier instrument than a judicious course of economical doctrine for tranquillizing the popular mind',[19] and the mechanics' institutes were natural sites in which the courses could be administered. The annual report of the Yorkshire union of mechanics' institutes for 1861 said that 'the greatest evil of the present day is the isolation between the employer and the employed. Indifference to each other's interests is the normal condition of their relation, and active hostility in the form of strikes has of late years become a painfully frequent feature of the time'.[20] An understanding of economics would help to end this hostility by bringing the employee to an understanding of the true position of his employer. It would also lead to an understanding that hardships, when they came, were inevitable, and had to be tolerated, but the discussion of these matters was constrained within the limits of 'orthodox' economics by

[17] J. F. C. Harrison, *Learning and living, 1790–1970* (London, Routledge and Kegan Paul, 1961), p. 67
[18] Berg, *The machinery question*, p. 170
[19] *ibid.*, p. 163
[20] Tylecote, *The mechanics' institutes*, p. 41

rules excluding politics and theology (always a dangerous body of doctrine).

Birkbeck, the founder of the institutes, had regarded them 'as agents of cultural education, as a means of liberating the mind and enriching the understanding' of working people.[21] Any discussion of the purpose of education or of the motivation of those providing it for the disadvantaged should, but often does not, include the disinterested belief in its value for its own sake or for the sake of truth. But the institutes had fallen from this ideal as they had become the instruments of those who can indeed be accurately described as seeking to further the interests of the ruling class. But the crudity of that single explanation of the educational process is demonstrated by the sequel to the story of the mechanics' institute. The attempt to instil social discipline into the working class failed. 'Down to the middle of the nineteenth century it seemed that the great middle-class effort to educate the workers had been only a partial success. It had, it appeared, reached only the upper crust of the working classes, leaving the great proletarian masses almost untouched. The middle classes themselves constantly lamented this fact.'[22]

One of the reasons for failure was 'a confused and inadequate idea of the character of the class in whose interest they were working. To speak of the "lower orders" or "the laborious classes" was to bring under one heading a number of quite incompatible elements.'[23] While the appetite of the artisans, clerks and shop keepers for education was often voracious the poor and the unskilled had not the time nor energy and little hope of self-improvement; some of the clients had not been vastly interested in the solution of their masters' problems. In the arguments leading to the establishment of the London Mechanics' Institute in 1823, Thomas Hodgskin had warned that 'men had better be without education – properly so called, for nature of herself teaches us many valuable truths – than be educated by their rulers; for their education is but the mere breaking in of the steer to the yoke'.[24] Education as a criticism of society had been established in the corresponding societies of the eighteenth century, and the Hampden clubs and Chartist educational activities of the

---

[21] Thomas Kelly, *A history of adult education in Great Britain* (Liverpool University Press, 1962), p. 123

[22] *ibid.*, p. 181

[23] David Wardle, *Education and society in nineteenth century Nottingham* (Cambridge University Press, 1971), p. 170

[24] Kelly, *History of adult education*, p. 121

nineteenth century. The Co-operative movement, too, encouraged educational activities from the 1820s. A new impetus was provided in 1842 by R. S. Bailey, minister of Howard Street Independent Chapel in Sheffield. His college for working men provided teaching in literature, history, Greek and Latin. The college survived, in different form until 1874, but Bailey's greatest influence may have been upon the minds and intentions of two Christian socialists, J. M. Ludlow and F. D. Maurice. Maurice acknowledged that 'we were plagiarists from the Sheffield people':

We heard in 1853 that the people of Sheffield had founded a People's College. The news seemed to us to make a new era in education. We had belonged to Colleges. They had not merely given us a certain amount of indoctrination in certain subjects, they had borne witness of a culture which is the highest of all cultures. We had formed in those Colleges friendships which we hoped to keep wherever we went – friendships that had had an influence upon our life and character through all the years that had passed since we left them . . . Was it not a glorious thing then that the working people should lay hold of this name, that they should say, 'we are determined we will have Colleges . . . because we want to connect all our education with our social life, with our fellowship as human beings'.[25]

The result of their 'plagiarism' was the establishment of the London Working Men's College. It was attended by workmen and radicals and, as in any genuinely educational process, the teachers learned from the pupils, in particular they learned for the first time about the reality of the lives of workmen. The knowledge was to have a profound effect upon their views on education.

This is the state, as well as we can describe it, of the relationship between education and the worker up to the time of Ruskin's involvement. The importance of education stems from his conception of true justice (as distinct from the everyday notion of justice which concerns a demand for 'rights', 'which if you could get them would turn out to be the deadliest wrongs' and which follows from an 'external mechanism' of envy and imitation). True justice means giving due aid to every human being in developing his faculties for action and enjoyment. Ruskin stresses that he means appropriate rather than equal; in education especially, true justice is curiously unequal:

if you chose to give it a hard name, iniquitous. The right law of it is that you are to take most pains with the best material. Many conscientious masters

[25] F. D. Maurice, *Learning and working* (London, Oxford University Press, 1968; first published 1855), pp. 4–5

will plead for the exactly contrary iniquity, and say you should take the most pains with the dullest boys. But that is not so (only you must be very careful that you know which *are* the dull boys; for the cleverest look often very like them). Never waste pains on bad ground, let it remain rough, though properly looked after and cared for.[26]

The first principle of education is that children should be rigorously selected for the appropriate kind.

Cook and Wedderburn point out that the importance attached by Ruskin to education is related to the view he took of it as an ethical rather than an intellectual process; 'you do not educate a man by telling him what he knew not, but by making him what he was not'.[27] 'Education does not mean making people to know what they do not know. It means teaching them to behave as they do not behave.'[28] The making or forming of moral habits is the key to social change in Ruskin and their formation is to be pursued in a vigorous fashion. The essential preliminary to education is 'the habit of instant, finely accurate, and totally unreasoning, obedience to their fathers, mothers and tutors', he says, in laying down the lines of his model communities of St George. This obedience is necessary to instil the understanding of the nature of honour and truth. He explains that the essential difference between what he is trying to teach and the prevailing popular science of economics is that he believes in attainable honesty in men and in the respect they can have for the interests of others. The received view among economists is, on the other hand, that men constantly have regard only for their own interest and can be expected to be honest only when their interest is secured. Honesty, says Ruskin, is an innate human quality. Honesty, obedience and honour 'are native in men, and the roots of them cannot wither, even under the dust-heap of modern liberal opinions'.[29] Honesty is a primary quality not based on religion or dependent upon policy for its production. 'If you ask why you are to be honest – you are, in the question itself dishonoured. "Because you are a man", is the only answer . . . to make your children capable *of honesty* is the beginning of education.' Honesty must not be based on self-interest, not even on religion, both policy and religion must follow from honesty and be based upon it; 'make the men first, and religious men afterwards, and

[26] Ruskin, *Fors Clavigera*, 27, p. 148
[27] Ruskin, *Munera Pulveris*, 17, p. 232
[28] Ruskin, *The Crown of Wild Olive*, 18, p. 502
[29] Ruskin, *Fors Clavigera*, 28, p. 21

all will be sound; but a knave's religion is always the rottenest thing about him'.[30]

Honesty for Ruskin is more than truth-telling; the 'teaching of trust as a habit will be the chief work the master has to do' and it is to be part of every aspect of education. 'First, you must accustom the children to close accuracy of statement; this both as a principle of honour, and as an accomplishment of language . . . carrying this accuracy into all habits of thought and observation also, so as always to think of things as they truly are, and to *see* them as they truly are.'[31]

The other great principle upon which education is to be based is compassion. Compassion should be made a matter of honour with children, collateral with courage, so that it should be held 'as shameful to have done a cruel thing as a cowardly one'. Ruskin was to emphasise more than once that the values held to be important by women were of great importance in determining the conduct of men; if women admired courage men would strive to be courageous; if women could be got to admire compassion men would strive to be compassionate. This is perhaps the main theme of *Sesame and Lilies*. By a similar process of influence teachers possessing these qualities must be chosen whom pupils will love and respect.

It is not always clear whether Ruskin sees these virtues as the object to be produced by education or whether he sees them as innate moral characteristics, or both. They are innate but they have to be developed, natural but choked by the present unnatural state of society which cannot be restored to health until they are restored to their proper place of influence. This restoration cannot be accomplished if education continues to be advertised as leading to success. It is a fallacy that men can be educated to become gentlemen and scholars so that, having been made both gentle and learned 'they are sure to attain in sequel the consummate beatitude of being rich'. Education is not an equaliser but a discerner of men. 'Even under the best training some will remain too selfish to refuse wealth, and some too dull to desire leisure.' But the proportions could be altered somewhat if we introduced some of the lower arts to university education and, even more important, if we extended the spirit of university education to the practice of the lower arts. Both steps would contribute to surrounding occupations with a degree of self-respect which would reduce the flight to abandon them and to use

[30] Ruskin, *Time and Tide*, 17, p. 348
[31] *ibid.*, p. 399

education as a means of escape from servitude to them. If the drudgery and self-contempt were removed from manual occupations we might bring about a condition in which no occupation would be unhappy or ignoble and when 'the chief object in the mind of every citizen may not be extrication from a condition admitted to be disgraceful, but fulfilment of a duty which shall also be a birthright'.[32]

Education fails because there is not desire for it in its proper form, 'the cry for it among the lower order is because they think that, when once they have got it, they must become the upper orders'.[33] The first requirement of education is that it cannot be seen as a means of getting on in the world. The danger of telling children that they can become as good as James Watt if they work as hard as he did is that all these 'candidates for distinction, finding themselves, after all their work, still indistinct, think it must be the fault of the police, and are riotous accordingly'.[34] And in a sense it *is* the fault of the police, he adds, or at least of our teachers of values and civic manners, of our leaders, because respect and obedience cannot be expected while there is none about who is worth obeying.

The purpose of education and the reason for its pursuit and its value are thus closely related to work, to kinds of work that are highly prized and to others that are generally despised. Ruskin is surely right in saying that any broader social purpose (assuming for the moment that education can achieve great social change) will be vitiated by its close association with a competitive struggle for place and privilege in which educational success is measured by financial reward and failure by drudgery and poverty. Such a state of affairs is an inversion of the kind of influence that education should have upon society and it serves to reinforce the values of a competitive commercial world. As Ruskin could justifiably be said to have already subjected those values to some telling criticisms, it follows that the educational process associated with them would need to be changed. This is yet one other respect in which Ruskin's influence has been widely acknowledged in the general attack upon competitive examination, selection and streaming. Once again the acknowledgement is totally misplaced. Ruskin insisted upon the most rigorous selection and careful streaming. As is so often the case, our educational technicians have got hold of the process and quite forgotten its content and

[32] Ruskin, *Lectures on Art*, 20, p. 21
[33] Ruskin, *Time and Tide*, 17, p. 394
[34] Ruskin, *Fors Clavigera*, 27, p. 152

purpose. Ruskin's major concern was that the disjunctions within the world of work should be less barbaric so that educational selection could be conducted without the implication of a judgment to a life of privilege on the one hand or of contemptible drudgery on the other. No educational process (even if it were well-founded) could bear the strain of such onerous implications without being warped by them. There is an intimate relation between education and the society for which it makes preparation.

Ruskin is, in fact, assaulting the two forces that have largely contributed to the development of present-day educational practice, egalitarianism associated with effort. It is the doctrine refined by Samuel Smiles out of his experience in the mechanics' institutes, that all the prizes are open to achievement through hard work. It is the ultimate justification for Victorian free competition that the traditional barriers of class can be overcome by merit. Ruskin sees the peculiar alliance between equality and competition:

the madness of the modern cram and examination system arises principally out of the struggle to get lucrative places; but partly also out of the radical blockheadism of supposing that all men are naturally equal, and can only make their way by elbowing; the facts being that every child is born with an accurately defined and absolutely limited capacity.[35]

The motivation underlying the pursuit of education established the relationship with work and its values but there were other respects in which Ruskin saw work and education as closely related. In 1867 in *Time and Tide* (subtitled 'Twenty-five letters to a working man of Sunderland on the laws of work') he hit upon a problem which he never satisfactorily solved, although frequently returning to its discussion. After outlining an ideal curriculum which would include history, natural science and mathematics, he adds that children should also be taught their trades. But what if, after learning riding, fencing, singing and natural history, they do not want to be tailors? He returns to the question in the next letter. All the wisest people have shown such contempt for useful occupations that there is no knowing who there will be to do them when education produces even more wise people or 'foolishly refined scholars'. The problem is so severe that many prudent people will look at his proposals for educational change and ask simply, 'is the man mad, or laughing at us to propose educating the working classes this way? He could not, if his wild scheme were possible, find a better method of making them acutely

[35] Ruskin, *Fors Clavigera*, 29, p. 496

wretched.'[36] There are two aspects of this problem, the first that educated people are going to shun degrading but necessary jobs, the second that, if they take them through necessity or some other form of compulsion, they are going to be made more miserable in their servitude by their education. It was a problem faced by Durkheim with callous candour when he concluded that broad education should be denied to those doing narrow jobs lest they find their constraint intolerable. Ruskin, not surprisingly, takes the opposite view.

The implication of believing that education for workers is dangerous and impractical because of its unsettling effect upon their mind is

that a certain proportion of mankind must be employed in degrading work, and that, to fit them for this work, it is necessary to limit their knowledge, their active powers, and their enjoyments from childhood upwards, so that they may not be able to conceive of any state better than the one they were born in, nor possess any knowledge, or acquirements inconsistent with the coarseness, or disturbing the monotony of their vulgar occupation. And by their labour in this contracted state of mind, we superior beings are to be maintained; and always to be curtseyed to by the properly ignorant little girls, and capped by the properly ignorant little boys whenever we pass by.[37]

This is nothing other than 'a very profound state of slavery, to be kept . . . low in the forehead, that I may not dislike low work'. But, again, Ruskin does not suggest a solution to the problem. The general development of his thought seems to suggest two possible conclusions, neither of which is really compatible with the other. The first is that dull work will be done by dull people but that the drudgery and self-contempt of it will be removed by several changes; the one in the general attitude to manual work, a change assisted by the proposal that all intellectuals and professionals should undertake some manual work (of which more anon), a second in a reduction in the great differences in differential reward, a third in reducing the extent of manual work so that it ceases to be associated with exhaustion. This Ruskin might call bringing to all work some proper measure of honour and dignity so that those confined to the worst kinds are not entirely despised. The second approach is a paradoxical development of his later years. Having come to see manual work as educative (and therefore necessary to the intellectual) he seems to have concluded

[36] Ruskin, *Time and Tide*, 17, p. 402
[37] *ibid.*, p. 403

that an intellectual education which threatened the efficacy of manual work should be avoided. It is not certain whether these strains of anti-intellectualism were the manifestations of jaundiced old age or whether they were the logical conclusion of a protestant suspicion of intellectual over-elaboration which had always been present and which was the source of the reminder to the economists that man was more than mere intellect, including 'a beastly part of him in a good sense; – that which makes him courageous by instinct . . . loving by instinct, as a Dog is, and therefore felicitously above, or below (whichever you like to call it), all questions of philosophy and divinity'.[38] The suspicion of reason and intellectual learning was a part of the old protestant tradition, reason was a 'thief within . . . which locks the door of every mind against the waft by the Holy Spirit'.[39]

Whatever the reason, his distrust of intellectual education seems to have grown as he got older. A modern education simply develops a man's capacity for error, whereas, if you 'leave him at his forge and plough, – and those teachers teach him his true value, indulge him in no error, and provoke him to no vice. But take him up to London, – give him her papers to read and low talk to hear and it is fifty to one' you will make a fool of him.[40] He had already concluded, in *Time and Tide*, that work is the 'primal half' of education. Years later, when discussing the educational programme for the communities of St George, he said he did not greatly care whether the children learned reading or writing 'because there are very few people in the world who get any good by either. Broadly and practically, whatever foolish people read, does them harm, and whatever they write, does other people harm.'[41]

Ruskin seems to have seen danger in intellectual work and at education aimed entirely at its pursuit. Education needed to be tempered or cleansed by work. Labour should always produce a useful result, 'the labour producing useful result was educational in its influence on temper . . . the first condition of education . . . is being put to wholesome and useful work'.[42] Ruskin repeatedly stressed, the more so as he got older, that manual work was in itself an educational

---

[38] Ruskin, *Fors Clavigera*, 27, p. 468
[39] Richard L. Greaves, *The puritan revolution and educational thought* (New Brunswick, Rutgers University Press, 1969), p. 120
[40] Ruskin, *The Storm Cloud of the Nineteenth Century*, 34, p. 75
[41] Ruskin, *Fors Clavigera*, 29, p. 479
[42] Ruskin, *Fors Clavigera*, 27, p. 38

process, it provided a singular discipline in observation, accuracy and control. Let a man 'once learn to take a straight shaving off a plank, or draw a fine curve without faltering, or lay a brick level in its mortar, and he has learned a multitude of other matters which no lips of man could teach him'.[43]

Ruskin's admiration for the qualities he saw in physical work has been widely shared, particularly by those who are not called upon to do very much of it. We have noted already the impact that the experience of meeting workers had on the tutors of the London Working Men's College. F. D. Maurice, in particular, elaborated a view of the place of work in learning which was to have an important influence on the course of adult education. There is also a striking similarity between Maurice's views and those of Ruskin, except that those of the former are, perhaps, more consistently worked out. Maurice dismissed the view that education was concerned with personal advancement as a 'pious fraud'. He was also concerned to reunite labour and learning in what he claimed was a traditional alliance. Adult education, in his view, had preceded juvenile education; it had formed a natural relationship with work in the training of craftsmen and in the life of the monasteries. 'Working and learning so far, not learning and leisure, went hand in hand. Or rather . . . the reading was the leisure. The work of the hands demanded this to quieten and sustain it. The reading demanded equally the work of the hands as the condition of its being healthy and nutritive to the mind.'[44] He acknowledged that there were great difficulties in the way of re-establishing a relationship between learning and work but he argued that the difficulties had to be faced because they were such as to threaten freedom, order and civilisation. Both learning and work would have to change;

we must raise Work to make it fit for association with Learning, as well as bring Learning to bear upon Work. But I am far indeed from thinking that these schemes, or any schemes have any virtue of their own. Their one use is, that they help to raise the workman to a sense of manhood and freedom; to the feeling that he is a person and not a thing, a citizen and not a slave.[45]

It is precisely this 'one use' that Ruskin noted as the problem of educating men beyond the requirements of their work in a society

[43] Ruskin, *Time and Tide*, 17, p. 426
[44] Maurice, *Learning and working*, p. 70
[45] *ibid.*, p. 101

which, if not based on slavery, is dependent upon involuntary labour. Both Maurice and Ruskin were prepared to face the consequences of emancipating labour: 'we must aim in all our teaching of the working classes, at making them free. We know that they feel themselves shackled in a thousand ways; that they ask to be delivered from their shackles. They may be wrong in some of their notions about the *nature* of their bondage; they are not wrong about the *fact* of it.'[46] In that both men agreed. The extent to which Maurice influenced Ruskin is uncertain, largely because of Ruskin's habit of giving a somewhat patronising acknowledgement of the influence of those whose views were closest to his own. The most notorious example is the dislike rather than acknowledgement which Ruskin expressed for Pugin whose views on the gothic were similar, although in this case there was the 'rational' explanation of Pugin's Catholicism in the period of Ruskin's most dogmatic puritanism. Amongst several references to Maurice there is a grudging statement of Ruskin's affection for him while he refuses to support a proposal for a memorial in Westminster Abbey, and, more to the point, a virtual dismissal of the value and influence of the London Working Men's College.[47] There is again, an inescapable hint of spitefulness whenever Ruskin describes an influential contemporary (except Turner), 'I loved Frederick Maurice, as everyone did who came near him; and have no doubt he did all that was in him to do of good in his day . . . but Maurice was by nature puzzle-headed... wrong-headed... egotistic... as insolent as any infidel of them all.' Within two pages he is attacking the deadly influence of working men's clubs as well as colleges and concluding that 'the only proper school for workmen is of the work their fathers bred them to, under masters able to do better than any of their men'.[48] Ruskin certainly differed from Maurice over Christian socialism, of course, but in other respects his judgment of Maurice may have been clouded. Cook and Wedderburn printed extracts from a letter from Ludlow and Thomas Hughes, in which they take Ruskin to task both for his version of a public argument between Ruskin and Maurice and for his verdict of 'puzzle-headed' – 'We, who knew him a good deal more intimately than yourself, used to find him while he lived the greatest solver of puzzles.'[49]

It is, of course, true that Ruskin reached his view of the importance

---

[46] *ibid.*, p. 114
[47] Ruskin, *Fors Clavigera*, 27, p. 388
[48] Ruskin, *Praeterita*, 35, p. 488
[49] *ibid.*, pp. 487–8

and the quality of human work quite independently of the influence of Maurice, but it is not so certain that his conclusions about its relationship to education did not depend greatly upon Maurice and on Ruskin's work for him at the London Working Men's College. Their association began at an early stage in the development of Ruskin's thought; the college was founded by Maurice in 1854 and Ruskin took the drawing classes there from that same year. His teaching duties were shared by D. G. Rossetti and Lowes Dickinson, and Ruskin continued more or less regular teaching there until 1860. There is no doubt that the experience was fruitful: 'the humble work of the drawing-classes . . . was teaching Ruskin even more than he taught his pupils'.[50] The expression of most of his conclusions on the relationship of work and education followed this experience and they reflect its significance and that of the views of Maurice. Ruskin, 'apart from any schemes of social reconstruction . . . held profoundly to the gospel of manual labour as a branch of education, both physical and mental'.[51]

Perhaps the best-known instance of Ruskin's belief in the efficacy of manual labour for intellectuals, was the repairing of the Hincksey road, outside Oxford. In 1874 he asked a local landowner for permission to repair the lane past Ferry Hincksey. He proposed the scheme to some Balliol men at breakfast on 24 March and the work began under the supervision of Ruskin's elderly gardener, David Downs (whom he asked to Oxford as Professor of Digging). Ruskin explained that 'even *digging*, rightly done, is at least as much an art as the more muscular art of rowing'. His gang of road-diggers included Alfred (later Viscount) Milner, Arnold Toynbee (promoted to foreman) and Oscar Wilde. The work was not particularly successful (Ruskin acknowledged it to be the worst road in the three kingdoms) and it attracted a great deal of amused attention from Oxford where its inspection was a favourite Sunday afternoon outing, and from the press of which only *Punch* and the *Spectator* seemed to have approved.

The comparison between manual work and athletics was made more than once by Ruskin; advising an audience to do something useful manually every day he reminds them that

in your own experience most of you will be able to recognise the wholesome effect, alike as body and mind, of striving within proper limits of time, to become either good batsmen or good oarsmen. But the bat and the rower's

[50] W. G. Collingwood, *The life of John Ruskin* (London, Methuen, 1922), p. 134
[51] Ruskin, editors' introduction, 27, p. lxiv

oars are children's toys. Resolve that you will become men in usefulness, as well as in strength, and you will find that then also, but not till then, you can become men in understanding.[52]

A little later he explains that fine art is essentially athletic, although we have forgotten the fact. Beautiful structures must be produced with tools that men can use because fine art 'involves the action and force of a strong man's arm from the shoulder, as well as the delicatest touch of his fingers: and it is the evidence that this full and fine strength has been spent on it which makes the art executively noble'.[53]

The athletic character of manual work and the skill called for in work much rougher than that of a craftsman is one of the elements that make work an essential part of education. Its inclusion also marks his concern at the separation into compartments of life which the specialisation of industrialisation encouraged. The first and most dangerous part of this process was the isolation of intelligence from work and consequent isolation of a thinking class from another class of doers. Ruskin would have agreed with Gramsci that the whole conception of an intellectual class or group is an invention of capitalism. Ruskin insists that the intellectuals should acquire some real *working* sympathy with the activities of manual work and with the condition of those who undertake it. One good reason for incorporating manual work into the education of all is that it will help to break down a social division of the most extreme and dangerous kind. Ruskin recognises that the division of humanity into thinkers and doers promotes the arrogance of the one and the self-contempt of the others, that it is a division far more vicious than that between rich and poor for the good reason that it seems to have been created by nature, while differences in wealth have always been made more tolerable because accompanied by the conviction that they were accidental, not entirely natural, inevitable and irreversible. Reformers can exaggerate the difference between thinkers and doers when, like Tawney, they argue that the first principle of industrial organisation under socialism would 'render the best service technically possible'. As a result 'there would be subordination, but it would be the subordination . . . of all men to the purpose for which industry is carried on . . . Under such an organization of industry the brain worker might expect, as never before, to come into his own.'[54]

[52] Ruskin, *Aratra Pentelici*, 20, p. 264
[53] *ibid.*, p. 304
[54] R. H. Tawney, *The acquisitive society* (London, Bell, 1930), p. 206

But the social consequence of the split between intellectual and manual work is not the only reason for Ruskin's attitude to work in education. He puts the two together because he believed that to separate them is unnatural and therefore unhealthy. His views in this respect were sometimes confused and even contradictory, but the conviction that intellectual education isolated from work was debased remained constant. The English preoccupation with games was in one sense sympathetic to this view and in another sense it was hostile. Arnold and Hughes had popularised the idea that intellectual effort without the interruption of healthy physical endeavour in games was unnatural and debilitating. But enthusiasm for cricket or football did not necessarily imply a place for brick-laying or road-making in Tom Brown's schooldays.[55] Ruskin suggested that putting muscles to work might be better than putting them to play and that not putting them to work was unnatural. Work provided a necessary accompaniment to learning, a relief from it and a balance in it. It also contributed discipline to lives that would otherwise come to be self-indulgent because those engaged in intellectual education would be, by selection if not by definition, predisposed to find intellectual work entirely enjoyable.

Another important reason for the inclusion of manual work in education was its utility. Ruskin's innate puritanical ascetism made him suspicious of purely (or merely) intellectual activity. What passed for intellectual work was often sheer amusement.

Our National wish and purpose are only to be amused, our National Religion is the performance of church ceremonies, and preaching of scientific truths (or untruths) to keep the mob quietly at work, while we amuse ourselves; and the necessity for this amusement is fastening on us, as a frivolous disease.

The alternative is that 'when men are rightly occupied, their amusement grows out of their work . . .'.[56]

Ruskin, like Maurice, pointed out that the association of work and learning was no rash, revolutionary proposal, that it had been an essential part of medieval education, a part of the life of the monastic orders. Ruskin saw the substitution of the association of work and

---

[55] The analogy between games and work and the comparison between the love for one and the hatred for the other had been drawn by Fourier. It is quite possible that this influence was brought to bear on Ruskin by Ludlow, who was an enthusiastic supporter of French communitarian experiments along lines recommended by Fourier (H. G. Wood, *Frederick Denison Maurice* (Cambridge University Press, 1950), p. 156)

[56] Ruskin, *Sesame and Lilies*, 18, p. 97

leisure for the relationship of work and learning as a part of the same falsity that divided the learned from the unlearned and intelligent work from drudgery. The association of work and learning was not only traditional, it was natural.

The possibility remains of one more massive misinterpretation of Ruskin. It emerged with the start of the 'great debate' on the relationship between education and work which opened with a speech by Mr James Callaghan at Ruskin College, Oxford, in 1976. The surface similarity to Ruskin's views about education require some discussion. The context within which the debate began was a conviction that there was a gap between the intentions and the achievements of the schools and the needs of industry. A battery of criticisms, much of them emanating from industrialists, the customers for the products of education, as they might describe themselves, suggested that the schools were failing to provide the basic accomplishments necessary to employment in an increasingly technical age. In short, school leavers were said to be deficient in reading, writing and arithmetic. A more general criticism was that the schools were failing to prepare children for work or for life (the charge frankly implying that the two were one as far as most people are concerned).

It was not only the alleged absence of the basic skills of literacy and arithmetic that caused the complaints of employers; they were as concerned about what the children knew as about their ignorance. In the words of a manager who must have given more satisfaction to his employers than to his teachers: 'school leavers are too often over-aspirated'. He would presumably argue for the advantages of keeping people 'low in the forehead' so that they do not become dissatisfied with their work.

The 'great debate' never took place. Mr Callaghan managed to make his demand for a closer relationship between school and work sound like a radical battle cry while at the same time stealing the opposition's washing. The Conservative Party and the CBI were not likely to rush to the defence of state comprehensive education or to argue for the separation of work and education. The 'debate' and the historical development of adult education reveal the constant confusion over the purpose of education, between its utilitarian and its humanitarian value. When the utilitarian aspect is presented in terms of self-improvement, individual advancement, improved living standards and increased gross natural product, all of them deemed to be good in themselves, then the confusion between utility and humanity is compounded.

Ruskin comes close to being drawn into this maelstrom. He will not separate work from education, he distrusts purely intellectual education, he regards manual work as itself education. Which side is he on? Ruskin's answer is that education is for life. If that is too vaporous an answer, in his own terms he says that a man entering life should know where he is ('that is to say, what sort of world he has got into'), where he is going ('that is to say, what chances or reports there are of any world besides this'), and what he had best do ('that is to say, what kind of faculties he possesses; what are the present states and wants of mankind; what is his place in society; and what are the readiest means in his power of attaining happiness and diffusing it').[57] The traditional orthodoxy is that education is for work. But to acknowledge that education unconfined to the demands of work will have a deleterious effect upon the worker or upon his work, is to confess that work is so unnatural, so perverted, an activity that it requires the virtual isolation of the worker from wider knowledge and from free intelligence.

If this orthodoxy is to be challenged it is because our faith in the future of work is becoming weaker. If work is to be replaced by higher technology the demand for the educational product may change and we will presumably begin to be told of the advantages of education for leisure in a new great debate. Whatever the situation with which we shall have to deal, with the aftermath of an industrial and industrious society or with a new automatic age, it is sad that the development and education of children is acknowledged to be determined by the manner in which they are to be put to work or not.

Ruskin believed that education should concern a knowledge of our physical and natural surroundings, with truth, with an understanding of our relationship and responsibility to others, with compassion. He is so far from the view that education must be a preparation for work that he insisted that work had to be changed in order to make education possible. In its present form work demands the destruction of education and, ultimately, of civilisation. In that and only in that sense does Ruskin put work before education.

[57] Ruskin, *The Stones of Venice*, II, p. 258

7

Work

We began this discussion of Ruskin by suggesting that a good reason for undertaking it was that no other writer revealed so well the complex quality of work. The extent to which this claim is justified deepens the problems at hand. It is not easy to understand what Ruskin makes of work because he seems never quite to make up his mind about it. He was often accused of self-contradiction and in his Cambridge inaugural address he appeared to have brushed the criticism aside with a genial confession:

I never met with a question yet, of any importance, which did not need, for the right solution of it, at least one positive and one negative answer, like an equation of the second degree. Mostly, matters of any consequence are three-sided, or four-sided, or polygonal; and the trotting around a polygon is severe work for people in any way stiff in their opinions. For myself, I am never satisfied that I have handled a subject properly till I have contradicted myself at least three times.[1]

The point is a serious one. He had some, perhaps slight, acquaintanceship with Hegel[2] but Ruskin differs from the German dialectical logic in his refusal to believe that the necessary closure of contradictions by synthesis is anything other than 'stiff'. Ruskin suggests that truth must embody contradicting statements so that it is itself likely to be contradicted by the superimposition of any simplifying synthesis.

We can have a definition of work, or at least of labour; it 'is the contest of the life of man with an opposite. Literally, it is the quantity of "Lapse", loss, or failure of human life, caused by any effort.' This view is both singularly bleak and unusual. Ruskin goes on to distinguish labour from effort, with which it is often confused, or with the application of power (*opera*);[3] but there is much effort which is merely a mode of recreation, or of pleasure. The most beautiful actions of the human

---

[1] Ruskin, *Cambridge Inaugural Address*, 16, p. 187
[2] Ruskin, *On the Old Road*, 34, p. 108
[3] The distinction between 'labour' and '*opera*' is important, at least much has been made of it
We shall return to it shortly

body, and the highest results of the human intelligence, are conditions or achievements of quite unlaborious, nay, of recreative, – effort. But labour is the *suffering* in effort. It is the negative quantity or quantity of de-feat, which has to be counted against every Feat or Deed of men. In brief, it is the quantity of our toil which we die in.[4]

All the contradictions in the experience of work are contained in this definition so it is a starting point rather than a resolution of the difficulty. Labour is loss, failure, defeat, death. But it is as facile to suggest that it should be avoided as it is to say that death must be avoided. It is so much a part of the human condition that to calculate its worth is impossible; it cannot be bought or sold, everything else is bought or sold for labour, labour itself is priceless. But labour is a measure of cost; 'it does not matter how much work a thing needs to produce it; it matters only how much distress... True labour, or spending of life is either of the body, in fatigue or pain; of the temper or heart . . . or of the intellect.'[5]

Some of Ruskin's best descriptions of the reality of work are, because of its very complexity, given in the form of parables. One of them is a description of a horse used on railway sidings to drag wagons uncoupled from the back of a train to the front of it, slipping

aside so deftly as the buffers meet; and, within eighteen inches of death every ten minutes, [fulfilling] his changeless duty all day long, content, for eternal reward, with his night's rest and his chopped mouthful of hay; anything more earnestly moral and beautiful one can never imagine – I never see the creature without a kind of worship.[6]

Another such parable or insight into the meaning of work comes in the introduction to *The Harbours of England*, perhaps one of the most splendid passages in Ruskin. He sets out to explain why it is that the bow of a boat, 'of all things, living or lifeless upon this strange earth' is the most miraculous and magical, why there is 'nothing else that man does, which is perfect, but that'. He explains that the one great thing that the nineteenth century had done, its great achievement, was the ship of the line,

the most honourable thing that man, as a gregarious animal, has ever produced . . . into that he has put as much of his human patience, common sense, forethought, experimental philosophy, self-control, habits of order and obedience, thoroughly wrought handwork, defiance of brute elements,

---

[4] Ruskin, *Munera Pulveris*, 17, p. 182
[5] *ibid.*, p. 184
[6] Ruskin, *Time and Tide*, 17, p. 355

careless courage, careful patriotism, and calm expectation of the judgment of God, as can well be put into a space of 300 feet long by 80 broad.[7]

The whole piece is a celebration of work although that is not its subject. Ruskin explains that the ships embodying the qualities he describes are warships, fishing boats, the smaller merchant brigs or schooners, the colliers and coasters. It is this last kind which inspires something like a hymn to work, first concerning the ships themselves:

there are few things more impressive to me than one of these ships lying up against some lonely quay in a black sea-fog, with the furrow traced under its tawny keel far in the harbour slime. The noble misery that there is in it, the might of its rent and stained unseemliness, its wave-worn melancholy, resting there for a little while in the comfortless ebb, unpitied and claiming no pity; still less honoured, least of all conscious of any claim to honour.[8]

And then, their crews, idle for the present,

the rest of human limbs and hearts, at utter need, not in sweet meadows or soft air but in harbour slime and biting fog; so drawing their breath once more, to go out again, without lament, from between the two skeletons of pierheads, vocal with wash of under-wave, into the grey troughs of tumbling brine; then as they can, with slacked rope, and patched sail, and leaky hull, again to roll and stagger far away amidst the wind and salt sleet, from dawn to dusk and dusk to dawn, winning day by day their daily bread; and for last reward, when their old hands, on some winter night, lose feeling along the frozen ropes, and their old eyes miss mark of the lighthouse quenched in foam, the so-long impossible Rest, that shall hunger no more, neither thirst any more, – their eyes and mouths filled with the brown sea sand.[9]

Any discussion and analysis of Ruskin's views about work must be set against the background of that passage in order to remind us that its constant ingradients are tragedy and pity. He certainly sees work as an inseparable part of the human condition and that it is therefore both blessed and cursed, 'human work must be done honourably and thoroughly, because we are now Men; – whether we ever expect to be angels or ever were slugs, being practically no matter'.[10] Human work is, he explains, affectionate, honest and earnest, and the resolution to do it well is the only sound foundation of any religion. Work has this ennobling, spiritual quality, precisely because it contains the opposite element of baseness and servility. A great number of jobs are accurately described as servile, that is 'they sink a man to the

---

[7] Ruskin, *The Harbours of England*, 13, p. 28
[8] *ibid.*, p. 26
[9] *ibid.*, p. 27
[10] Ruskin, *Fors Clavigera*, 29, p. 88

condition of a serf . . . the proper state of an animal, but more or less unworthy of men; nay, unholy in some sense, so that a day is made "holy" by the fact of its being commanded, "Thou shalt do no servile work therein".'[11] But not entirely so, such work could be the holiest of all particularly if it were undertaken by clerics or if they made the taking up of some disagreeable, despised but useful trade, an earnest of their conversion. The suggestion was not entirely ironic; it was made repeatedly, along with the proposal that a proportion of rough manual work should be done by the upper classes.[12] He refers to the opinion of a clerical friend who had been much affected by the degenerate state of brickmakers: 'Let him go and make and burn a pile or two with his own hands; he will thereby receive apocalyptic visions of a nature novel to his soul.' Brickmaking will bring you quite as near God as writing lawyers' letters at five shillings a time, the only difference is that 'instead of getting five shillings for writing a letter, you will only get it for a day and a half's sweat of the brow'.[13] Christian duty demanded more than church attendance and the forms of prayer, it might require that the richman's children should sweep street crossings on alternate Sundays, and to the predictable objection that providence has called us all to our various stations Ruskin asks the rich whether it was they or providence that had brought about the allocation of stations in life: 'You knock a man into a ditch and then you tell him to remain content in the "position in which Providence has placed him". That's modern Christianity.'[14]   He insists that the suggestion is not strange (despite the episode of the Hincksey road); the experience of manual work is, after all, the life of most people, but that is a measure of the falsity of modern society that it should find the idea strange, or wild, or radical. To share in the work of the poor or to undertake their work on their behalf would provide priests and gentlemen with some of their strength, their ability to endure sorrow, that quality which has given them peace and 'till now rendered their oppression possible. Only the idle among them might revolt against their state; the brave workers die passively, young and old – and make no sign.'[15]

This dignified passivity is brought only by work. In the midst of 'this yelping, carnivorous crowd, mad for money and lust, tearing

[11] Ruskin, *Time and Tide*, 17, p. 417
[12] *ibid.*, p. 335
[13] Ruskin, *Fors Clavigera*, 28, p. 566
[14] Ruskin, *The Crown of Wild Olive*, 18, p. 422
[15] Ruskin, *Fors Clavigera*, 29, p. 473

each other to pieces, and starving each other to death, and leaving heaps of their dung and ponds of their spittle on every palace floor and altar stone, – it is impossible for us, except in the labour of hands, not to go mad'.[16] But it must be manual work, 'it is only the peace which comes necessarily from manual work which in all time has kept the honest country people patient in their task of maintaining the rascals who live in towns'. Much of modern Marxist theory has come to agree, to its own despair, that the socialisation of the proletariat takes place in work, that the experience of work forms an aspect of the deep structures through which the authority of capitalism is communicated through rules unquestioned by its subordinates. But Ruskin's insight is that it is work itself rather than industrialised work which contributes this passive stability to society and which serves as a moral bond.

Ruskin is, of course, perilously close to a dilemma in this respect. Why should labourers display such heroic passivity in maintaining the rascals who live in the towns? If they are truly rascals and the system which creates them is so wicked, should not they and it be brought down? And how can those features which cement and support it be regarded as admirable rather than contemptible? Before arriving at conclusions about the consistency or otherwise of his reasoning, we may notice that his explanation of the consequences of manual work may be a lot more accurate than predictions about its revolutionary implications in capitalist society. Manual work binds men together, contributes to a morality of acceptance and quietism. It is non-work, the withdrawal of work, which breeds trouble. The intensely divided machine work of capitalist industry may have the effect of promoting demoralisation and disorder which will bring about the downfall of a system essentially founded in corruption, a downfall more complete than any predicted revolt of a proletariat simply demanding its shares of the spoils. In anticipation of what is now dismissed as economism Ruskin at one point taunts workers with their claim that they are free men: 'Much good may that do you as you must do whatever I like, or die by starvation. "Strike!" – will you . . . And when you are forced to work again, will not your masters choose again, as they have chosen hitherto, what work you are to do?'[17] Engels also saw that one of the consequences of mechanisation was that, in freeing man from physical labour, it deprived him of the

---

[16] Ruskin, *Fors Clavigera*, 27, p. 207
[17] *ibid.*, p. 515

pride in muscular prowess which had made his work acceptable simply because it was demanding or dangerous. The rascals who live in the towns may cease to be maintained when everyone is brought to share in their rascality, when their exploitation of labour ceases to provide labour of any moral quality.

We have noted before that Ruskin came close on occasions to making somewhat obscure indirect suggestions that working men might actually consider doing something about their condition. He asks the trade unions, 'What talk you of wages? Whose is the Wealth of the World but yours? Where is the Virtue? Do you mean to go on for ever, leaving your wealth to be consumed by the idle, and your virtue to be mocked by the vile.'[18] But Ruskin's invitations to workers that they should consider the possibility of a sudden change in their affairs are alway hesitant and uncertain, lacking the urgent conviction of an organiser of barricades. For the most part, one of the virtues of manual labour is that is is necessarily accompanied by tranquility. His point is that it is the capitalist's destruction of manual work that is likely to promote a general collapse in the order manual work produces.

Ruskin's defence of the subordination and order which he sees accompanying manual work is rigorous in the extreme. He begins his defence, characteristically, at the weakest point, with a description of some kind of subordinate work as menial, their being no word that people more dislike being applied to them. But there is nothing in itself dishonourable about being menial, the word derives from 'meinie' or 'many', 'the attendant company of anyone worth attending to'. The important question is '*whose* many you belong to, and whether he is a person worth belonging to, or even safe to be belonged'. It is also important to know the cause in which you follow, 'if you follow for love it is good to be menial – if for honour, good also; – if for ten per cent, – as a railway company follows its Director, it is not good to be menial'.[19] Ruskin often illustrated the value of menial work by the loyalty of domestic servants and on this occasion he illustrates his point with a reference to the novels of Dickens who, although he was as likely to worship success as much as any hack from the *Eatanswill Independent*, left as his best portraits, as the characters he loved most, menials like 'Sam, Mark, Kit, Peggotty . . . Is not the entire testimony of Dickens traced in its true

[18] *ibid.*, p. 515
[19] *ibid.*, p. 517

force, that no position is so *good* for men and women, none so likely to bring out their best human character, as that of a dependent or menial.'

And yet the ambiguity remains. Ruskin reported in *Time and Tide* that some of his readers had been offended by his statement that manual work is degrading. He repeated it: 'simply, or totally manual work alone *is* degrading, though often in measure refreshing, wholesome and necessary. So it is highly necessary and wholesome to eat sometimes; but degrading to eat all day, as to labour with the hands all day. But it is not degrading to think all day – if you can.'[20]

This is the first of several important qualifications about the value of work; it must be of limited duration otherwise it becomes a form of torture. The second is that it should not be so thoroughly divided that it becomes the life task of a special class who are allowed no respite from it and are permitted to do nothing else. But rough work will remain to be done by rough men and

it is of no use to try to conceal this sorrowful fact by fine words, and to talk to the workman about the honourableness of manual labour and the dignity of humanity. Rough work, honourable or not, takes the life out of us; and the man who has been heaving clay out of a ditch all day, or driving an express train against the north wind all night, or holding a collier's helm in a gale on a lee shore, or working white-hot iron at a furnace mouth, is not the same man at the end of his day, or night, as one who has been sitting in a quiet room . . . reading books. If it is any comfort to you to be told that the rough work is the more honourable of the two, I should be sorry to take that consolation from you; and in some sense I need not. The rough work is at all events real, honest, and, generally, though not always, useful; while the fine work is, a great deal of it, foolish and false . . . and therefore dishonourable; but when both kinds are equally well and worthily done, the head's is the noble work, and the hand's the ignoble . . . The inherent nature of hard work is one of calamity.[21]

It is the fact that rough work is heavy, painful, arduous, that gives it the power to provide moral quality in the men who undertake it. But it is dangerous in every sense because it can stupefy and ruin, it can kill. For that reason we must examine carefully how the manual worker is to be 'comforted, redeemed and rewarded'. One important consideration is the principle by which those who do it are selected for it, it must not be an arbitrary process as the present arrangements make it because when those who do the rough work are those who

[20] Ruskin, *Time and Tide*, 17, p. 423
[21] Ruskin, *The Crown of Wild Olive*, 18, p. 417

chance to have fallen into it, it cannot be done well nor with a will. No one can have a sound will for it unless he knows that he is doing what he should 'and is in his place'. This meets Durkheim's requirement for the establishment of moral order in industrial society, that there should be some consonance between the distribution of talents and tasks. Yet this alone would make for the most brutal meritocracy in which the superior position of the masters would be legitimated by their superior abilities and the subordination of the servants enforced by their acknowledged inferiority.

Ruskin never blinks at the severity of the distinction and never produces cosmetic disguises to comfort those who are disadvantaged by their own nature. First, he says, labour should be taken seriously, trained for, not merely in terms of the mastery of the necessary techniques but made analogous with military service, enlisted, trained, dressed and praised; 'teach the plough exercise as carefully as you do the sword exercise and let the officers of troops of life be held as much gentlemen as the officers of troops of death'.[22] But, above all, a relationship of justice must exist between them. The idea of honouring those who undertake the important and dangerous (it can stupefy as well as kill) labour of society seems impractical and absurd in our own social setting. Yet the Soviet Union and China have demonstrated that it is at least as consistent and sensible (for whatever devious reason) to give state honours for a collier's output as for political services or military distinction.

And Ruskin demonstrates that the honour due to labour is no mere question of managerial or political strategy directed at achieving both passivity and productivity. The labourer is never sufficiently stupefied as to be unable to see through such sophisticated deceptions as are recommended in modern management texts. Ruskin says that the honour in labour is simply a reflection of the bifurcated nature of man, the poor forked animal:

the initial virtue of the race consists in the acknowledgement of their own lowly nature and submission to the laws of higher being. 'Dust thou art, and unto dust shalt thou return', is the first truth we have to learn of ourselves; and to till the earth out of which we were taken, our first duty: in that labour, and in the relations which it establishes between us and the lower animals, are founded the conditions of our highest faculties and felicities: and without the labour, neither reason, art, nor peace, are possible to men.

But in that labour, accepting bodily death, appointed to us in common with the lower creatures, in noble humility; and kindling day by day the spiritual life, granted to us beyond that of the lower creatures, in noble pride, all wisdom, peace and unselfish hope and love, may be reached on earth as in heaven, and our lives be but a little lessened from those of the angels.[23]

So Ruskin reveals the complexity of his view of work and suggests some reasons why it is an essential part of the process of education and why it is not simply a matter of giving honour to those who undertake it but of seeking honour by its voluntary undertaking. Labour is a vital part of the human condition. For that reason the active pursuit of its diminution must be undertaken with some care. If labour carries with it these connotations of nobility and humanity, the substitution for labour by machinery must be suspect. William Morris showed little respect for the argument that machinery was introduced to ease the burden of the worker: if it was employed to increase productivity and profit it was more than likely to make the condition of the worker worse. Braverman[24] and Berg[25] have argued that machines are used to rob the worker of the control of his work and so to threaten his humanity and independence. Ruskin, as we shall see, took a remarkably modern view in his scepticisicm about machines. Morris, while seeing through the purpose of machine utilisation, is quite ambivalent over the question of whether machines *should* be used to substitute for labour, or what was to be done about hard and unpleasant tasks. Morris is in fact praised in some quarters for his 'enlightened' attitude to the machinery question in order to establish that he was no 'mere medievalist'. The matter of his ambivalence to noxious tasks is discussed at a little more length elsewhere.[26] The passage in Morris always quoted to demonstrate his positive attitude to machinery ('wonders of invention', etc. from *News From Nowhere*, 1890) is not as impressive as that passage in Ruskin in which he asks 'what may be the real dignity of mechanical Art?' before going on to describe a locomotive engine: 'these glittering cylinders and timely respondent valves, and fine ribbed rods, which touch each other as a serpent writhes in noiseless gliding, and omnipotence of grasp: infinitely complex anatomy of active steel'. And of the men who made it he asks what 'would these Iron-dominant Genie think of me? and what ought I to think of them?'[27] Ruskin, too, admired machines but saw more clearly than Morris what they could do to men. Ruskin says

[23] Ruskin, *Fors Clavigera*, 27, p. 332
[24] Harry Braverman, *Labour and monopoly capitalism* (New York, Monthly Review Press, 1974)
[25] Berg, *The machinery question*
[26] P. D. Anthony, *The ideology of work* (London, Tavistock, 1977), pp. 279–81
[27] Ruskin, *The Cestus of Aglaia*, 19, p. 61

unpleasant tasks should not be avoided and that the employment of machines to perform them threatens the human condition because labour is an essential part of it. Ruskin inverts the values that see labour as something to be avoided without in any sense refusing to acknowledge the character of labour itself. And he sees the most unpleasant characteristic of labour as being essentially what is mechanical about it. While manual work, because of the negative character of the task, can promote positive qualities in the worker, mechanical work is devoid of this power:

foul or mechanical work is always reduced by a noble race to the minimum in quantity . . . The highest conditions of human society reached hitherto have cast such work to slaves; but supposing slavery of a politically defined kind to be done away with, mechanical and foul employment must, in all highly organized states, take the aspect of either punishment or probation.[28]

The reason for the superiority of manual over mechanical work emerges from a carefully drawn distinction between machines and tools: 'any instrument is a machine so far as its action is, in any particular or moment, beyond the control of the human hand. A violin, a pencil, and a plough, are tools, not machines. A grinding organ, or a windmill is a machine not a tool . . . a lathe is a machine, and the workman's chisel used at it is a tool.'[29] Mechanical work is to be avoided, because its performance entails a loss of control by the workman over his operations. If its avoidance is impossible, the simplest forms of machinery must be used first.

Powerlessness or loss of control is given by Blauner as one of the features of alienated work and there is a spirited controversy over whether this is brought about by technical development in the production process or whether it and they are the result of capitalism and its drive for productive efficiency. Ruskin does not recognise the distinction, but his remedy takes the form of some sort of legal or social proscription of mechanical work. We can distinguish what he has to say about manual work from mechanical labour. Manual work is necessary but degrading in excessive amounts; it must be controlled in its duration, must be the more or less specialised activity of manual workers except insofar as that specialisation is mediated by the sharing of manual work with the priesthood, intellectuals and upper classes. Because it is necessary and dangerous its performance should be honoured. Mechanical work is entirely dangerous and is to be

[28] Ruskin, *Munera Pulveris*, 17, p. 234
[29] Ruskin, *Fors Clavigera*, 27, pp. 644–5

avoided wherever possible because it implies a loss of control which is always entirely bad in its effects. If it must be done it should be confined to the simplest forms of machine work and its performance be regarded as criminal punishment.

Machines should not be used as substitution for human labour because that is wasteful, they should be used to perform useful tasks of a kind (such as great irrigation schemes) too colossal for human labour to accomplish by itself.[30] Machines never 'increase the possibility of life. They only increase the possibilities of idleness.' The power of a machine is only in enabling the people whose labour it saves to be idle, it is not likely that they will remain as happy as they were but even if we assume that, in future, 'idleness is to be the mother of all good, the machine will not enable them to live better than they did before nor to live in greater numbers . . . Out of so much ground, only so much living is to be got, with or without machinery.'

Ruskin lays down such proscriptions sometimes in relation to his model communities of St George, sometimes in advice for the restructuring of society as a whole. He appears to take the view that law or customary regulation will determine the limits of the permissible in terms of tasks, machines and hours. This was the method of regulation described by Marx as limiting the too intensive development of the division of labour in the guilds and medieval towns. It was also the method preferred by Comte; Durkheim was probably right to say that no law or authority could possibly control in sufficient detail, the division of jobs in multitudes of workplaces. We must acknowledge that Ruskin was best when the practical arrangements to be made to introduce his proposals were left in the vaguest form. He also engaged in exhortation to bring about a reduction in mechanical work by attempting to reduce the demand for its product. The consumers of the products of labour must exercise care in the pains they put on those on whom their comfort rests.

Who is to do the pleasant and clean work, and for what pay? Who is to do no work, and for what pay? And there are curious moral and religious questions connected with these. How far is it lawful to suck a portion of the soul out of a great many persons, in order to put the abstracted psychical qualities together and make one very beautiful or ideal soul?...we live, we gentlemen, on delicatest prey, after the manner of weasels; that is to say, we keep a certain number of clowns digging and ditching, and generally stupefied, in order that we, being fed gratis, may have all the thinking and feeling to ourselves.[31]

[30] Ruskin, *Munera Pulveris*, 17, p. 156
[31] Ruskin, *Sesame and Lilies*, 18, p. 107

He more than once lectured his women readers about the distress caused by their tastes in hats and jewellery (reinforcing the general impression of a constant affinity between radicalism and puritanical self-denial). To the extent that manual work is degrading it is the duty of the middle classes 'to diminish the demand for this kind of work' and to live with as few wants as they can, remembering that they are maintained by the labour of others; 'the less your keep costs the better. It does not cost money only, it costs degradation. You do not merely employ these people you also *tread* upon them. It cannot be helped; – you have your place, and they have theirs; but see that you tread as lightly as possible, and on as few as possible.'[32]

Ruskin frequently tells his readers that it is difficult for them to imagine the kind of tasks done and lives led by those who support them in their privilege.

Infinite nonsense is talked about the 'work done' by the upper classes. I have done a little myself, in my day, of the kind of work they boast of; but mine, at least, has been all play. Even lawyers', which is, on the whole, the hardest, you may observe to be essentially grim play, made more jovial to themselves by conditions which make it somewhat dismal to other people. Here and there we have a real worker among soldiers, or no soldiering would long be possible; nevertheless, young men don't go into the [army] with any primal or essential idea of work.[33]

The cost of real labour is so high that it cannot be regarded as a commodity to be bought or sold; the true object

of Political Economy is not to buy, nor to sell labour, but to spare it. Every attempt to buy or sell it is, in the outcome, ineffectual; so far as successful, it is not sale but betrayal; and the purchase-money is a part of that thirty pieces which bought, first the greatest of labourers, and afterwards the burial-field of the Stranger's, the purchase money in its very smallness being the measured opposite of the *villis annona amicorum* and making all men strangers to each other.[34]

Ruskin is quite clear that the payment for labour involves the payment for a part of the life of the labourer. 'Labour is the contest of the life of men with an opposite; – the term "life" including his intellect, soul, and physical power, contending with question,

---

[32] Ruskin, *Time and Tide*, 17, p. 424
[33] The remark about soldiering as an alternative to working seems singularly perceptive. While unemployment or the absence of work has always produced a high proportion of soldiers, the remainder always seemed to have preferred discipline, privation and the prospect of death as an alternative to the discipline of work. It is akin to the choice of 'freedom' of the seafarer as against the routine of the landsman
[34] Ruskin, *Munera Pulveris*, 17, p. 183

difficulty or material force.'[35] Labour is of a higher or lower order 'as it includes more or fewer of the elements of life'. He adds that the Greeks distinguished between worthy and false labour. The former was regarded as a divine thing and its price was an honourable estimate or an honorarium, it was to be honoured with the kind of respect paid to the gods. False labour was that which led away from life and was paid with vengeance, an execution in which the goddess Tisiphone was an expert, 'a person versed in the highest branches of arithmetic, and punctual in her habits'.[36]

There is more than a suggestion here that the intrinsic value of work is destroyed in employment when it becomes the subject of close calculation, precise measurement and wary bargaining. The purchase money makes work into the measured opposite of its proper function and sets men against each other. Ruskin is saying that the calculation of the employment relationship produces alienation and that this condition is further exaggerated when the sacrifice entailed by labour is unnecessarily squandered on the production of worthless goods. While Alan Fox is quite right in saying that social values have been transferred from the process of production to consumption,[37] Ruskin insists upon a balance between the two, consumption 'is the end, crown, and perfection of production'.[38] So, labour is of a higher or lower order 'as it includes more or fewer of the elements of life' and as to whether it is constructive, nugatory or destructive;[39] 'finally, I believe nearly all labour may be shortly divided into positive and negative labour: positive, that which produces life; negative, that which produces death'.[40]

Is there, then, any clear distinction between a kind of labour that is intrinsically valuable to the labourer and the rest, the foul and mechanical kind of labour? What is it that makes some labour 'false', its component tasks or the fact that it is done only for calculated reward, the kind that is rewarded by Tisiphone? Is there good work and bad work?

Sherburne, one of the best modern commentators upon Ruskin's social theory, says that he 'stresses the distinction between *opera* which "recreates" and labour, work which corrupts or destroys'. Labour,

[35] Ruskin, *Unto this Last*, 17, p. 85
[36] *ibid.*, pp. 95–6
[37] Alan Fox, *A sociology of work in industry* (London, Collier-Macmillan, 1971)
[38] Ruskin, *Unto this Last*, 17, p. 98
[39] *ibid.*, p. 96
[40] *ibid.*, p. 97

he continues, 'is the suffering in effort . . . *Opera* is happy, creative work.' Sherburne goes on to say that this 'distinction between labor and *opera* is basic to his thinking. It has its source in his vision of the Gothic builder and his own creative experience in art and authorship. Ruskin's belief in positive work separates him sharply from the classical economists and from many of his Victorian contemporaries.'[41] Sherburne finally seeks to establish a relationship between Ruskin's vision of positive labour and his 'assumption of abundance'. We have already briefly examined the reliability of this alleged concern with abundance; the present assertion of creative work, of *opera* as distinct from labour, is a more serious error. Let us examine it.

Unlike the classical economists and most Victorians who, says Sherburne, distinguished simply between labour and its opposite, non-work or leisure, Ruskin sees the future as a society, not of leisure, but as one in which happy work is maximised and degrading labour is minimised. This is surely not the case. Ruskin does *not* simply distinguish between happy work and degrading work. It is not merely the feelings induced in the worker by the tasks he performs that makes the work *opera* or labour. Ruskin is no mere job enlarger. He recognises, as we have surely seen, that work contains both positive and negative elements, that it is precisely this duality that makes it important, that its importance cannot lead to a programme for its progressive reduction, that the danger of machinery is that it replaces it, and that its positive or negative quality depends as much upon what it is for as upon what composes it. Ruskin does not consistently distinguish between the terms 'work' and 'labour', he seems to use them interchangeably and he certainly does not use them with the precise and carefully distinguished meanings accorded them by Hannah Arendt[42] or in the broadly different sense which Engels attributed, falsely or otherwise, to Marx's usage in *Capital*. As Ollman points out, both terms are, in any case, covered in German by the single term '*arbeit*'.[43]

It is less clear whether Ruskin distinguishes between labour (or work) and *opera*. The second term does not appear (except in the sense of musical drama) in Cook and Wedderburn's general index. Ruskin uses it in *Munera Pulveris* when he is defining labour and when he says that labour 'is usually confused with effort itself, or the application of

[41] Sherburne, *Ambiguities of abundance*, p. 130
[42] Hannah Arendt, *The human condition* (University of Chicago Press, 1958)
[43] Bertell Ollman, *Alienation, Marx's conception of man in capitalist society* (Cambridge University Press, 1971), p. 100

power (*opera*), but there is much effort which is merely a mode of recreation, or of pleasure'. And Ruskin goes on to say that the most beautiful actions of the body and the highest results of the mind are achievements 'of quite unlaborious, nay, of recreative, – effort. But labour is the *suffering* in effort.'[44] The cost of anything is measured in labour, not effort or power, the cost of 'winning it, moving it, coming at it', and cost is therefore measured in labour, not in *opera*; what matters is how much *distress* the production of a thing takes. Now this may seem to point in the direction of a difference between good and bad work, between happiness and misery, but Ruskin is not talking of happy work, he is discussing something that is not work or labour at all and the distinction is certainly not to be confused with the very superficial and modern view that 'creative', or 'meaningful', or 'self-actualising' work is different from labour. Ruskin clearly makes the point that 'operative dexterity is necessary in all the higher arts; but the cost of [that is, surely, the labour necessary to produce] this dexterity is incalculable'.[45] The opposite of this is unlaborious, recreative effort, a mode of recreation, which produces the highest human achievements. It is also the pleasurable effort that goes into games and into those middle-class intellectual professions that are game-like ('even lawyer's work . . .'). One of the characteristics that distinguish the gothic for Ruskin is not its nobility, or the 'creative' work that went into it, it is the vulgarity, its coarseness, the contribution of labouring men at play, the comic and the grotesque. Ruskin acknowledges the distinctions that we are fond of making about levels of creativity and that Sherburne tries to distinguish from *opera*, but he says these are distinctions within labour itself, not apart from it. Labour of good quality 'includes always as much intellect and feeling as will fully and harmoniously regulate the physical force' and the highest and most worthy labour was regarded by the Greeks as a divine thing, to be honoured rather than paid for. And it is purposeful, directed at a fit and worthy goal. Indeed Ruskin's savage criticism of what Sherburne sees as 'happy work' and what we have learned to call 'creative work' is well-illustrated by his comments on the ill-directed but highly skilled lithographies of the Parisienne pornography trade and on the technically assured but morally debased work of Gustav Doré.

The point is worth examination because it is important to establish

---

[44] Ruskin, *Munera Pulveris*, 17, p. 183
[45] *ibid.*, pp. 184–5

that Ruskin is not putting work or labour, an essentially ugly thing, into one category, and *opera* or creative work, a beautiful thing, into another. Sherburne's distinction may well apply to William Morris and his judgment that the distinction arises from 'his own creative experience and authorship' is true of Morris, but not of Ruskin.

Ruskin not only refused to raise technical accomplishment and skill to an exalted level, he actually warned that it carried its own special dangers. Fine art was the result of a balanced application of strength, dexterity and intellect involving 'the action and force of a strong man's arm from the shoulder as well as the delicatest touch of his fingers'. The dangers in technical proficiency he represents by Daedalus, 'the type of practically executive craftsmen'. One danger is a delight in semblance rather than the form of truth, the other and more serious is that ingenuity may 'become bestial, an instinct for mechanical labour only, strangely involved with a feverish and ghostly cruelty . . . rebellious, finally against the laws of nature and honour, and building labyrinths for monsters, – not combs for bees'.[46] Ruskin frequently referred to Daedalus to illustrate 'whatever good there is and whatever evil in the labour of the hands, separated from that of the souls'.[47] It is not machine work or machine making that is dangerous, it is craftsmanship and the pride that is taken in it which overcomes its proper relationship with moral good. Ruskin illustrates the danger in re-telling the story of Arachne whose weaving was technically perfect but whose tapestry was impious, composed of base and abominable things and so was 'Fault . . . of a poisonous and degrading kind, sensual, insolent and foul: so that she is changed by Athena into the meanest of animals, and the most loathsomely venomous; whose work instead of being an honour to the palaces of kings is to be a disgrace to the room of the simplest cottager'.[48]

It is not true to conclude that Ruskin looked forward to a society in which happy work is maximised and degrading work is minimised. Morris did, although he was never quite sure how it could be done except by the magic transformation of a socialist revolution. Ruskin distinguishes between power and work. Power is the attribute of God, 'it is only for God to create without toil; that which man can create without toil is worthless'.[49] Ruskin also believed that power was the characteristic of genius ('sound and colour wait on them from their

[46] Ruskin, *The Queen of the Air*, 19, p. 353
[47] Ruskin, *Fors Clavigera*, 27, p. 403
[48] Ruskin, *The Story of Arachne*, 20, p. 377
[49] Ruskin, *The Stones of Venice*, 9, p. 454

youth'), the work of whom no amount of emulation, education and hard work could parallel. The work of great painters, musicians and poets is indeed *'opera'* but this is something very different from 'happy' or meaningful or craft work. Ruskin cannot be understood to mean that the work of the world is to be reduced while its *'opera'* is to be increased. To begin with, no conceivable programme of training or deliberate reallocation of resources could considerably increase it because those capable of producing it cannot be stopped (neither can they be paid) and those incapable cannot be brought to it. Ruskin is frankly contemptuous of the attempt to imitate those capable of *'opera'*. There are a few in any generation who cannot be stopped writing or painting even if they are to starve,

but the people who take to writing or painting as a means of livelihood because they think it genteel, are just by so much more contemptible than common beggars . . . Whatever in literature, art or religion, is done for money is poisonous itself, and doubly deadly, in preventing the hearing or seeing of the noble literature and art which have been done for love and truth. If people cannot make their bread by honest labour, let them at least make no noise about the street.[50]

Even those 'powerful' artists, the latent geniuses upon whom sound and colour wait, must be trained and developed and that is a process remarkably close to labour.

And labour is irreplaceable in the world, so vital that it cannot be bought, the measure of all value, labour is life itself. Writing of Turner's treatment of a windmill, Ruskin says:

there is a dim type of all melancholy human labour in it . . . Turning around a couple of stones, for the mere pulverization of human food, is not noble work for the winds. So, also, of all low labour to which one sets human souls. It is better than no labour; and, in a still higher degree, better than destructive wandering of imagination; but yet that grinding in the darkness, for mere food's sake, must be melancholy work enough for many a living creature. All men have felt it so . . . Turner has no joy of his mill. It shall be dark against the sky, yet proud, and on the hill-top not ashamed of its labour, and brightened from beyond, the golden clouds stopping over it, and the calm summer sun going down behind, far away to his rest.[51]

There is a distinction to be made between labour and *opera*, but the almost effortless application of power (however laboriously acquired) is such a rare thing as not to be characteristic of the work of most men

---

[50] Ruskin, *Fors Clavigera*, 28, p. 646
[51] Ruskin, *Modern Painters*, 6, p. 18

and women. In any case, it is not the same as the difference between labour and creative work. Morris regarded craft work as the model for general imitation, he could not be happy until all men could take as much pleasure in their work as he took in his own. Morris has contributed to the obfuscation of the discussion of work by the promotion of what has always been a small part of men's work to be the model for human activity. We cannot rest until we can all be engaged upon hand-loom weaving or the carving of love spoons,[52] and this at a time when craft work seems to have already left the world. In this respect Morris, despite his protestations to the contrary, remains something of an unreal medievalist. Ruskin, like Morris after him, believed that men could not be happy if their working lives were miserable but he did not suggest that this change could be achieved by providing creative work for all.

To 'create' cannot be said of man's labour unless it is the work of imaginative invention, to create anything in reality is to put life into it . . . A poet, or creator, is therefore a person who puts things together . . . His work is essentially this: it is the gathering and arranging of material by imagination, so as to have in it at least the harmony or helpfulness of life, and the passion or emotion of life. Mere fitting and adjustment is nothing; that is watchmaking.[53]

A great deal of what we call craft work would not pass this test of creativity and a great deal more work of the world has to be done that could even approximate to this standard if it were to be made the pattern for happy work. Much of Ruskin's conception of labour is that it is important precisely because it is miserable, hard, necessary, dangerous. The proposition that the world should be populated by workers engaged in happy work would seem to Ruskin monstrous and unpractical. But the workers might yet be happy, many of them, and the rest have their misery reduced.

The confusion over *work* and *opera*, or rather the significance of the distinction between them is easy to understand. We have all been taught for a very long time that work is an important matter because it represents the way man makes his mark upon the world or creates

---

[52] The manufacture of Welsh love spoons illustrates the inanity of much of the concern with the restoration of craftsmanship. They were made as an act of recreation and as an earnest of love. Love spoons can be made but they cannot be manufactured and people cannot be employed to make them; if they are, then however intricate the product and however much 'craft' has gone into it, it cannot be a love spoon. The development of rural industry and crafts to 'restore' the manufacture of love spoons is a meaningless contradiction and its products can have utility only in the tourist trade

[53] Ruskin, *Modern Painters*, 7, p. 215

his life. Capitalist and communist agree about the absolute importance of *homo faber*. The attitude comes to be summarised in the
modern world as an emphasis upon self-actualising work, the kind in
which we can express ourselves, through which our personalities can
grow, interesting, demanding, challenging work. The rest, repetitive
and senseless operations, are measured against this standard of
meaningful or good work and, to the extent that they are deficient,
they are dismissed as 'alienating' or 'anomic'. The distinction is
clearly made by Blauner who, as Sherburne suggests of Ruskin, is
anxious to discover the features of 'good' jobs so that they can be
imitated at the expense of jobs that are not 'self-actualising'. The
importance of work, of all work, for Ruskin, is thus confused with a
quite different intention to make jobs meaningful (sometimes in a
badly disguised effort to satisfy the interest of those who manage
them).

The distinction between Ruskin's view of work and the modern can
be illustrated by the contrast he drew between the gothic and the
renaissance. For Walter Pater, the renaissance spirit concerned the
high dignity of man 'bringing the dust under his feet into sensible
communion with the thoughts and affections of the angels . . . not as
renewed by religious system, but by his own natural right', it was man
asserting himself in 'that rehabilitation of human nature, the body,
the senses, the heart, the intelligence, which the Renaissance
fulfills'.[54] It is this assertion of high dignity of man creating his world,
his life and his destiny which informs the view that work must be
meaningful. Ruskin's conception is not to be confused with it simply
on the ground that he saw work as the most vitally important activity
in which men engaged. Ruskin's is nearer to a medieval conception of
work, that it represents man's imperfection, his animal-like nature as
well as his divine aspiration, his grotesque crudity as well as his spirit,
his suffering as well as his salvation. It is ironic that, contrasted with
the high idealism of the modern view, it is Ruskin's realistic view of
work and of human nature that has been called utopian and
idealistic.

We have seen the proscriptions that Ruskin would impose. Because
work entails suffering (the quantity of toil which we die in) it must be
controlled in its amount both by the restriction of the demand that is
made for it and in the restriction of the hours that those who provide it
must endure. It must not be made mechanical, not because of some

---

[54] Walter Pater, *The renaissance* (London, Macmillan, 1910), p. 41

blind prejudice against machines but because as much intelligence and judgment or discretion as possible must be left in it. Ruskin saw what a number of contemporary Marxists have seen, that the purpose of mechanisation may not simply be to raise productivity but to seize control over the worker so as to rob him of independence. This is never better accomplished than when the worker is left to labour at a task in which every element of intelligence has been extracted so as to make it the special work of some management functionary. Ruskin saw this as not only deadly in terms of its effect upon the worker, but as dangerously divisive and possibly irredeemable in its consequences for society. For this reason Ruskin inverts the judgments by which the use of machines is normally regarded as possible and praiseworthy; the first priority was to use muscle power, only if this was insufficient for the provision of the population's well-being should natural mechanical power be next used, and only as a last resort should there be recourse to artificially produced mechanical power. It is wasteful to use machines while men are idle and are, because of their idleness, corrupted and polluted.[55] Ruskin believed that labour was an essential part of the educational process because of the moral quality that accompanied it and that therefore work should form part of the activity of all people. Finally, he attached such importance to labour in the life of a community or a nation that he believed its organisation, the values that were attached to it, the honour that should be paid to it, was perhaps the most important affair to which the nation should pay attention.

This then is, in brief, a summary of the attitude that Ruskin took to labour and its place in the life of mankind. What view did he take of its present place in the world? We have followed his argument that the decline or corruption of morality and justice in society had been reflected in the decay of art and architecture, that the process had been celebrated and hastened by the doctrine of the economists, a doctrine which had, for the first time, required the universal veneration of selfishness. The precise point at which immoral doctrine caused social decay was in its impact on work. We have seen (in Chapter 3) his account of the immediate consequence in terms of the division of labour, or as he preferred it, in the division of men. The destruction of morality and justice is translated into physical and social consequences through the loss of meaning in work. The process begins with the substitution of rational calculation for traditional

[55] Ruskin, *Time and Tide*, 17, p. 543

relationships; Ruskin makes the renaissance stand for the transformation, subsequently to be described by Max Weber as the
development of rational bureaucracy. The process reaches its climax
of degradation under capitalism when employment is substituted for
service and when work both expands to an unknown scale and is
reduced to an inhuman precision.

Generally speaking, Ruskin regards all forms of employment under
capitalism as corrupted. It would be pressing him too far to make the
distinction absolute, but he usually regards the model of working
relationships as a form of service, the highest form of which can be
found in the domestic servant and in the soldier. Employment
without service and deprived of the bond of mutual dependence
between master and servant[56] becomes an exploitative and calculating relationship. For this reason Ruskin suggested that workers
should consider self-employment rather than employment by 'capitalist supporters of labour'.[57] What we might these days call one of the
fundamental contradictions of the capitalist employment relationship rests, in Ruskin's view, on the fact that as labour is the life of man,
it cannot be bought and the attempts to buy it 'makes all men
strangers to each other'.

The worst consequence of that contradiction is that it forces the
labourers who suffer from it to take action to defend themselves,
which serves only to deepen the contradiction and to encourage the
further refinement of its cause. It becomes, therefore, a contradiction
without hope of resolution. The unions may tell themselves that they
are well able to defend their members against the capitalist but

you may shorten your hours of labour as much as you please; – no minute of
them will be merry, till you are serving truly: that is to say until the bond of
constant relationship – service to death – is again established between your
masters and you. It has been broken by their sin, but may yet be recovered
by your virtue.[58]

Trade unions react to the impact of capital only in terms of 'its effect
upon their immediate interest; never in the far more terrific power of

[56] The terms 'master' and 'servant' have become, except perhaps in law, archaic, because of the
unacceptable suggestion of servility. Ruskin would not abandon them. He generally preferred
to call a spade a spade, not out of unthinking obedience to common usage, but because he saw
the name as denoting a most honourable instrument of the highest form of labour,
agricultural work. For the same reasons he suggested that a much more proper name for trade
unions was 'labour unions'. 'Men don't live by trade but by work.' For Ruskin these are not
pedantic matters; the readiness with which we look for euphemisms for such terms of work
reveals our barely concealed loathing for what it has become and our contempt for those who
do it. It reveals the extent to which it has been dishonoured
[57] Ruskin, Fors Clavigera, 28, p. 67
[58] Ruskin, Fors Clavigera, 27, p. 600

its appointment of the kind and the object of labour. It matters little, ultimately, how much a labourer is paid for making anything; but it matters fearfully what the thing is, which he is compelled to make.'[59] This is precisely the burden of the criticism that emerges within the Marxist view of trade unions, that they are subject to what Lenin called 'economism', incapable of mounting a general resistance to capitalism, riven by sectionalist representation and rivalry. The criticism continues with the argument that collective bargaining is a device for social control which protects its structure from damage by encouraging the negotiation of trivia, with 'bargaining at the margins'. Ultimately the debate sinks into the pessimism of the conclusion that the deep structures of a capitalist hegemony are unshakeable, that the very structure of thought and criticism are permeated by capitalist perceptions and assumptions, that technology and science are simply the ideological constructions of bourgeois society.

Ruskin believed that the roots of this destruction lay in the capitalist conception of work which poisoned moral and responsible relationships between men and women. The calculated relationship which it holds up as a model for general imitation leads to estrangement between one man and another and it therefore threatens the stability and meaning of social relationships. In its destruction of labour it threatens more total damage. In labouring upon the earth we recall our animal nature, establish relationships with nature and build the foundation of our higher culture. If labour is destroyed man becomes alienated from nature and the foundations of culture are destroyed.

What are we to make of Ruskin's view of work and the contrast he draws with its present condition? It is not a unique view. Its rugged Protestant character was no doubt learned at his mother's knee, reinforced by his father's sound practical business sense and given literary expression by Carlyle, whose work he admired. It is easy to conclude that Ruskin inherited and exemplified the Protestant ethic.

But the Protestant ethic, by the time it came down to Victorian manufacturing England, had almost forgotten whatever radical character it had once possessed[60] and was concerned to ensure that the doctrine of work meant zealous application to the needs and

[59] Ruskin, *The Crown of Wild Olive*, 18, p. 391
[60] There were exceptions, see the Chartist sermons preached in 1838 by the Methodist J. R. Stephens, imprisoned for sedition in 1839 (Louis James, *Print and the people* (London, Allen Lane, 1976)). But generally speaking it was the object of subsequent developments in Methodism to put aside its radical past. J. R. Stephens was expelled from Methodism (Bernard Semmel, *The Methodist revolution* (London, Heinemann, 1973))

requirements of the employers. It was also losing ground for, although Thompson describes its continuing utility,[61] its appeal was in some measure being replaced by more secular exhortations to effort. In any case, Ruskin had no early interest in doctrines of work, Protestant or any other, he came to the subject through art and architecture and developed a sympathetic understanding of the conditions of working men and women. The social question then acquired overwhelming significance for him, no doubt developed not only by his own experience but by acquaintance with the widespread literary and ecclesiastical criticism of existing conditions. Ruskin, as we have acknowledged, was by no means alone in finding the conditions and the values of manufacturing England unacceptable. But his understanding of their impact upon the worker and his labour was perhaps unique. He saw labour as having fundamental significance for man. He brought back to it a classical conception that had been carried over into the doctrine of the Christian Church in the middle ages. It is almost certain his classical and Christian background (rather than romanticism) that contributed the values against which he could measure the realities of business society. It is also, paradoxically, the success of his father in that society that exempted and protected him from direct experience of it until he had acquired the values that would subsequently reject it. His 'marsupial' upbringing, his parents' conviction that he should be educated first for the Church, second for poetry and always, to be a gentleman, quite accidentally resulted in his having developed in intellectual terms somewhat independently from the world in which he lived. When he finally entered the world it shocked him and he spent the rest of his life in a powerful and independent analysis of the manner and extent to which it failed to meet the principles upon which his education had been founded.

One peculiarity about Ruskin's doctrine of work deserves some attention. In two important respects it is similar to the conceptions of Marx. There is, as far as I know, no single reference to Marx in the whole of Ruskin's work. The solitary reference to him by the editors in their general index is in a brief footnote explanation of a sardonic comment by Ruskin about the International of 1864.[62] Yet both evolved distinctive explanations of the significance of work. The first similarity is in respect of the notion of alienation. Its significance in Marx is now a question that has grown to epic proportions and we do

[61] E. P. Thompson, *The making of the English working class* (Harmondsworth, Penguin Books, 1968)
[62] Ruskin, *Fors Clavigera*, 27, pp. 381–2

not have the time or occasion to go into it here, except to observe that
it is an idea of remarkable richness, some obscurity and not a little
ambiguity. Ruskin, without using the term, speaks of separation from
the world of nature and of other men. Both ideas are developed by
Marx. In both Ruskin and Marx the idea of separation or of
destruction of an ideal relationship is dependent upon the second
theme which the two have in common, the idea that work is the
distinctively human, significant, in Ruskin, spiritual, activity of man.
In Marx, the theme is expounded in the Economic and Philosophical
Manuscripts of 1844. He says that the worker can create nothing
without nature, the sensous exterior world. The relationship with
nature is fundamental: 'that man lives from nature means that nature
is his body with which he must maintain a constant interchange so as
not to die. That man's physical and intellectual life depends on nature
merely means that nature depends on itself, for man is a part of
nature.'[63] Labour or work (unlike Ruskin, Marx possibly sees a
difference between the two, but this view as we have seen, is
contested) is the essential activity of mankind, it is in work that man
affirms himself as a species. Ollman, among others, has argued that
the idea of alienation depends upon the supreme importance which
Marx attaches to work: 'alienation can only be grasped as the
absence of unalienation, each state serving as a point of reference for
the other. And, for Marx, unalienation is the life man leads in
communism. Without some knowledge of the future millennium
alienation remains a reproach that can never be clarified.'[64] Ruskin
has no faith in an imminent millennium, in a new Jerusalem, but his
conception of alienated work certainly depends upon a shattered
ideal, a society once based upon community, trust and justice, in
which work related men to each other and to nature. It is clear that
for Ruskin labour has the most considerable moral significance. It is
clear that for Marx labour has absolute economic and social
significance – the significance of ethics in Marx is a matter of
considerable scholarly and even greater polemical contemporary
debate. The matter to be explained is how these two very different
writers independently arrived at positions which gave unparalleled
significance to the importance of work, not merely on a practical, but
on a philosophical plane.

Ruskin did not much like what he knew of German philosophy.

---

[63] David McLellan (ed.), *Karl Marx: early texts* (Oxford, Blackwell, 1971), p. 139
[64] Ollman, *Alienation*, p. 132

Modern Painters contained an amusing parody of the high style of German philosophers,[65] and Ruskin added later that he was often told that ten or twelve years' study of it would do little harm but that busy men are best persuaded not to meddle with German books.[66] It may be that he was better acquainted with it than he acknowledged. He had studied German in 1861 and he had read Kant. The widespread influence of German culture on English writers of the nineteenth century has been well documented.[67] Two of its most influential interpreters, Coleridge and Carlyle, were thoroughly familiar to Ruskin and he would thus have been introduced, if indirectly, to the formative philosophical influence upon Marx. There is also an interesting suggestion that the traffic between German and English culture was by no means one-way. Berki, arguing that 'Marx's concept of labor owes nothing to the notion of labor in Hegel's own writings'[68] suggests the greater influence of English economists and early English socialists and, more significantly, of Carlyle. Marx knew Carlyle's *Past and Present* which had appeared in 1843 and had been appreciated by Engels in a long review printed in Marx and Ruge's *Jahrbuecher*.

Ruskin had probably read more widely in Simond de Sismondi, but how far his study had extended beyond the *History of the Italian Republics* to Sismondi's economic studies is undertain. The similarity of some of their views is so startling that it is unlikely that Ruskin had no acquaintanceship with Sismondi's wider work.[69] Sismondi might well have been a source common to both Marx and Ruskin. There is, however, little purpose in speculating about the influences that might have been in common to both. The more vital question concerns the quite different conclusions they reached concerning the consequences of capitalism and the similarities between so many of their criticisms. For the first part of the answer to this question we shall turn to Ruskin's proposals for practical reform.

[65] Ruskin, *Modern Painters*, 5, pp. 203–4
[66] *ibid.*, pp. 424–6
[67] Rosemary Ashton, *The German idea* (Cambridge University Press, 1980)
[68] R. N. Berki, 'On the nature and origins of Marx's concept of labour', *Political Theory*, 7, no. 1 (1979), 35–6
[69] For example, 'The accumulation of wealth *in abstracto* is not the aim of the government, but the participation by all its citizens in the pleasure of life which the wealth represents' (Charles Gide and Charles Rist, *A history of economic doctrines* (London, Harrap, 1948), pp. 191–2).

8

Revolution

Because of the association falsely ascribed to Ruskin in some quarters, and in case the title of this chapter is misleading, it is necessary to assert, once again, that Ruskin was not a socialist. Indeed, one of the outcomes of present tendencies that he most desperately wanted to avert was socialism. He saw it as continuing, even exaggerating the worst characteristics of contemporary capitalism and as emerging as a result of the inexorable development of capitalism. In this sense, again, Ruskin's analysis is akin to that of Marx. But whereas Marx sees socialism as a welcome and inevitable consequence of capitalism, almost as its consummation, Ruskin sees it as a disaster. Socialism 'is simply chaos – a chaos towards which the believers in modern political economy are fast tending and from which I am trying to save them'.[1]

And yet Ruskin came to take an attitude that was at best equivocal about the prospect of revolution, and there is more than a hint of populism, even anarchism, in his later opinions. One of the reasons for his equivocation and uncertainty was that he could not accept the facile conclusion (for which so many other radicals have been praised in terms of their 'realism') that change must be assured by political action. Political discussion was useless partly because of an absence of definition of terms. There is no opposition between liberals and conservatives. 'There is opposition between Liberals and Illiberals. I am a violent Illiberal; but it does not follow that I must be a Conservative.' A conservative is opposed to a destructive, who wishes to destroy things as they are, but, 'though I am an Illiberal there are many things I should like to destroy';[2] Ruskin's short list includes most English and all Welsh railways, the Houses of Parliament, the East End of London, the new town of Edinburgh, the north suburb of Geneva and the city of New York.

[1] Ruskin, *Munera Pulveris*, 17, pp. 106–7
[2] Ruskin, *Fors Clavigera*, 27, p. 14

As the facile conclusion of political action is unacceptable and as the problem of achieving change is bigger and more complex, Ruskin cannot allow himself to come to an easy conclusion as to how it is to be brought about. But let us first recall what is to be changed or what is to be achieved before we examine the methods to be used. First, any right form of human society must exist in relationship with nature and must be in tune with that balance and harmony that Ruskin saw evident in all things perceivable by the senses or conceivable by the mind: 'the desert has its appointed place and work; the eternal engine, whose beam is the earth's axle, whose heart is its year, and whose breath is the ocean, will still divide imperiously to the desert kingdoms . . . As the art of life is learned, it will be found at last that all lovely things are also necessary.'[3] This is perhaps the first element of a society that is to be stable, that is a part of or in relationship to what we could now call an ecological system which encompasses the universe. In this respect, as we have seen, Ruskin is distinguished from that aspect of Marxism and of science which sees man as paramount, living upon the world rather than in relationship with it.

Ruskin is as concerned as any post-Durkheimian sociologist with the 'problem of order' with the pre-eminent necessity that man should live in an orderly and protected community in which the strong are responsible for the defence and well-being of the weak. But the establishment of order must depend upon the substitution of a moral relationship of care and responsibility for an economic relationship of competitive selfishness. We cannot begin by preaching at others that they should be content with their station in order to produce a more stable society. 'That your neighbour should, or should not remain content with *his* position is not your business; but it is very much your business to remain content with your own.'[4] It is, however, entirely insolent to preach contentment to a labourer on thirty shillings a week 'while we suppose an active and plotting covetousness to be meritorious in a man who has three thousand a year'.[5]

This characteristic of stability is an aspect of the need to impart honour and morality into economic relationships; an honourable man of business will give as much for his customer's money as he can, the rogue as little, and one way to bring about this considerable change in affairs is to consistently honour the one kind of businessman and as constantly to call the other a rogue. Employment is likely to be

[3] Ruskin, *Unto this Last*, 17, p. 111
[4] *ibid.*, p. 112
[5] *ibid.*, p. 322

subject and similar to slavery to the extent that it is endured entirely for the wages that reward or compensate it: those employed become less abject 'in proportion to the degrees of love and of wisdom which enter into their duty, or can enter into it'.[6]

Ruskin demands, if not a just and moral society, at least that the reference points for conduct, the operating values of society, should be those of justice and morality. At least, he says, if we are to have a society which will not sink into corruption, poison its relationships along with its environment and bring to an end the art and architecture which we have come to associate with civilisation, then we must transform the values upon which social behaviour is founded. Ruskin demands, in short, the most complete revolution imaginable, a revolution so total as to make the most cataclysmic political convulsions appear by comparison to be merely transitory political tremors. He looks for the re-establishment of the fundamental order which he saw as uniting the beautiful, the moral and the practical in nature, as an order which man destroyed in his own society.

The first obstacle in the way of bringing about such a transformation is the practical objection that it cannot be done, that the proposal is utopian, romantic, idealistic.[7] Ruskin had several counters to an attack that was well-known to him. First, he said, the values he demanded were none other than those of the religion of our state; to dismiss them as unreal was to confess that we lived in an official conspiracy of hypocrisy. Second, he said, they were the values by which our greatest mythical, historical and fictional heroes had lived. Third, they were rational values, their abandonment would mean death, physical or spiritual. Fourth, they were values founded in the greatest and most consistent philosophies that we had been taught, they were, therefore, the moral standards by which conduct was measured. Their suspension was a temporary or, at least, a recent aberration by which economists had succeeded in convincing us that pathology was health. Ruskin frequently illustrated this point by referring to areas of activity in which it was still quite normal for men to live by standards abandoned in business as archaic or unreal. If you make men soldiers and give them the choice 'of a bullet through their heart, and of wife and children being left desolate, for their pride's

---

[6] *ibid.*, p. 269
[7] It will be necessary to examine, in the next chapter, what E. P. Thompson ultimately came to make of precisely the same charges laid against William Morris, not least by Thompson himself in the first edition of his biography of Morris.

sake, they will do it gaily, without thinking twice, but if you ask them for their country's sake to spend a hundred pounds without security of getting back a hundred-and-five, they will laugh in your face'.[8]

If the revolution that Ruskin wished to achieve could be brought about, how would it be done? It would have been perfectly consistent and sufficient if he had gone no further in answering this question than outlining the sound basis of moral and social relationships, reinforced through education and in work, which were to form the outlook and habits of every citizen. If the revolution was to entail an overturning of accepted moral values then that could be accomplished, perhaps could only be accomplished, by the reformation of the individual through the remodelling of the principal influences upon him; the rich, the employer, the institutions of employment, the family (through the forming influence of women), the Church and the school. But Ruskin was trapped in the same dilemma as Robert Owen and every other grand reformer of human behaviour. Political change was irrelevant if men did not first change their values; but without something remarkably like political activity the change would either not take place or, in much the same way, would be too gradual to be apparent. Reformers, like the rest of us, want to see some results for their efforts; the more ambitious their intentions the more anxious they are likely to become. Ruskin's own explanation of his recurrent periods of mental breakdown was rage and disappointment at the fact that no one would listen and nothing was done. The reasoned appeal that men should change, should follow the paths of righteousness, and the rational claim that a reasoned appeal would be sufficient to bring about such change breaks against the inconsistent but human desire to accelerate a process that, while it might be inevitable, is likely to be measured in generations or centuries. So, Owen, believing that persuasion and appeal would be sufficient, is persuaded to industrial experiment, to community planning, to trade union organisation, to innovative banking, to lobbying on an international scale. And while his argument for environmental conditioning remains enormously influential, his practical experiments in reform, designed to demonstrate the truths of his views and to accelerate their universal application are, for the most part, written off as disasters. William Morris, fired by a more poetic and vivid version of Ruskin's ideal world, latterly descends into political action and becomes absorbed and consumed by the viperous

[8] Ruskin, *Unto this Last*, p. 270

intrigues of the Socialist Democratic Federation and the sectarian establishment of the Socialist League.

Ruskin, despite his contempt for politics, could not avoid meeting the challenge of unpracticality by action, nonetheless political because it was conducted outside the area of parliamentary parties. It seems possible to divide his practical or political activity (as opposed to his preaching, as it has often been called) into three areas: the first is the elaboration of a political programme which, despite its untarnished unreality, resembles a manifesto; the second is a practical experiment in the establishment of an ideal community, the League of St George; the third is the suggestion, the innuendo, implicit rather than explicit, of a theory of political action. My contention is that Ruskin's temptation into political activity, as in the case of almost every radical critic (with the baleful exception of Marx and, even here, practical success must be set against historical disaster), was a fiasco. The theoretical suggestions are, however, more interesting and significant.

The practical programme is shaped at every point by moral law and it is to be applied with Presbyterian severity. Ruskin had no time for the liberal-Christian fashion in which 'to be an extremely useful sinner is the best qualifications for becoming an extremely Christian Christian'.[9] He refers to a jury's mercy for a man who had beaten his wife to death; they were possessed of a cowardly fear of commanding death, your 'modern conscience will not incur the responsibility of shortening the hourly more guilty life of a single rogue; but will contentedly fire a salvo of *mitrailleuses* into a regiment of honest men'.[10] Submission to moral law must be absolute and, once again, Ruskin emphasises that good work is essential to the process. In his essential instruction to workmen he tells them that they are to do good work, whether they live or die and they are to die rather than produce any 'destroying machinery'; they are to seek to revenge no injury ('I do not say, seek to punish no crime'); they are to learn to obey good laws until they 'reach the better learning – how to obey good Men'.[11] The enforcement of law must be directed at the acquisition of habitually orderly and moral life, the prejudice against interfering with individual liberty must be overcome, 'make your educational

[9] Ruskin, *Fors Clavigera*, 28, p. 99
[10] *ibid.*, p. 100
[11] *ibid.*, p. 129

laws strict, and your criminal ones may be gentle; but leave youth its liberty, and you will have to dig dungeons for age'.[12]

Ruskin divides law into three general categories: 'archic' law defines what is and is not to be done about the arrangement of rewards and penalties; 'meristic' law determines what is and is not to be possessed, what every person possesses by right and secures it to him, and what every person possesses by wrong and deprives him of it, its object is 'to secure for every man his rightful share of wealth, what he has worked for, produced, or received by gift' while enforcing conditions of possession, that land should not be wasted or air polluted; 'critic' law determines questions of injury and assigns reward and punishment to conduct. Ruskin points out, rather ominously, that we normally understand by injury or harm only that of which the sufferer is conscious, 'whereas much the worst injuries are those he is *unconscious* of'.[13] This is no doubt true, but the determination of the area of unconscious injury has been the cause of great suffering despotically imposed. Injury, says Ruskin, is the violation of a man's right or claim not to be hindered from doing what he should do and to be hindered from doing what he should not, these two forms of hindrance being applied by reward and help on the one side and by punishment, impediment and even death on the other. Ruskin adds that the application of 'critic' law entails the establishment of the worth of a man as well as his want of worth but that this more interesting and vital aspect of law is commonly ignored.

In *Munera Pulveris*, Ruskin goes on to outline the essential features of government. All government is necessarily by some form of council because even dictators have to voluntarily or otherwise, submit themselves to the influence of others. All government is always both visible and invisible. Visible government nominally carries on rational business. Invisible government 'is that exercised by all energetic and intelligent men, each in his sphere, regulating the inner will and secret ways of the people, essentially forming the character, and preparing its fate'.[14] It is, of course, only visible government that is usually regarded as the proper study of the political theorist and constitutional lawyer, but Ruskin's distinction between the two forms is of the greatest possible significance. It is, ironically, his concision as well as his unfashionableness that explains his lack of reputation as a social critic. That one sentence, unelaborated except by an unrelated

[12] Ruskin, *Munera Pulveris*, 17, p. 236
[13] *ibid.*, p. 242
[14] *ibid.*, p. 244

broadside against the United States of America as representing the perfect practice of economics ('total ignorance of the finer arts . . . the discontent of energetic minds unoccupied, frantic with hope of uncomprehended change . . . it is not collapse, but collision, the greatest railroad accident on record'), evokes the subsequent development of the discussion of hegemony and of conscious and unconscious influence in the political process. 'Invisible government' comes to embrace the influence of consumerism, of trade unions and collective bargaining as instruments of conformity and the structural influence of language itself. But, as far as I know, Ruskin, having made this vital distinction has no more to say about it.

Visible governments take one of three forms: they are monarchies (that is, authority is invested in one person); oligarchies (where authority is vested in a minority); or democracies (where authority is vested in a majority). There are many variations of these types and the terminology used to distinguish them is deceptive and confusing rather than clear, so that no man using the terms can be sure that he understands or is understood. The particular form of government in any instance is neither to be praised or condemned: 'all forms of government are good just so far as they attain this one vital necessity of policy – *that the wise and kind, few or many, shall govern the unwise and unkind*'.[15] The form of government is entirely without significance except in relation to its firmness and adaptation to this need; if there are few wise and many foolish in a State then the few should govern the many, if many wise and few foolish then the many should govern the few (at this point Ruskin tells the tale of the 'elytric' democracy of the Lake Zug beetles which we mentioned in Chapter 2).

More than once Ruskin insists that the institution of slavery cannot be singled out for solitary condemnation without knowing what it is that makes it especially abominable. The compulsion of one man by another is not in itself evil.

It is wrong to scourge a man unnecessarily. So it is to shoot him. Both must be done on occasion; and it is better and kinder to flog a man to his work, than to leave him idle till he rots, and flog him afterwards. The essential thing for all creatures is to be made to do right; how they are made to do it – by pleasant promises, or hard necessities, pathetic oratory, or the whip – is comparatively immaterial.[16]

Ruskin is not only stressing the necessity of compulsion but the

---

[15] *ibid.*, p. 248
[16] *ibid.*, p. 255

degradation of the hidden or disguised form of compulsion which liberal denunciations of slavery refuse to acknowledge as existing in free societies. Ruskin is not condemning the one more than the other, he is saying that both are an inevitable condition, 'slavery is not a political institution at all, *but an inherent, natural, and eternal inheritance* of a large portion of the human race – to whom, the more you give of their own free will, the more slaves they will make themselves'.[17] This most unacceptably illiberal conclusion is reinforced when Ruskin goes on to recommend a system of proportional representation based upon plural voting. Representation must be proportionate to the age, income, office and position of the voter. Wealth (as long as it is the reward of sagacity and industry), age and every sign of office and authority 'implying trustworthiness and intellect, should have its known proportional number of votes attached to it'.[18]

In whatever way the citizenry chose to exercise those votes, there is no doubt that Ruskin's prescriptions for a society based upon moral law would contain a good deal of compulsion (perhaps it is entailed by the recognition of the importance of 'invisible government') and a degree of direction of private and public life unacceptable even to those well used to the benevolent responsibilities of the Welfare State. Ruskin agreed with Plato that the State should regulate the right to marry, partly out of regard for eugenic principles and partly as a reward to youth bestowed by the State as a 'national attestation that the first portion of their lives had been rightly fulfilled'.[19] The right to marry would be an honour and it would be celebrated, according to one of Ruskin's sillier accounts, in one of two annual festivals. Poor newly-weds would be entitled to claim a fixed state income for seven years for the setting up of homes and, for the same period, would be subject to a controlled maximum income, the surplus to be accumulated in trust for them by the State. His intention was that rich and poor should not, at the outset of adult life, be distinctly cast into classes until the one had been supported long enough to secure their footing while the other was 'trained somewhat in the use of moderate means, before they were permitted to have the command of abundant ones'.[20]

For the rest, the moral State would rest upon compulsory and free education which would teach and sift or select children in terms of the

[17] *ibid.*, p. 256
[18] *ibid.*, p. 254
[19] *ibid.*, p. 420
[20] *ibid.*, p. 422

pursuits appropriate to their abilities. Subsequently, wages would be
fixed, merchants would be paid salaries rather than depending upon
profit and they would be officials of trade guilds. Other occupations
would be organised into guilds but were not to be set up as
monopolies, tradesmen would volunteer to join them, the public
could go to the guilds or to the free tradesmen, but the guilds would
guarantee quality and content. Men, women, land, water and air
must not be bought and sold but they may be bound to particular
people under certain conditions. The State will secure its land to those
of its citizens who deserve to be trusted with it according to their
desires and capacities and the State will subsequently leave them free,
but will interfere in cases of gross mismanagement and abuse of power
and will pay the landholders a fixed income; land, rather than a
source of income, should be a cost to the landholder. Ruskin sketched
in *Time and Tide*, the hierarchy of an upper class (landowners,
soldiers, commercial leaders, professionals and intellectuals), officers
of law, of public service, of war, of Church and of public education.
He acknowledged that his outline might be seen as impractical and
unrealistic but he engaged upon it and addressed it to workmen at
Sunderland, he said, because 'the working men of England must, for
some time, be the only body to which we can look for resistance to the
deadly influence of managed power'.[21]

Ruskin's practical proposals, if such they can be called, have
excited little sympathy among even his more devoted admirers. The
best that can be made of them by Lord Clarke, for example, is a
dutiful description, an acknowledgement that they are out of
sympathy with the age and an embarrassed and hasty escape into
safer ground. The sheer daftness of many of them is exemplified by
what Ruskin has to say about the new role for the bishops. Over every
hundred families a bishop should be appointed to give an account to
the State of the life of every individual and to have care for their
interests and their conduct so that it will be impossible for anyone to
suffer from unknown want or to live in unrecognised crime. This
overseeing is to be carried out within limits set by law and patient,
gentle and Christian pastoral care. These bishops are to be 'the
biographers of the people', recording the principal events in the life of
each family, the records forming the basis on which is determined
which family is to be advanced in position or distinguished with
honour. The records would become the true record of a nation and

people would prefer to 'obtain some conspicuous place in those honourable annals, than to shrink behind closed shutters from public sight'. Ruskin's protestations that these proposals are neither 'un-English' nor spying are not convincing and it is hardly necessary to dwell upon the dangers. But let us recall that Ruskin has specifically and flatly denied that trade, manufacture and economic relationships can form the basis of a decent and orderly society. Ruskin's difficulty is that he must begin with the enormous prejudicial advantage enjoyed by the *status quo*, the belief that what *is* is what is natural and proper. He has been at great pains to convince us that it is unnatural and improper. However we conduct our business (and we do not conduct it well or decently) we cannot conclude that it will magically provide a formula for coincidentally running our lives, our families, our cities and our State. *Laissez-faire* is dangerous enough confined to the conduct of business, it cannot be extended to our social relationships without the certainty of disaster.

Now, if the economic nexus is denied, as the provision of the founding framework of society, some other must be found. Ruskin is proposing that honour and virtue should be substituted for greed and gain. Careful and deliberate attempts must be made to reinforce those values in the lives of ordinary people if there is to be hope of substituting them for the values that are constantly emphasised in their daily lives by the irrefragable network of 'hidden government'. And if the values are to be nurtured in the roots of society some means must be found of making them permeate its entire system. They must be reinforced, not by a competitive scramble for advantage in which the successful are rewarded by material gain and by national honours, but by the careful observance of characteristics which, because they are valuable, are likely to be unadvertised and unrewarded. The honours system that will actually reward honour rather than graft will have to depend upon a local intelligence network and it will have to be universal in its scope. In practical terms, Ruskin's bishops may be a necessary innovation and no more fanciful than the Soviet system of honouring factory workers (except that the Soviets continue to reward economic performance on the capitalist premise that what is good for Moskvitch motors is good for the USSR).

Ruskin came to believe that he would have to demonstrate that all this could work.

In the fifth letter of *Fors Clavigera* Ruskin announced a fund (into which, in a matter of months, he paid £7,000, a tithe of his own possessions) for the purchase of land to be cultivated by Englishmen with their own hands. A 'company' was established which, by 1877, had become the Guild of St George. Articles of association were drawn up with the greatest care. The first report to the members was made by the Master (Ruskin) in February 1879. In the second report Ruskin is anxiously seeking for someone else to undertake the work of direction. Shortly afterwards the rule that members had to contribute a tenth of their income was relaxed. By 1885 there were 57 members or companions. Ruskin's last report was dated January 1886, he complained in it of the lack of general and financial support for the Guild's activities.

Cook and Wedderburn point out that the Guild of St George is both a study in utopia and an actual record of practical arrangements and things done.[22] The principles that the Guild was to embody emerge from those that we have discussed. It was to demonstrate that sufficient food could be produced by well-directed labour on barren and neglected land (there were shades of the Digger experiment here), only machines driven by natural forces were to be used, rents and wages would be fixed. Government would be ordered, under the absolute power of the Master by '*Comites Ministrantes*', '*Comites Militantes*', and '*Comites Consilie*'. Children would be taught appropriate crafts and each community would be provided with Shepherd's Libraries and model schools. Ruskin's direction of affairs would have been sufficiently precise to have concerned itself with the details of dress, the design of coinage and the provision of the finest Yorkshire pies. The Guild was to spread throughout Europe as the Society of Mont Rose.

Even Ruskin's loyal editors cannot avoid irony: 'Such was the ideal. The actual realisation was a Master who, when wanted to discuss legal deeds, was often drawing leaves of *anagallis tenella*; a society of Companions, few and uninfluential; some cottages in Wales; twenty acres of partly cleared woodland in Worcestershire; a few bleak acres in Yorkshire; and a single museum.'

With even greater irony, the land cultivation undertaking in Tatley ultimately failed, to give way to a commercial and financially successful market garden. Some satellite activities were more successful. A substantial St George's Museum was established at Walkley, subsequently moved to Meersbrook Park, Sheffield. A hand-weaving mill was established at Laxey in the Isle of Man inspired by Guild

[22] They give an account of the Guild's history and affairs in their introdution to vol. 30 which is entirely concerned with affairs of the Guild and the Museum of St George.

enthusiasm, encouragement and money. Longdale home-spun linen was re-established at Coniston and Keswick. A co-operative mill was established by a disciple of the Guild, George Thomson, at Huddersfield. Among the more permanent of Ruskin's practical arrangements was the engagement of his pupil and engraver, George Allen, to publish *Fors Clavigera*; his protégé was the founder of the publishing house now known as George Allen and Unwin. Among the more socially significant was his engagement of Octavia Hill to manage property he owned in Marylebone and which was the beginning of Miss Hill's influential pioneering of 'model' worker housing.

The Guild of St George still exists, its activities little publicised and far less crusading, as a charitable educational trust, receiving applications for financial support, promoting through scholarships and awards, appropriate schemes, crafts and research. Its profession of an active commitment to the principles of 'the Founder' might seem a little out of key with its present Master's assertion that the 'earlier' Ruskin who had written philosophical writings on art and architecture had given way 'to the active reformer, the abstract thinker to the educational pragmatist'.[23] Presumably it requires the confidence of a Master to accuse Ruskin of pragmatism.

Little more need be said about the practical reformer and that little can be postponed until we attempt an assessment of his influence upon the world. To return to the far more significant area of Ruskin's abstract thought we shall examine the suggestions he threw out concerning the mode of action by which workers might influence their own future.

We have repeated to the point of tedium that Ruskin was not a socialist; he despaired of egalitarianism and levelling and he deplored the fiction that equality of rights was based upon equality of capacity, talent and strength. The tale of the beetles of Zug reminds us of his contempt for the democracy of collective decision making. He sometimes called himself an old tory. He sometimes called himself a communist, 'reddest also of the red . . . we Communists of the old school think that our property belongs to everybody and everybody's property to us'.[24] True (as opposed to 'baby', or 'pink') communism means:

1 that everyone must work in common and do common or simple work for his dinner, or have no dinner;

[23] J. B. Thomson, *Ruskin's vision* (The Guild of St George, undated)
[24] Ruskin, *Fors Clavigera*, 27, p. 117

2 that public property shall be grander and more extensive than private wealth;

3 that the fortunes of private persons should be small and of little account in the State while the common wealth of the State should be great, that instead of a common poverty and national debt there should be public wealth.

The pink communists are more concerned to protect the property of their neighbours from injury, 'more anxious for the safety of the possessions of other people (especially their masters)', the true reds 'cannot rest unless we are giving what we can spare of our own; and the more precious it is, the more we want to divide it with somebody'.[25]

Old tory or old communist, Ruskin's criticism of contemporary society is consistently radical; it is the very depth of his uprooting that makes his proposals for episcopal surveillance seem so absurd. One of his strengths is his realism, his insistence that human nature must be recognised for the damaged and imperfect thing that it is. He rounds upon Carlyle's 'benevolent' critics for denouncing him as a worshipper of force: 'What else . . . *is* to be worshipped? Force of brains, Force of heart, Force of hand: – will you dethrone these, and worship apoplexy?'[26] His defence of the old landed lords had always rested upon the historical basis of their wealth, that they had grabbed what they had; his criticism of their current decline was that they no longer had the strength, physical or moral to hold it. His appeal, in *Time and Tide* and *Fors Clavigera*, to the workmen of England was addressed to them in part because they had the power to influence events, 'the only body to which we can look for resistance to the deadly influence of managed power'. Ruskin, in this respect, follows a radical tradition laid down by Saint-Simon and Robert Owen, of turning to the workers as a potential agent of change, a social lever for the application of approved policies, if once convinced of their efficacy (an agent chosen almost in despair after bishops, lords, manufacturers and monarchs had failed either to be moved or to move). But Ruskin's approach grows out of an initial sympathy with the condition of workers (manifested to begin with in *Modern Painters* and *The Seven Lamps of Architecture*), an appreciation of their crucial role as producers in society and a real respect for the power they possess. In a sense, Ruskin appealed to no one other than workers except, in a

---

[25] *ibid.*, p. 123
[26] *ibid.*, p. 230

different context and because he thought them equally influential, women. Ruskin addressed workmen because they had both the power and the right to act; there is no question of what is right and wrong for survivors in an open boat and the matter is equally clear but more important in the context of a nation: 'the right of restraint vested in those who labour, over those who would impede their labour, is as absolute in the large as in the small society'.[27] Ruskin's growing pessimism is caused by the convictions that nothing will or can be done to prevent an inevitable and violent social upheaval. It was Ruskin, not Marx nor Engels, who wrote:

Occult Theft. – Theft which hides itself even from itself, and is legal, respectable, and cowardly, – corrupts the body and soul of man . . . And the guilty Thieves of Europe, the real sources of all deadly war in it, are the Capitalists – that is to say, people who live by percentages on the labour of them; instead of by fair wages for their own. The *Real* war in Europe, of which this fighting in Paris is the Inauguration, is between these and the workman, such as they have made him. They have kept him poor, ignorant, and sinful, that they might, without his knowledge, gather for themselves the produce of his toil. At last a dim insight into the fact of this dawns on him; and such as they have made him he meets them, and *will* meet.[28]

'*Will* meet'; the confrontation is not pleasant in prospect to Ruskin, it is inevitable. It is in this sense that there is an element of anarchism in his primitive communism. He has done what he can to avert the coming crisis, he has warned the landowners, preached to the priests and berated the economists. Subsequently he settles into sullen despair and looks forward without joy to what *will* happen. There is the same conviction of historical inevitability that provides the energy behind the argument of *Capital* and the *Communist Manifesto*. But in Ruskin's case the energy is not dissipated by the paraphernalia of economic calculation or the contradiction of exhortation and political action. The conviction is reluctantly borne in on Ruskin by the moral corruption of capitalist society (the cause of breakdown) and the anarchic facts of power (the remedy). His attempts at action are pathetic efforts, such as the Guild of St George and occasional messages of restraint ('the victory cannot be by violence')[29] to stave off the disaster which he ultimately comes to accept as unavoidable.

Ruskin's explanation of the political response to capitalism is, in part, an acknowledgement of power misused and corrected, its

[27] Ruskin, *Time and Tide*, 17, p. 373
[28] Ruskin, *Fors Clavigera*, 27, p. 127
[29] Ruskin, *Fors Clavigera*, 29, p. 257

inevitability is a matter of the reality of force and it discounts the necessity of political action (except in a vain attempt to avert the consequence of force). It is also, in a literal sense, a matter of faith. The relationship of nineteenth-century cataclysmic social prediction, particularly in Marx, to chiliastic imagery has been observed before. In Ruskin's case the metaphor is frequently and explicitly drawn with biblical references, often from Revelation. Professor Harrison, while not addressing himself to Ruskin's position inside this tradition provides evidence of a fairly direct link between Ruskin and the survival of millenarianism in the nineteenth century by establishing first, a relationship between millenarian teaching (reinforced by references to the Books of Daniel and of Revelation) and radicalism; 'Dig into the history of popular radicalism almost anywhere before 1850 and the chances are good that a millenarian reference will be unearthed';[30] and second, the friendship of the millenarian preacher, Edward Irving, with Thomas Carlyle, Ruskin's 'master'.

The millenarian metaphor can be pressed a little further in order to resolve an inconsistency that has been observed in Ruskin's social theory. Sherburne suggests that Ruskin's work exhibits an 'unresolved conflict' between an admiration for the grand disorder of nature or the gothic and a dislike of *laissez-faire* freedom in society.[31] The existence of a conflict depends upon our accepting that Ruskin perceived nature, and for that matter, the gothic, as disorderly. The argument of Chapter 1 and of other commentators is that Ruskin's conception is of essential order. Indeed, the heart of the attack on *laissez-faire* is that it represents an ugly, competitive unnatural scramble, quite out of tune with the balance to be observed around us. Ruskin sees the times and human society as so far out of joint that they will, by reason of the extent of their disorder, produce and require a millenarian disturbance in order to restore something like the Kingdom of God on earth. Ruskin's view of mankind is too realistic to suppose that this will lead to a utopian transformation in human affairs; he does not expect the lion to lie down with the lamb but the revolution, when it comes, will at least restore the rule (in the sense of a standard of reference) of justice rather than injustice, right rather than wrong, order rather than disorder. To maintain an 'unresolved conflict' between approval of natural disorder and disapproval of *laissez-faire* competition would require a belief in Ruskin's allegiance

---

[30] J. F. C. Harrison, *The second coming: popular millenarianism, 1780–1850* (London, Routledge and Kegan Paul, 1979), p. 224
[31] Sherburne, *Ambiguities of abundance*, p. p. 84

to 'the goose', Herbert Spencer's analogy between natural selection and social competition. As it happens, Ruskin rejected Darwin on the one hand, Mill on the other and Spencer cohabiting with both.

The greatest indictment of Ruskin's revolution is that he did nothing to bring it about. In broader terms the criticism is that his concentration upon moral reformation, however radical, depends upon individual transformation which cannot be achieved without widespread social and institutional change brought about by political action. Raymond Williams' sensitive exposition of Ruskin's outlook ends with the judgment that his value was as a negative critic of industrial society, his was 'an image without energy, because the necessary social commitment could not or would not be made', unlike Morris, he could not go beyond a criticism of the values of his own society because he could not relate values to 'an actual and growing social force: that of the organized working class'.[32] To judge the force of this criticism we must first try to assess Ruskin's influence upon the world and upon his successors.

[32] Raymond Williams, *Culture and society, 1780–1950* (Harmondsworth, Penguin Books, 1961), pp. 152–3

9

The legacy

Ruskin's fall has been grandiose and complete. His influence once rested upon the respect paid him by the most powerful and influential. Tolstoy, Morris, Shaw, Tawney, Proust, Gandhi and a host of figures of more ordinary standing demonstrated or acknowledged their debt. For socialists, once, Ruskin, had become a part of the sacred writing, not always understood but to be regarded with reverence. Quentin Bell reported that when the British Labour Party was established in 1906, 'it was found that the book which had exerted the greatest influence on the members of the young party was "Unto This Last"'.[1] He added that a 'veteran of the movement' had doubted whether any of them had read it although they might have felt that they should have done. Bell said that Ruskin 'could be accommodated in the Pantheon of British Socialism. Whether he still has a place there may well be doubted.' Even that element of doubt has by now been removed.

The case for re-establishing the importance of Ruskin's social criticism faces formidable difficulties. It is out of touch with the times. Contemporary society, if it is not wedded to the capitalist economics of industrial growth, is concerned with centralised planning to achieve the same ends, or with egalitarianism. Ruskin stands against all these objectives. In terms of current influence, Ruskin is dead.

Let us begin the attempt at resuscitation (for that is what it will amount to, rather than the more detached essay in appraisal or assessment) in the least ambitious manner. Ruskin exercised a direct influence upon a body of economic doctrine so remote from the main current of theory and so impractical in its consequences that it was described by Keynes as 'an underworld'. The denizens of this region have been illuminated by Finlay, who modestly begins his account of the social credit movement by acknowledging that it 'was a minor

[1] Quentin Bell, *Ruskin* (London, The Hogarth Press, 1978), p. 147

phenomenon and ultimately a failure'.[2] Social credit, says Finlay was a part of that underworld whose adherents 'felt that socialism was not a sufficient break with liberalism, that it was a mere tampering with the mechanism. Such critics pointed to socialism's clinging to the Rousseauesque notion of the atomised society of free individuals, to its retention of profit as the test of any course of action even if the profit motive itself was abandoned, to its willingness to make use of a purged parliamentary system.'[3]

This characteristic of a rejection of prevailing economic orthodoxy whether in its capitalist or its socialist manifestation, the very reason for Keynes' consignment of it to the nether regions, is precisely the force of Ruskin's attack and of his assertion that socialism would make no difference, that it would make things worse because it would exaggerate the inhuman characteristics of capitalism, it would be capitalism rationally extended throughout human affairs, deprived of its saving weakness of inefficiency and error. And it emerges from Finlay's account that this is no mere matter of a coincidence of doctrine; that Ruskin exercised a direct influence upon the underworld's leaders. The relationship is established in several ways, in his beginning a tradition of the subordination of economic affairs to moral guidance, in the inseparable unity of aesthetic and social considerations, both of which were to a greater or lesser extent shared by these thinkers, and in the direct debt which many of them acknowledged to Ruskin's thought. Finlay's description of the network of inter-connecting lines that relate some of the secondary radical movements of the early twentieth century is fascinating and clear. Three movements, in particular, show the inheritance from Ruskin: distributism, social credit and guild socialism.

Distributism is a notably catholic perspective of social criticism. Its most famous representatives, G. K. Chesterton and Hilaire Belloc, maintained an implacable offensive against both capitalism and socialism. The values and preferences stressed in distributism are for generalised property ownership as against monopoly, a high regard for peasant holding, land-based ruralism and for the aesthetic. While Chesterton's novels are pointed and witty illustrations of the principles of distributism (of local autonomy and character in *The Napoleon of Notting Hill*, of the awfulness of the administrative mind and centralised do-goodery in *The Flying Inn*), Belloc's *The Servile State*

---

[2] John L. Finlay, *Social credit* (Montreal, McGill-Queen's University Press, 1972), p. 1
[3] *ibid.*, p. 2

remains a clear and powerful indictment of the protection given to capitalist power by socialist principles. Ruskin's influence is apparent: 'wealth is matter which has been consciously and intelligently transformed from a condition in which it is less to a condition in which it is more serviceable to human need', 'wealth can only be produced by the application of human energy, mental and physical, to the forces of nature'.[4] The thesis of the book is that while the anarchy of capitalism cannot continue, socialism and rationalisation will merely increase the dependence of the community upon the capitalist class, and that industrial society will, unless checked, guarantee subsistence and security to the proletariat 'at the expense of the old political freedom and by the establishment of that Proletariat in a status really, though not nominally, servile. At the same time, the Owners will be guaranteed in their profits.'[5] The theme has recently been revived in less distinguished literary, that is, in sociological, form in a discussion of the growing influence of corporatism.

The relationship between Ruskin and guild socialism is even more direct. Ashbee's Ruskin reading class at Whitechapel turned itself into the Guild of Handcraft, one of many looking back to the Guild of St George and sharing 'an idea which was to surface again and again, and is indeed still with us – that men were out of tune with their surroundings. Industrialization had destroyed all creativity. Division of labour took away responsibility. Capitalism, the tyrannical "cash nexus", had a terrible effect on the British workman's soul.'[6] More significant than those practical experiments in restoring community and creative life to work, most of which, like Ashbee's ultimately failed, was the attempt 'to devise a means for giving Ruskin's guild ideas a practical basis' based on 'the use of the trade unions in a way which implied forms of workers' control'.[7] The guild movement, elaborated by A. J. Penty with the help of Orage, grew not only from Ruskin and Morris, but from the same philosophical ground cultivated by Ruskin: 'Christian belief formed the groundwork of his [Penty's] thought and most of his judgments in connection with the guild movement were developed from Christian, and especially medieval, ethics.' The development of guild socialism was not so much a direct and immediate consequence of Ruskin's teaching, as a

---

[4] Hilaire Belloc, *The Servile State* (London and Edinburgh, T. N. Foulis, 1912), p. 11
[5] *ibid.*, p. 183
[6] Fiona MacCarthy, *The simple life, C. R. Ashbee in the Cotswolds* (London, Humphries, 1981), p. 22
[7] Frank Mathews, 'The ladder of becoming', in David E. Martin and David Rubinstein (eds.), *Ideology and the labour movement* (London, Croom Helm, 1979), p. 156

development from a network of thinkers sharing to some degree his ideas, encouraged in their exchanges by the general determination to create a better world and by the aesthetic drive of the arts and craft movement. Chief of the contributors in influencing the development of guild socialism was A. J. Penty, an architect who broke with the Fabians, says Finlay, after he learned that the winner of the competition for the design of the new London School of Economics would be the architect whose plan got the greatest room space into the available area. Penty was greatly influenced by Ruskin and by Morris and attracted by way of a general love of medievalism to think of a system of guilds, associations of producers which would allow them to compete only in terms of excellence. He followed Ruskin in abominating the renaissance and, in particular, the view deriving from it that man was naturally good and perfectible; guilds, as Ruskin saw the gothic, would represent man's imperfect nature marked by original sin. The practical significance of his view depended upon the connection he made with the trade unions. Despite the superficial similarity of the view to syndicalism he, and his colleague and editor, Orage, were at pains to emphasise that '"The fathers that Begat us" were not French Syndicalists, but English Socialists.'[8]

The early guild socialists were concerned to produce not only an alternative system of industrial administration which would provide access to control for industrial employees, they possessed a deep philosophical and spiritual conviction of the need for 'a complete spiritual regeneration of the nation. Only this could give the whole people the will to change the social and economic structure.'[9] Because of it, or in spite of it, the movement had a considerable effect on the official policies of some of the largest trade unions and, for a time, on the Labour Party. It was a major influence on the Independent Labour Party and its influence was one of the explanations of the disturbances in Glasgow during and after the first world war. The miners, the post office workers and the engineers, until the general strike and the depression of the 1930s, adopted policies closely parallel to guild socialism. A substantial and effective national building league was established. Some of the best and brightest members of the Labour Party adopted, at least temporarily, a guild programme and outlook; guild socialism was, perhaps the only

[8] *ibid.*, p. 154
[9] *ibid.*, p. 158

serious challenge to the ultimate domination exercised by the Webbs and Fabianism. R. H. Tawney was, for a time, a member of the National Guilds League but the chief influence was exercised by G. D. H. Cole. Cole believed that 'a National Guild would be an association of all the workers by hand and brain concerned in the carrying on of a particular industry or service, and its function would be to carry on that industry or service on behalf of the whole community'.[10] Guild organisation would be based upon the workshop, officials would be chosen by those under them, the arrangement of work would be the result of collective agreement rather than hierarchical command. Guild socialism developed to allow for the special representation of consumers' interests and to engage the principle of 'encroaching control' as a method of gradualist achievement of complete worker control in employment.

Guild socialism did not survive the twin blows to idealism, the economic depression and the access to power of the Labour Party. By 1944 the trade unions had accepted the legitimacy of managerial rights claiming for themselves only recognition and access to collective bargaining. The only discernible practical impact on British industrial relations was the establishment of joint consultation in the public sector which, despite its extent, must be regarded as a poor thing by any standards. The principles of guild socialism ran into the sands of administrative responsibility and the post-war addiction to economic planning, it left the ground of idealism ultimately to the dafter fringes of that fertile legacy of Ruskin, to movements like the Kibbo Kif, the Green Shirts, anarchist groups and, by a strange association, the fascists.

Yet Cole, to his death in 1958, was unrepentant in his commitment to guild socialist principles. Carpenter sums up their influence: 'Guild Socialism was an important restatement of the libertarian features of British Socialism. Cole did far more than merely repeat these features. He embedded them in institutions, creating an important model of decent society. In short, he created a Utopia – perhaps the last Socialist Utopia – and gave it much more contemporary relevance than most Utopias ever obtain.'[11] But it is Ruskin, not Cole, whose influence we are evaluating. Cole is important because of his considerable influence upon practical politics, perhaps the last discernible moral influence that British politics has experienced, and

[10] L. P. Carpenter, *G. D. H. Cole, an intellectual biography* (Cambridge University Press, 1973), p. 58
[11] *ibid.*, p. 45

because he exhibits the strongest evidence of Ruskin's influence. Cole is one of two important figures. The other, if not by now apparent, is shortly to be presented.

Cole's concern with industrial as well as political democracy contradicts Ruskin's scepticism on the ultimate value of that political characteristic. But his reasons for emphasising its importance reveal the same values and concern as Ruskin and his conception of democracy was not dissimilar. It did not mean 'that I want all men to have everything the majority of them would vote for now . . . I do not stand for that kind of democracy.' Democracy is a sense of community, it 'means loving your neighbours, or at any rate being ready to love them when you do not happen to dislike them much – and even then, when they are in trouble and come to you looking for help and sympathy'.[12] Above all else, Cole seems to have been a moralist. Social theory was, for him, a normative study aimed at telling 'people how to be socially good, and to aim at social goods and avoid social evils'.[13] His concern, he said, was with 'social theory as the social complement of ethics, with "ought" rather than with "is" with questions of right rather than of fact'.[14] None of this is far from Ruskin but he does not seem to have got it from Ruskin. The early influence that Cole acknowledged was Morris; he was converted when, as a schoolboy, he read Morris's *News from Nowhere*, 'I became a Socialist, as many others did in those days, on grounds of morals and decency and aesthetic sensibility.'[15]

The 'many others' were as likely to have been brought to socialism by Morris as by Ruskin; Mrs Abse rightly suggests that the Fabians, 'pursuing policies of social efficiency', owed little to Ruskin (although more arguably, she puts the guild socialists in the same camp) and she points out that Morris, 'his greatest disciple', differed from him in turning to political action.[16] Morris's influence was direct, overtly political and multi-faceted in its effect. E. P. Thompson gives a moving account of the unity of his personality and his work in explaining the 'growing stature which he assumes in the perspective of history'.[17] Morris adds a dimension of imaginative reality to Ruskin's moral criticism of capitalism which Ruskin could not have

[12] *ibid.*, p. 247
[13] *ibid.*, p. 221
[14] *ibid.*, p. 230
[15] *ibid.*, p. 5
[16] Joan Abse, *John Ruskin, the passionate moralist* (London, Quartet Books, 1980), p. 238
[17] E. P. Thompson, *William Morris, romantic to revolutionary* (London, Merlin Press, 1977), p. 717

contributed; Morris provides a vision of a socialist future which succeeded in inspiring English socialism until it was submerged by economism and administrative reform. Morris may well provide the 'critical break' between moral outrage and political action. The question then becomes important as to the source and direction of Morris's vision.

It is a question which has become the subject of some particularly arid, not to say polemical debate. Fortunately, Thompson himself provides a detailed account of the argument in which he both personified one of the combative positions and, subsequently, a significant abandonment (or at least qualification) in that stance. (It is also one of the most interesting and honest autobiographical accounts of intellectual development and adjustment written in recent years.) Thompson's explanation of Marx's significance is worth following in some detail because it summarises, in itself, the claims and counter-claims that have been made for Morris's allegiance. It is also an issue which takes the influence of Ruskin some distance beyond his relationship to the 'underworld' of economic doctrine. If this second connection is established we can claim that Ruskin's significance is considerable.

There are two editions of Thompson's exhaustive and scholarly biography of Morris, the first published in 1955, the second in 1977. In the second appendix to the first edition, Thompson reviews the argument and evidence and concludes, counter to the opinion prevailing at that time, that Morris was a Marxist. He blames two early authorities on the life and opinions of Morris for the mistaken view that he was a romantic, anti-Marxist utopian. Mackail in his biography had improperly emphasised Morris's statements of exasperation over Marx's economics and had imposed his own prejudice against socialism, believing that 'Morris took to Socialism, as Poe took to drink'. The second was Glasier, an idealist and a romantic, the prophet of 'moral' socialism, who insisted that Morris should fit into his own romantic myth. Thompson finally cites Paul Meier as providing a conclusive examination which demonstrates that Morris's political writing draws upon and is consistent with a Marxist tradition.

In the postscript dated 1976 to the second edition, Thompson turns to those critics who had accused him of Marxist dogmatism and bias in the first. He acknowledges that 'in 1955 I allowed some hectoring political moralism as well as a few Stalinist pieties, to intrude upon the text', and that he then had a 'somewhat reverent notion of Marxism

as a received orthodoxy'.[18] Despite these confessions it was clear, he
says, that it was Morris's political commitment rather than his own
treatment of him that drew the critics' fire. His book was type-cast as
demonstrating the Morris/Marx equation. Sensitive readers should
have detected, because of the stress upon 'Morris's genius as a
moralist, that there was a submerged argument within the orthodoxy
to which I then belonged'. The sensitive reader would have had to
overcome, of course, the author's splenetic tone and Marxist bias
(both phrases he honestly cites from his critics) and the contemptuous
treatment he meted out to those who had claimed Morris for an older,
romantic, idealist, utopian tradition. And what is the submerged
argument of 1955 that emerges clear and uncluttered by dogmatism
in 1976? It is that the English romantic tradition was tougher than it
was supposed to be, independently (of Marx and Engels) capable of
mounting a moral criticism of capitalism, that it 'was pressing
forward to conclusions consonant with Marx's critique and it was
Morris's particular genius to think through this transformation, effect
this juncture and seal it with action'.[19] And now, in order to rebut the
old criticism that Morris was a romantic, utopian, regressive socialist,
Thompson turns on 'orthodox' Marxism for having seen it in this way
and for turning 'its back upon a juncture which it neglected to its own
peril and subsequent disgrace'. Paul Meier who had, in 1955, been
cited as providing a conclusive examination to demonstrate that
Morris's political writing drew upon and was consistent with the
Marxist tradition is, in 1976, described as having 'only written out at
large pieties and excisions in my own original treatment'.[20] and is
then criticised for offering 'Morris to us as an orthodox Marxist, and
his notion of this orthodoxy is heavily influenced by its subsequent
Marxist-Leninist definitions . . . The notion of Marxism as a correct
truth is assumed throughout, and Morris is judged approvingly in
terms of his approximation to this.'[21]

This appears to Thompson in 1976, as it had appeared to others
before, to be error. The error lies, he says, in the Marxist tradition
itself, 'narrowed' by Engels to exclude the romantic tradition which is
condemned as 'moralism' and 'utopianism'. It is more important to
understand Morris as a transformed romantic than as a conforming
Marxist; more important than his adhesion to the Marxist tradition is

[18] *ibid.*, p. 769
[19] *ibid.*, p. 779
[20] *ibid.*, p. 802
[21] *ibid.*, p. 780

'the Marxist "absences" or failures to meet the adhesion half-way'.[22]
'The question of Morris's relation to Marxism raises acutely the
question, not as to whether Marxists should criticise Morris, but
whether Marxism should criticise itself.'[23] Morris 'may be assimilated
to Marxism only in the course of a process of self-criticism and re-
ordering within Marxism itself'. This truly rigorous reappraisal of the
earlier position ends with the conclusion that Morris was a communist utopian 'with the full force of the transformed Romantic
tradition behind him'.[24] The answer to the question as to whether
Morris was a Marxist or not is that 'he was somewhere else, doing
something else, and the question is not so much wrong as
inappropriate'.[25]

The question remains an important one, however, because of what
has been made of it by that very Marxist tradition. Until the claim
was made that Morris was a Marxist, he was derided and it is possible
that, without that claim, his stature as a social critic would have been
diminished and that he would not have been acknowledged as a
serious radical critic of capitalism. Before that claim Laidler dismissed
him: 'he wrote more as a poet than a scientist', these pseudo-utopians
'have many flaws from the standpoint of economic science';[26] Pierson
described his socialism as 'regressive', a relapse, a reversion to
utopianism;[27] Pevsner wrote that 'Morris's Socialism is far from
correct according to the standards established in the later nineteenth
century.'[28] For some people it seems to have been necessary to claim
that Morris was a Marxist in order to take him seriously.

The evidence for the claim always rested upon interpretation of
what he wrote in order to assert that his views coincided with, or
could have developed only as the result of, a sympathetic understanding of Marx. The interpretation followed and built upon three
foundations: the unchallengeable fact that he was a revolutionary
communist, his acceptance of 'central tenets' (class conflict, exploitation and alienation), and that he acknowledged the influence of
Marx and of 'that great work' *Capital*. As to the first, Morris's
communism does not demonstrate his Marxism, the *genus* is larger
than the *species*. As to the second, class conflict and exploitation are

[22] *ibid.*, p. 786
[23] *ibid.*, p. 788
[24] *ibid.*, p. 792
[25] *ibid.*, p. 791
[26] H. W. Laidler, *History of socialism* (London, Crowell, 1968), p. 116
[27] *ibid.*, p. 791
[28] N. Pevsner, *Pioneers of modern design* (Harmondsworth, Penguin Books, 1960), p. 24

notions older than Marx and the idea of alienation can be traced in Ruskin and is acknowledged by Thompson to derive from the romantic tradition. As to the third, Morris's references (if we discount his exasperation) to Marx certainly demonstrate admiration, even awe, but they can well be explained by his late introduction to socialism and socialists. His latter-day companions included Hyndman, Aveling, Bax, Shaw, who were anxious to complete or begin his political education; he may well have been as anxious to please his new colleagues and teachers, although he retained, to the last, a natural impatience with high-flown intellectual discussion. That characteristic alone might be sufficient to separate him from the Marxist tradition.

We have followed (believe it or not, briefly) the labyrinthine argument that Morris was a Marxist and its qualified rejection by Thompson because it leaves out of account a fact central to our present purpose, that the chief influence upon Morris, acknowledged by him as accounting for his own development, was John Ruskin. Thompson acknowledges it briefly, quoting Morris: 'The essence of what Ruskin taught us . . . was really nothing more recondite than this, that the art of any epoch must of necessity be the expression of its social life.' Please note, says Thompson, it was what Ruskin taught, not Marx, and before he had even heard Marx's name. The important question is not whether or not Morris was a Marxist but the significance of the difference that Thompson finally acknowledges between Morris and Marxism. The difference represents the measure of Morris's attachment to an English, romantic, utopian, moralistic tradition. The difference lies in Ruskin.

Those qualities for which Morris was once berated and for which he came to be praised, of moralism, idealism, utopianism, are his inheritance from Ruskin. What he got and acknowledged from Ruskin was moral criticism of capitalist values added to despair at the prospects for art in a capitalist world. Everyone acknowledged that Morris came to social and political criticisms by way of art and architecture, so did Ruskin. Morris followed a trial laid by Ruskin. Morris's famous denunciations are remarkably similar to Ruskin's, except that Ruskin's are more savage, sometimes, coarser, and were made first. It is impossible to read both without being struck by the similarity of language, imagery and thought. There are differences. On the one hand, the claim that Morris was a 'genius as a moralist' would be difficult to sustain and has not, I believe, ever been advanced by a moral philosopher; his moral standpoint is largely derived from Ruskin except that it lacks Ruskin's consistency and depth. Morris's ethics are probably shallower than Ruskin's constant elaboration of the essential unity of moral, aesthetic and social questions. While Ruskin derives his own position from Christian doctrine and classical philosophy it is not at all certain from where Morris gets his own position unless it be, simply, from Ruskin. Even Morris's determination to see the death of art rather than its survival in a capitalist setting (which Thompson uses to rebut a charge of aestheticism) is an echo of precisely the same conviction in Ruskin.

The other source acknowledged for Morris is, of course, 'romanticism', tougher than it was once acknowledged to be. The attribution of Ruskin to romanticism was made by Raymond Williams, by Sherburne, and by Rosenberg. It is doubtful if that loose and generic label is of very great descriptive value. Marilyn Butler's brilliant analysis, for example, seriously questions the very existence of a 'romantic movement' other than as an intellectual artifact:

'Romanticism' is inchoate because it is not a single intellectual movement but a complex of responses to certain conditions which Western society has experienced and continues to experience since the beginning of the eighteenth century. There seems small chance of understanding how social pressures worked upon the artistic process except by making careful discrimination between the atmosphere of different cultures . . . and different times.[29]

There are elements in Ruskin's 'romanticism' which are classical, conservative and reactionary, but all those features, Butler demonstrates, can be found in aspects of 'romanticism'. He can also be clearly related to an ancient tradition of English radicalism. Raymond Williams concludes, however, that valuable as Ruskin was as a destructive social critic 'there was no force to which Ruskin could appeal . . . His society was an image without energy, because the necessary social commitment could not or would not be made.'[30] He rightly concludes that Ruskin's small-scale local experiments were absurd. It took Morris, says Williams, to relate the influence of Ruskin and 'to attach its general values to an actual growing force: that of the organized working class. This was the most remarkable attempt that had so far been made to break the general deadlock.'

Was it a break-out or a renewal of the impasse? The other side of the coin in the relationship of Morris to Ruskin is that the pupil

---

[29] Marilyn Butler, *Romantics, rebels and reactionaries* (Oxford University Press, 1981), p. 184
[30] Williams, *Culture and Society*, p. 152

contributed energy and imagination to the master's doctrine. The doctrine is much the same except in the important respect for which Morris is praised and Ruskin criticised. Morris engaged in practical politics, saw the working class as the agent of political struggle and set about the task of bringing it to political action. Morris, unlike Ruskin, believed in the possibility of political action. His political intentions were also different; as J. A. Hobson pointed out:

a society in which everyone at once does what he likes, and likes what he does, is the ideal that is presented [by Morris]. All sense of pain and irksomeness is brushed away from labour; duty either towards oneself, one's neighbours, or society nowhere presents itself as a necessary motive. The artist even now likes what he does; therefore, place all work on the footing of an art, the necessary work will be done for its own sake, and for the sake of the pleasure got from doing it. Now Mr. Ruskin is at once more definitely moral and more practical.[31]

More moral *and* more practical? Surely the terms are contradictory? But it was Ruskin's unshakable conviction that moral change is the only conceivable means for the achievement of practical change. What is commonly called the practical action of political organisation, the decisive step for which Morris is congratulated, of hitching the moral engine to the wagon of the working class, is precisely what Ruskin saw as impractical. It would not work because it would slip into the same rut of ineffectuality as we saw at the end of guild socialism, a movement which left G. D. H. Cole at the end of his life with moral convictions unchanged while he concerned himself with the Labour Party's programme of planning. It would not work because it would be impelled towards consensus with the values it set out to overthrow, because political action requires collaboration and because political action requires the abandonment of irreconcilable ethical positions. Ruskin saw that the only conceivably 'practical' course was the moral reformation of society and the only way to achieve it was by a revolution of values achieved in individuals by the teaching, preaching and precept of influential social leaders.

Paradoxically, while Morris's political engagement (for which he is now applauded) was largely ineffective in that the long-term effect on the political process has been negligible, he did advance the thrust of Ruskin's moral appeal because he added to it his own imaginative and creative energy. While Ruskin preaches, however beautifully, Morris, in *News from Nowhere* creates a moving vision of a noble future.

[31] Hobson, *John Ruskin*, p. 30

It is the utopian moralist in Morris, not the political activist, that provides the decisive link between Ruskin and the practical possibility of a revolutionary change in the world's values. Morris should be valued for quite the opposite reason than that for which he has been lately taken up by Marxists. It is indeed, as Thompson has come to see, the deficiency of Marxism that Morris (and Ruskin) reveals. Conversely, Morris's weakness is what has been claimed as his strength, he failed to understand Ruskin's warning that a proletariat schooled in capitalism's values will, if it acts politically, exaggerate capitalism's faults.

The relevance of Ruskin's moral criticism of capitalism and of Morris's imaginative extension of it is taken up and applied to the contemporary world by a new school of social criticism. It bears a remarkable similarity to Ruskin, not least in its rejection of the belief in material progress and irreversible economic growth. It has won considerable influence, particularly among the educated young of developed countries, for its scepticism about the value of science and technology and their analogues of social and political planning. Ivan Illich, demanding a natural balance between man and the tools with which he works, warns that 'if the balance is upset, the tools and the technology come to dominate man until it becomes irrelevant whether an enterprise is nominally owned by individuals, corporations, or the state, because no form of management can make such fundamental destruction serve a social purpose'.[32] The crisis, he says, is in the industrial mode of production itself, but that mode so restricts our imagination and so influences our intelligence that alternatives to mass production seem unreal, 'like a Utopian design for noble savages'. Arguing that we are trapped (or almost trapped) in a circle in which technology produces problems which seem to demand more technology to cure them ('the cure for bad management is more management . . . the cure for polluted rivers is more costly non-polluting detergents'), that machines cannot replace slaves because they enslave men, he demands a 'new politics' for a post-industrial society. The essence of this position must be an enforced limit on the development of technology so that 'no one person's ability to express himself or herself in work will require as a condition the enforced labor or the enforced learning or the enforced consumption of another'.[33] Unless man is able to limit the interference of the tools that

---

[32] Ivan Illich, *Tools of conviviality* (London, Calder and Boyers, 1973), p. xi
[33] *ibid.*, p. 13

have mastered him there will be an apocalypse. Even if it could 'work', 'the bureaucratic management of human survival is un-acceptable on both ethical and political grounds'.[34] The only acceptable alternative is a political process in which decisions are taken about the quantity of any resource or energy which any member of society can claim; the only possible solution is a frugal society. The new politics of the new society, quite clearly must depend upon the creation of a new moral awareness, it is that which it is Illich's purpose to achieve.

Theodor Roszak stresses different aspects of the same dark view of industrialised society. Dismissing Marxist-Leninism as a 'cosmic caricature of nineteenth-century bourgeois scientism',[35] he claims that there is a 'strange new radicalism' abroad, a religious renewal. Standing counter to this development is the prevailing rationalist culture maintaining a divided and unnatural conception of man. This 'single-vision', this ruling perception of science, has become the boundary condition of industrial culture, so dominant that it is equated with reality and sanity. This is the perceptual framework, the 'psychic style', upon which the technocracy depends. Like Illich, he argues that the perception is self-feeding and self-perpetuating; 'the economy of the artificial environment is a fabric of waste, extrava-gance, compulsive consumption, and purely technogenic necessities. The pressure which we tend to interpret wholly as population pressure is largely the produce of a sick lifestyle.'[36] In demanding an economics of permanence, Roszak says that we must first engage in a searching examination of work which will require questions about, not whether industrial plant saves work, but how much it saves in the production of things unwanted; and how much work it would be better to do by hand or by intermediate technology in the con-servation of other values. Machines have replaced work with leisure, with nothing but 'a vacuum rapidly filled with cheerless, obsessive getting and spending, with idiocies like pre-packaged tourism'.[37] But work could be what it once was, 'a form of prayer'.

Schumacher also begins and ends with work, pointing out that we have no theory of work. We might add that we also have no *study* of work; 'work study' means, if anything, the study of the avoidance of work, or its close measurement. 'Industrial relations' is largely

[34] ibid., p. 100
[35] Theodor Roszak, *Where the wasteland ends* (London, Faber, 1973), p. 21
[36] ibid., p. 419
[37] ibid., p. 234

concerned with representative institutions in work and the formal and informal arrangements for its control. We need a study of work but the first difficulty is in finding a name for it. Ergonomics, like work study, has already claimed a special meaning and will not do. The Latinised 'lavorology' would be absurd. The best inception I can arrive at would be a Saxon construction, 'swink-lore', but it would not go down well in the universities. In the absence of a proper study of work, says Schumacher, we never ask what the work does to the worker and usually insist that the worker adapts to the needs of the work, and that usually means to the needs of the machine. He derives three fundamental purposes of human work:

First, to provide necessary and useful goods and services.

Second, to enable every one of us to use and thereby perfect our gifts like good stewards.

Third, to do so in service to, and in cooperation with, others, so as to liberate ourselves from our inborn egocentricity.[38]

The qualities thus contained in work are so central to human life that it is impossible to conceive of human life devoid of work. Its fundamental importance makes the damage done to work by large-scale industrial processes all the more dangerous, more damaging, more divorced from nature. 'The basic aim of modern industrialism is not to make work satisfying but to raise productivity; its proudest achievement is labour saving, whereby labour is stamped with the mask of undesirability. But what is undesirable cannot confer dignity.'[39] Industrial society is also based upon and exaggerates autocracy, complexity, envy and avarice, and is therefore bound to end in disaster; 'now that it has adopted cumulative growth as its principal aim, the end cannot be far off'. Schumacher, lapsed or saved economist as he was, goes on to catalogue some very real and uncomfortable forms that this disaster is likely to take; the disruption of organic relationships so as to promote population growth beyond the means of subsistence, a threat to the means themselves, the depletion of non-renewable mineral resources, the degradation of morality and intelligence while creating a way of life demanding greater moral and intellectual qualities, the encouragement of violence.

Schumacher says that education ought to prepare people for acting as spiritual beings, in accordance with their moral impulses; for

[38] E. F. Schumacher, *Good work* (London, Abacus, 1980), pp. 3–4
[39] *ibid.*, p. 119

acting as neighbours rendering service to each other; for acting as persons creatively engaged in developing the gifts they have been given. But education cannot do these things if we cannot distinguish between good and bad work, if human life on earth has no meaning or purpose. Good for what, for making money, for promotion or for achieving power? If education is to distinguish between good and bad work, as it should, it must encourage young people not to accept bad work: 'they should be encouraged to *reject* meaningless, boring, stultifying, or nerve-racking work in which a man (or woman) is made the servant of a machine or a system. They should be taught that work is the joy of life and is needed for our development, but that meaningless work is an abomination.'[40] Education for good work means challenging utilitarianism and the utilitarian idea of work, that it is an unpleasant necessity and that the less there is of it the better.

These three criticisms of the prevailing society have several characteristics in common and, although the several representatives would differ from each other in important respects, it would not be unfair to concentrate upon what they have in common and to suggest that it presents a coherent, recognisable attack upon the prevailing industrial order and its value systems. All three make a central point of the pervasiveness of that system, of its boundary-forming perspectives. One is reminded of 'invisible government'. The same stress on the influence of the material base of society upon our thought patterns, of the monopolistic influence of scientific-rational logic emerges in some forms of structuralism and in the work of Stewart Clegg. In its extreme form the analysis is so pessimistic about the rational domination of capitalism or industrialism that the analysis falls into a philosophical impasse: the thing that is hated is shown to be so powerful that there can be no escape from it, a logical enough conclusion except that it is often unacceptable to the analyst's intentions.

The movement, often called the counter-culture, also shows some dangerous characteristics of a political kind. It offers an uncertain vision of a future which we will have to construct before we are able to judge whether we like it or prefer it to the present. It is idealistic, resting upon a somewhat exemplary view of human nature. It is often criticised for being impractical; how are we to get off the materialist band-wagon short of some ecological disaster (and will that disaster

[40] *ibid.*

be welcome or not)? It is, in a very dangerous sense, romantic, anti-rational, and it can lead to strong and awful extremes, to drugs, violence and atrocities justified because of the prevailing social 'atrocity' that 'provokes' them. It often demonstrates a degree of moral rectitude, it rests upon an intellectual's view of what his fellow-man's life should be like, it has coercive characteristics.

It is not our business to judge it or to subject it to close analysis. It has several characteristics which closely identify it with Ruskin. One is that very air of rectitude, that authority that prompted Shaw to say that the society most closely representing Ruskin's views in practice was the Bolshevik regime of the Soviet Union. The second, perhaps associated characteristic, is its moralism, the subjection of economic relationships to moral scrutiny, the insistence by Ruskin that relationships of business and employment must be based upon justice rather than greed. The third is that it presents a positive conception of the nature of man, it is therefore ideal if not utopian in its outlook. Finally, it concerns work as an important manifestation of human behaviour on earth.

It is to be hoped that it was unnecessary and superfluous to point to the close similarities in these three writers to Ruskin. Schumacher, in particular, demonstrates a quite remarkable coincidence in values and in argument to be explained by the fact that, like Ruskin, his criticism is derived from Christian doctrine. But even if the association is accepted we may still be left having made no great claim for the influence of Ruskin upon the contemporary world. The case amounts to a contestable degree of influence upon Morris, himself a figure of dubious significance, a fairly clear relationship to the 'underworld' of economic theory, generally judged to be without influence, and a close affinity to the contemporary counter-culture, dismissible as operating at the fringes of present-day political consciousness. That, in effect, may be as far as the case for Ruskin's relevance can go. It is possible also that it need go no further.

First, in a world in which economic orthodoxy prevails, un-orthodox attacks upon it will, by definition, appear to be impractical and, if they are noticed, be pronounced anathema. The charge of irrelevance is the price paid for the severity of the attack. Let us examine the significance of the attack. If we take the reassessment of Morris latterly arrived at by E. P. Thompson we see that he not only makes large claims for Morris (which, we argue, would be more properly related to Ruskin so that, in this context, we can say, for Morris read Ruskin), but he also makes large acknowledgements of the needs of Marxism. If we accept Thompson's final verdict (and in this case we could not have a more expert witness) then the potential contribution of Ruskin (or Morris) to contemporary Marxism is vast. The necessary infusion of moral and aesthetic concern, of idealism, promises yet one more version of communism with a human face with, this time, the possibility of synthesis with a significant and new contribution; no mere scholarly revisionism of established dogma but a fusion of two tributaries. If that 'junction' were to be established, if the materialist ideology that dominates one half of the world while posing some threat to the other were to be infused by a moral influence then the case for Ruskin's relevance would be assured.

The reader would be right to interject that all that is as may be. In the meantime there remains the more immediate question of whether Ruskin's criticisms of nineteenth-century industrial society are relevant to the twentieth century. Our representatives of the counter-culture demonstrate that they are but there is no sign of their views capturing the allegiance of a majority at the polls and no major party has championed them. The 'victims' of industrial society, the factory workers, are not disaffected, the nature of their work does not prevent them being envied by the growing number of those that have no work at all. What is Ruskin's relevance to the society of space-age technology and the micro-chip?

The problem of assessing his criticism is ultimately the same as that of any intellectual outsider, contemplating at a distance the manufacturing process, expressing his own revulsion and extending it to a universal condemnation. Marx, Morris and Ruskin all say: 'I could not live like that; no one should.' The question is whether the indisputable fact that most people do live like that, apparently happily, is a refutation of their view. It is to be doubted in the first place, whether an expression of moral revulsion can ever be refuted, it remains true or untrue as a communication of the judgment of the critic. The practical question is whether that judgment influences the outlook of others, whether they are brought to agree with the criticism launched against their surroundings. The practical question is not only one of real political possibilities, it concerns the resonance of the criticism. Can others, in the face of the conforming pressures of the everyday world, come to agree that there is something wrong with the world and with their lives which should be put right?

Ruskin tells us that there is, and his ultimate escape is that if others will not agree, it is because their moral judgment has been distorted by the immoral reality that we have created. Ruskin comes close, in this respect, to an argument from false consciousness. The people must be made, by the best means, to do right. Ultimately, he escapes from the test of the ballot box by the assertion that industrial society is so manifestly contrary to the laws of God and to the accumulated moral judgment of civilisation that it will destroy itself or that it must be destroyed. These alternative conclusions that the world must be changed and that it will change, as in Marx, are puzzlingly contradictory; there is never any certainty that wickedness does not work. The real question is whether industrial or capitalist society is wicked and whether those that see it so are right.

It is at this point that any reader of Ruskin (or, more particularly, any writer) must get off the fence. Let us attempt a summary. Capitalism provides an affluent society but at the expense of growing poverty in the third world and of relative and painful poverty in advanced societies. While it demonstrates great flexibility in its ability to adjust to moral and social demands upon it and to ameliorate conditions demonstrated to be wrong, these demands always remain outside its own domain, it meets them only while it can be profitable; it is not preoccupied with morality. Capitalism, as writers on the American business system acknowledged, has no sympathy with the understanding of aesthetic considerations; this is enough in itself to determine those who believe that artistic creativity is the highest human accomplishment that capitalism is inadequate. Capitalism is careless of the preservation of resources or the pollution of the environment unless it is controlled by law or public outcry; its responsibility is a measured response to an external set of considerations or powers. Capitalism is concerned about the conditions of its employees only to the extent that they are relevant to productivity or to the extent that they are controlled by the law or trade unions. This is perhaps Ruskin's major criticism, but all the charges against capitalism would demonstrate, for him, that a moral concern which ought to be a central preoccupation of the most powerful agencies of societies is, for business, always, at best, peripheral, or, at worst, alien to it.

It is in the area of employment conditions that most change has taken place since Ruskin's day and it is this same area in which he makes his most damaging attack. The working day has been shortened, not in Britain by law (except for women and juveniles), but largely as a consequence of union pressure. The working life has been shortened, partly as the result of expanded education and partly as a response to economic conditions. The dangers of industrial disease and accident have been reduced by legislation and inspection although much remains to be done. In other respects we seem to have achieved the outcome that Kropotkin promised of technology, where 'factories, forge and mine *can* be as healthy and magnificent as the finest laboratories in modern universities'. Further improvements are promised in the development of electronically controlled production processes which may reach the point at which some of us, an increasing number, are excused from the necessity of work at all.

The exclusion from work would be, for Ruskin, the biggest problem, a commentary in itself on what we had made of labour in that its cessation would come to be seen as a blessing. Work was for Ruskin, as for Schumacher, a necessary and natural activity, without any of the cant associated with its 'dignity'; a world in which substantial proportions of society would never have useful work to do would be an abomination. Predictions about the future of leisure and work are currently uncertain but it seems likely that we may face the gravest problems in continuing to value the increasingly important and complex work of some highly, while we have to persuade the rest that they will have no need of it. Predictions about the consequences of robotics and the new production processes veer from the pessimistic (mass unemployment made tolerable by compulsory leisure) to the optimistic (decentralisation of managerial control and authority and a return to a kind of cottage industry, a working day of five hours with the possibility of greater social control of the production objectives), but all such predictions are uncertain and unreliable. What does seem certain in the interim is that those still at work in the future will be subjected to a further intensification of detailed control of the kind which has already become familiar. A recent report suggested that the competitive demands of the international economy on industrialised nations will require more complex work with closer attention to detail.

To reduce the possibility of mistakes all the discrete operations will be detailed minutely in order to have predictability and control. The corollary of this is that the worker will have less and less possibility of introducing variability into his or her actual work . . . workers will have less chance to exercise their authority over the execution of tasks and operations; their discretion will be further limited.[41]

The micro-processor may release many people from the opportunity

[41] European Foundation for the Improvement of Living and Working Conditions, *Physical and psychological stress at work* (Dublin, 1982), p. 98

of employment but those that retain it may do so only by demonstrating that they are cheaper or more reliable than robots.

The evidence on the existing state of affairs already suggests that manufacturing, assembly, service and managerial work produce physical and psychological symptoms of stress. One aspect of this evidence helps us to answer the question concerning the seriousness with which we should regard Ruskin's criticisms of the inhuman character of work and whether his humanity was merely the result of his own sensibility, shocked at the condition of others who find no cause for complaint in their working lives. The report on physical and psychological stress at work concludes that 'a large majority of people tend to ignore perceptions of discomfort or stress for as long as possible'. After seven to nine years, in one industry studied, the first symptoms of 'wear and tear' appear, often denied in terms of their cause but associated with cardiac, circulatory and ophthalmic problems. This phase is followed by a loss of personal control, a state of hopelessness or reactive depression and, finally, to generalised neurasthenic behaviour.[42] The tragic fact is, it seems, that people find their disabling work natural and are not disposed to complain even when it begins to damage them. As far as we can tell, nothing has changed. If that is so, Ruskin's rage is as justified now as it was in the nineteenth century.

Our case is that Ruskin's influence, although it has often not been identified or acknowledged, is clear and consistent in a living tradition which attempts to explain man's productive life in the world. Whether that tradition is to be influential or not, the question of the meaning of work and of the relationship that it establishes with other men and with nature, as long as it is conceived to be a moral rather than merely an economic question, must return to its treatment in Ruskin.

Whatever the measure of the influence he has exerted upon our times, his continuing relevance is assured by the essential features of his work. His moral concern with the ends and object of production, with the conditions that it imposes upon men and women and the values that it incorporates, bring his criticism to the central activity in the life of society and of its inhabitants. If we are to see developments take place which enable us to produce in some measure without working, in which more people are freed from the necessity of labour, we must continue to ask what are the costs of the affluence of some and

[42] *ibid.*, pp. 153–4

the idleness of others and how many we are continuing to 'tread upon'. The prospects of new technology, however far they extend, may in fact make it more possible to measure work against the standards Ruskin set and to require that its replacement by machines should not be too casually undertaken without thought for human and social consequences. The tests Ruskin set may be more applicable now than they were in his own society because we are more free. There is as much optimistic hope as fear in the prospects of the new economy with some prospect of freedom from the conformity of centralised bureaucratic decisions and constraint.

In one respect Ruskin's concern for the values of labour and its relationship to art and thought seems to meet with a more sympathetic response in the contemporary world than in his own. The movement which he pioneered, with Morris's example to follow, which became known as the arts and craft movement, survived the contempt with which it was received by the functionalist establishment and has become a respectable phase in English architecture. It was associated with marked social and political characteristics. The signs are that, in the vast proliferation of DIY, gardening, fishing and crafts, we are returning to the practice of doing and making, that we are becoming a more active, constructive and creative people as the demands of a diminished concept of employment begin to recede. We may even succeed in substituting work, socially useful, performed for the community and related at last to education, for the stultifying experience of employment.[43]

It is the political aspect of that essentially English tradition which is at its weakest at the present time. We do not need to return to the imbroglio over the precise position taken up by Morris to observe that the relationship claimed for him to Marxism, if conceded, ends that 'romantic' tradition which he is supposed to have related to it. The paradox of the claim of a 'juncture' established between the English 'romantic' tradition and Marxism is that its relevance to Marxism can be established only by demanding a re-interpretation so thorough as to make it unrecognisable to Marx.

A re-examination of the English radical tradition, finding perhaps the clearest and certainly its most moving expression in the work of Ruskin and Morris, reminds us of what we have lost and of what we still need. In terms of contemporary political thought, it is the tragedy of politics, not of Ruskin, that he seems no longer to speak to us. His

---

[43] David Bleakley, *In place of work . . . the sufficient society* (London, SCM Press, 1981)

assertion of the inseparable relationship of work, beauty and morality is, for the present, a vanished ideal. In terms more acceptable to common English usage, he reminds us of the ideal of a decent society. In that sense he may well prove to be more important tomorrow than today.

Bibliography

Abse, Joan, *John Ruskin, the passionate moralist*, London, Quartet Books, 1980
Anthony, P. D., *The ideology of work*, London, Tavistock, 1977
Arendt, Hannah, *The human condition*, University of Chicago Press, 1958
Ashton, Rosemary, *The German idea*, Cambridge University Press, 1980
Bell, Quentin, *Ruskin*, London, The Hogarth Press, 1978
Belloc, Hilaire, *The Servile State*, London and Edinburgh, T. N. Foulis, 1912
Berg, Maxine, *The machinery question and the making of political economy, 1815–1848*, Cambridge University Press, 1980
Berki, R. N., 'On the nature and origins of Marx's concept of labour', *Political Theory*, 7, no. 1 (1979), 35–6
Bleakley, David, *In place of work . . . the sufficient society*, London, SCM Press, 1981
Bourdieu, Pierre, 'Systems of education and systems of thought', in M. F. D. Young (ed.), *Knowledge and control*, London, Collier-Macmillan, 1971
Braverman, Harry, *Labour and monopoly capitalism*, New York, Monthly Review Press, 1974
Burnett, John, *A history of the cost of living*, Harmondsworth, Penguin Books, 1969
Butler, Marilyn, *Peacock displayed*, London, Routledge and Kegan Paul, 1979
Carpenter, L. P., *G. D. H. Cole, an intellectual biography*, Cambridge University Press, 1973
Checkland, S. G., *The rise of industrial society in England, 1815–1885*, London, Longmans, 1971
Collingwood, W. G., *The life of John Ruskin*, London, Methuen, 1922
Colls, Robert, *The collier's rant: song and culture in the industrial village*, London, Croom Helm, 1977
Conner, P. R. M., 'Pugin and Ruskin', *Journal of the Warburg and Courtald Institute*, XLI (1978), 344–50
Cook, E. T. and Wedderburn, A. (eds.), *The works of John Ruskin*, 39 vols., London, George Allen, 1903–12
Dearden, James S., *Facets of Ruskin*, London, Charles Skilton, 1970
Eastlake, Charles, *A history of the gothic revival*, New York, Leicester University Press, second edition, 1970
European Foundation for the Improvement of Living and Working Conditions, *Physical and psychological stress at work*, Dublin, 1982

Fain, John Tyree, *Ruskin and the economists*, Nashville, Vanderbilt University Press, 1956

Finlay, John L., *Social credit*, Montreal, McGill-Queen's University Press, 1972

Flanders, Alan, *Collective bargaining*, Harmondsworth, Penguin Books, 1969

Flinn, M. W., 'Social theory and the industrial revolution', in T. Burns and S. B. Saul (eds.), *Social theory and economic change*, London, Tavistock, 1967

Ford, Henry, *Moving forward*, London Heinemann, 1931

Fox, Alan, *A sociology of work in industry*, London, Collier-Macmillan, 1971
Beyond contract: work, power and trust relations, London, Faber and Faber, 1974

Garrigan, Kristine Ottesen, *Ruskin on architecture, his thought and influence*, Madison, University of Wisconsin Press, 1973

Gash, Norman, *Aristocracy and people*, London, Edward Arnold, 1979

Gide, Charles and Rist, Charles, *A history of economic doctrines*, London, Harrap, 1948

Gouldner, Alvin, W., 'The norm of reciprocity', *American Sociological Review*, xxv (1960), 161–79

Greaves, Richard L., *The puritan revolution and educational thought*, New Brunswick, Rutgers University Press, 1969

Harrison, J. F. C., *Learning and living, 1790–1970*, London, Routledge and Kegan Paul, 1961
The second coming: popular millenarianism, 1780–1850, London, Routledge and Kegan Paul, 1979

Harvey, John, *The master builders*, London, Thames and Hudson, 1971

Hoare, Quinton and Smith, Geoffrey Nowell (eds.), *Selections from the prison notebooks of Antonio Gramsci*, London, Lawrence and Wishart, 1971

Hobsbawm, E. J., *Industry and empire*, Harmondsworth, Penguin Books, 1969

Hobson, J. A., *John Ruskin, social reformer*, London, James Nisbet, 1898

Illich, Ivan, *Tools of conviviality*, London, Calder and Boyers, 1973

James, Louis, *Print and the people*, London, Allen Lane, 1973

Jaques, Elliot, *Equitable payment*, London, Heinemann, 1961

Johnson, Richard, 'Educating the educators', in A. P. Donajgrodski (ed.), *Social control in nineteenth century Britain*, London, Croom Helm, 1977

Kelly, Thomas, *A history of adult education in Great Britain*, Liverpool University Press, 1962

Laidler, H. W., *History of socialism*, London, Crowell, 1968

Leon, Derrick, *Ruskin, the great Victorian*, London, Routledge and Kegan Paul, 1949

Lindsay, A. D., *The Republic of Plato*, London, J. M. Dent, 1950

Lindsay, Jack, *William Morris, his life and work*, London, Constable, 1975

Lutyens, Mary, *The Ruskins and the Grays*, London, John Murray, 1972

MacCarthy, Fiona, *The simple life, C. R. Ashbee in the Cotswolds*, London Humphries, 1981

Macrae, Donald (ed.), *Herbert Spencer, the man versus the State*, Harmondsworth, Penguin Books, 1969

Mathews, Frank, 'The ladder of becoming', in David E. Martin and David Rubinstein (eds.), *Ideology and the labour movement*, London Croom Helm, 1979

Maurice, F. D., *Learning and working*, London, Oxford University Press, 1968

McLellan, David (ed.), *Karl Marx: early tests*, Oxford, Blackwell, 1971

Meynell, Mrs *John Ruskin*, Edinburgh, Blackwood, 1890

Myrdal, Gunnar, *Against the stream, critical essays on economics*, London, Macmillan, 1974

Oakeshott, Michael, *On human conduct*, Oxford University Press, 1975

Ollman, Bertell, *Alienation, Marx's conception of man in capitalist society*, Cambridge University Press, 1971

Pater, Walter, *The renaissance*, London, Macmillan, 1910

Pevsner, N., *Pioneers of modern design*, Hardmondsworth, Penguin Books, 1960

Ruskin, John *Modern Painters* (1843–60), in E. T. Cook and A. Wedderburn (eds.), *The works of John Ruskin* (39 vols., London, George Allen, 1903–12), vols. 3–7 (1903–53)

> *The Seven Lamps of Architecture* (1849), *Works*, vol. 8 (1903)
> *The Stones of Venice* (1851–3), *Works*, vols. 9–11 (1903–4)
> *Pre-Raphaelitism* (1851), *Works*, vol. 12 (1904)
> *The Harbours of England* (1856), *Works*, vol. 13 (1904)
> *Inaugural Address at the Cambridge School of Art* (1858), *Works*, vol. 16 (1905)
> *The Oxford Museum* (1859), *Works*, vol. 16 (1905)
> *The Two Paths* (1859), *Works*, vol. 16 (1905)
> *Unto this Last* (1862), *Works*, vol. 17 (1905)
> *Sesame and Lilies* (1865), *Works*, vol. 18 (1905)
> *The Study of Architecture in Schools* (1865), *Works*, vol. 19 (1905)
> *The Cestus of Aglaia* (1865–6), *Works*, vol. 19 (1905)
> *The Crown of Wild Olive* (1866), *Works*, vol. 18 (1905)
> *Time and Tide* (1867), *Works*, vol. 17 (1905)
> *The Queen of the Air* (1869), *Works*, vol. 19 (1905)
> *The Flamboyant Architecture of the Valley of the Somme* (1869), *Works*, vol. 19 (1905)
> *Lectures on Art* (1870), *Works*, vol. 20 (1905)
> *Fors Clavigera, letters to the workmen and labourers of Great Britain* (1871–84), *Works*, vols. 27–9 (1907)
> *Aratra Pentelici* (1872), *Works*, vol. 20 (1905)
> *Munera Pulveris* (1872), *Works*, vol. 17 (1905)
> *Love's Meinie* (1873), *Works*, vol. 25 (1906)
> *The Laws of Fesole* (1877–8), *Works*, vol. 15 (1904)
> *A Joy for Ever* (1880), *Works*, vol. 16 (1905)
> *Fiction, Fair and Foul* (1880–1), *Works*, vol. 34 (1908)
> *The Storm Cloud of the Nineteenth Century* (1884), *Works*, vol. 34 (1908)
> *On the Old Road* (1885), *Works*, vol. 34 (1908)
> *Praeterita, outlines of scenes and thoughts perhaps worthy of memory in my past life* (1885–9), *Works*, vol. 35 (1908)
> *The Story of Arachne* (1894), *Works*, vol. 20 (1905)

Salzman, L. F., *Building in England*, Oxford University Press, 1952

Schumacher, E. F., *Good Work*, London, Abacus, 1980

Scott, Geoffrey, *The architecture of humanism*, London Methuen, 1961

Semmel, Bernard, *The Methodist revolution*, London, Heinemann, 1973

Shaw, George Bernard, *Ruskin's politics*, London, Christophers, 1921

Sherburne, J. S., *John Ruskin or the ambiguities of abundance*, Cambridge, Mass., Harvard University Press, 1972

Sheridan, Ronald and Ross, Anne, *Gargoyles and grotesques, paganism in the medieval church*, Boston, New York Graphic Society, 1975

Shrimpton, Nick, '"Rust and dust"; Ruskin's pivotal work', in Robert Hewison (ed.), *New approaches to Ruskin*, London, Routledge and Kegan Paul, 1981

Simpson, D. H., 'Is there an economics of industrial relations?', paper presented to University of Wales Colloquium, Duffryn House, July 1980

Tawney, R. H., *The acquisitive society*, London, Bell, 1930

Thompson, E. P., *The making of the English working class*, Harmondsworth, Penguin Books, 1968

William Morris, romantic to revolutionary, London, Merlin Press, 1977

Thomson, J. B., *Ruskin's vision*, The Guild of St George, undated

Tylecote, M., *The mechanics' institutes of Lancashire and Yorkshire before 1851*, Manchester University Press, 1957

Unrau, John, 'Ruskin, the workmen and the savageness of gothic', in Robert Hewison (ed.), *New approaches to Ruskin*, London, Routledge and Kegan Paul, 1981

Wardle, David *Education and society in nineteenth century Nottingham*, Cambridge University Press, 1971

Watkin, David, *Morality and architecture*, Oxford, Clarendon Press, 1977

Wilenski, R. H., *John Ruskin: an introduction to further study of his life and work*, London, Faber and Faber, 1933

Williams, Raymond, *Culture and society, 1780–1950*, Harmondsworth, Penguin Books, 1961

Wood, H. G., *Frederick Denison Maurice*, Cambridge University Press, 1950

Wootton, Barbara, *The social foundations of wage policy*, London, Allen and Unwin, 1955

Index